Computing Texts

A Course in Programming with QBASIC

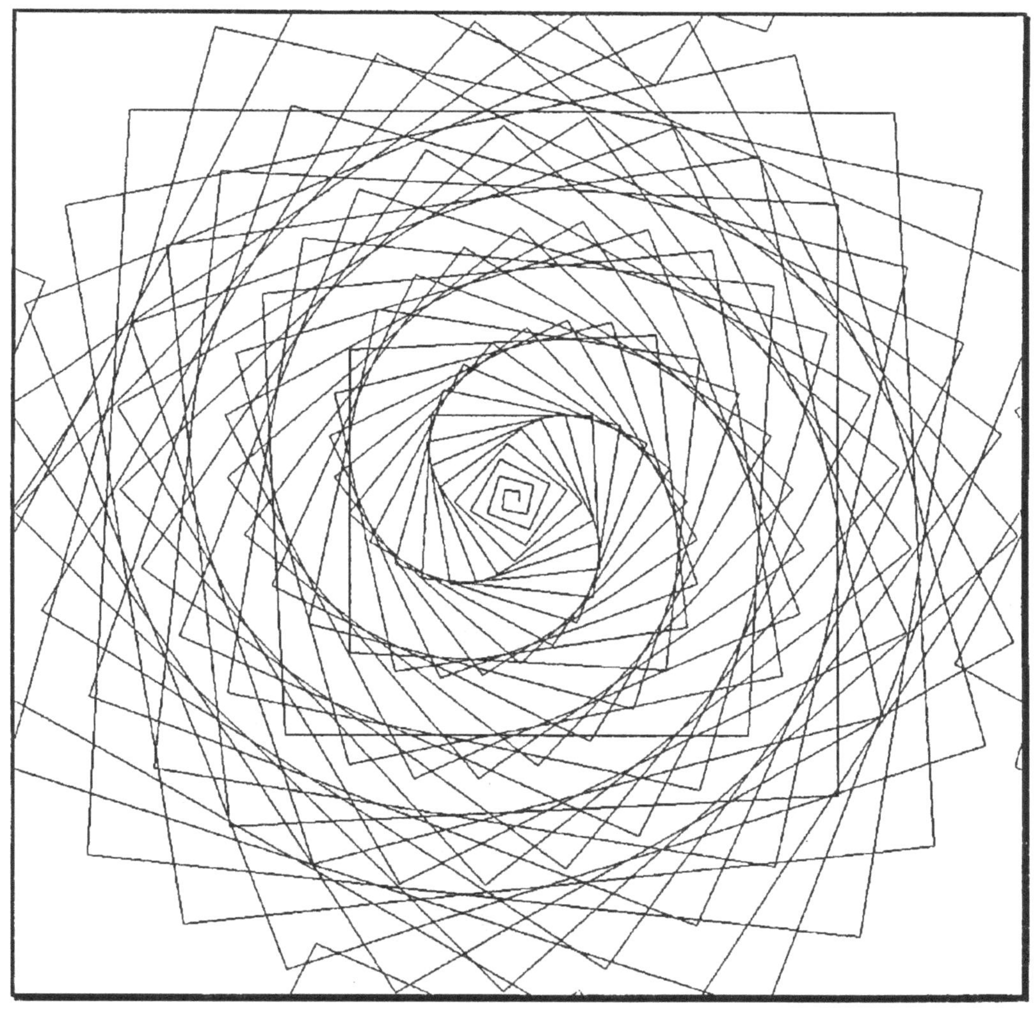

Tony Hawken

This English edition was first published in 2009

ISBN: 978-1-4452-4069-5

This book was originally published in Chinese (Mandarin) in 1995 as

QBASIC 编程入门

Tony Hawken（英）

哈尔滨船舶工程大学出版社出版
新华书店首都发行所发行
黑龙江商学院刷厂印制

开本 787×1092 1/16 印张 16 字数 150 千字
1995 年 8 月 第 1 版 1995 年 11 月 第 17 次 印刷
印数：1001—4000 册

ISBN 7-81007-585-3 / TP・33

定价：16.00 元

Preface

Aim

The aim of this book is to introduce structured programming to students who possibly haven't programmed before. It is also my intention to appeal to people who have computing experience and wish to extend their knowledge or move from another programming environment.

Need

BASIC is still one of the most popular programming languages in the world. This is so because it is easy to learn and yet has powerful features that compare very well with so called "serious" languages that the professional programmer uses.

There are very few books that are at the same time accessible to a beginner but at the same time treat the subject in a comprehensive and serious manner. BASIC for a long time suffered a bad reputation as being a language that encourages unstructured programming. QBASIC provides the constructs which make such programming unnecessary. What is needed is a book that encourages good practice.

Approach

The material in this book is at the same time designed to be informal and easy to use as well as treating the subject in more depth by including advanced topics.

It provides :-

- Introductory material to get a beginner started
- Extensive exercises to encourage the reader to write programs
- A logical progression from one topic to the next
- Advanced topics for the more serious reader
- An extensive bibliography for further study

Ways of using the book

The book can be read from cover to cover to provide a comprehensive study of programming using QBASIC. Alternatively if it is to be used as a basis for a programming course. The teacher can select chapters to teach as self-contained units.

If this is the case a core course would consist of the first 8 chapters. Then other chapters can be selected as required.

A suitable path for progression through the book follows on the next page

Logical Progression for study

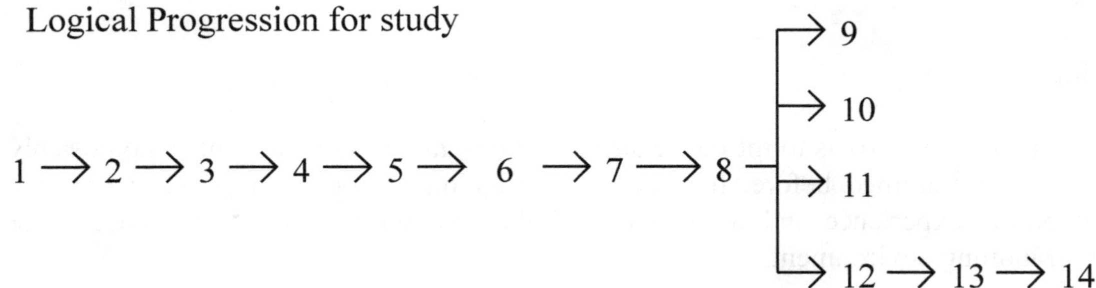

Other more knowledgable readers may want to browse through the book looking at bits that interest them. They may for instance wish to use the book to compare how things are done in QBASIC compared to the language they are used to.

Where next?

By the time you have finished this book you will have learnt a lot and realised that QBASIC is an excellent vehicle for learning programming.

You may also find out where QBASIC is deficient. In particular :-

- It cannot produce a standalone executable program
- It has a limite range of datatypes
- It does not have pointers

You will however have developed useful skills which can be applied in other areas. In particular you may wish to try out the following :-

1. Microsoft QuickBASIC — This will run any QBASIC program. In addition it has extra commands and can produce standalone executable programs.

2. Microsoft BASIC PDS — This is an extension of QuickBASIC. In addition it provides database management facilities.

3. Microsoft Visual BASIC — Retains most of the features of QBASIC and QuickBASIC and provides the facilities for developing windows applications.

At some time or other you may find yourself using either Microsoft Word for Windows or Excel. Both of these products have a built in macro language which resembles BASIC.

Table of Contents

Page

1. Getting Started with QBASIC

1.1 A bit of DOS

The assumption that I am making in this first chapter is that there are some of you who may never have used a computer and need to have some guidance on how to get started.

If you are using an IBM compatible computer MS-DOS is the Operating System that you will be using. This is a program which manages the resources on your computer. It also has a command language interface which enables you to talk to the computer.

When you switch on your computer MS-DOS is loaded into memory and after a few seconds you will end up with a prompt like this:

C:/>

This prompt is an invitation for you to type in an MS-DOS command.

When you enter a command remember to press the **<Return>** key after each command

To get you going I am inviting you to try out these commands:

DATE	-- Outputs the current System date
TIME	-- Outputs the current system time
DIR	-- Lists files in the current directory

Hopefully you will have a machine that has both a Hard drive designated as **C:** and also a floppy drive designated as **A:** .You may also have a second drive called the **B:** drive. If you have two drives one may be a 3½ inch disk and the other a 5¼ inch disk.

To change to the floppy drive type:

A:

To change back to the hard-disk type:

C:

The hard disk is typically there to store all of your application software. I am going to suggest that you store all of your programs on a floppy disk. If you are writing your programs on a computer at college you will probably have to do that anyway.

It is a good idea to get yourself organised from day one. You will need a box of 3½ inch or 5¼ inch floppy disks, preferably high density disks. Actually you will probably fit all of your programs on one disk, but I am going to encourage you to have more disks so that you can take the precaution of making backups.

Note high density disks have **HD** written on them, and double density disks **DS/DD**.

Before you can use a disk you will need to format them.

If you have high density disks all you need to type from the C: is:

```
format a:
```

For 3½ inch disks, if you want to format double density disks you will need to type:

```
format a: /f:720
```

The option /f: 720 is an instruction to format the disk as 720k bytes instead of the 1.44Mbyte capacity of a high density disk.

Now that you have done this you can organise your disk into directories. Directories make it much easier to locate your files and see what you have got using the DIR command.

I suggest that you create a directory for each chapter in this book. That way if you want to go back to a program which you wrote when you were reading chapter 4 you will know where to find it. Call the directories P1, P2, P3 ... etc.

As you can see from fig 1.1 the directory structure is hierarchical. The top of the directory is called the root or \. Directories underneath the root are called \p1, \p2 etc. That is the directory name is obtained by naming every directory that you have to pass through to get to the desired directory.

Right at the bottom we have the directories \p2\progs and \p2\docs.

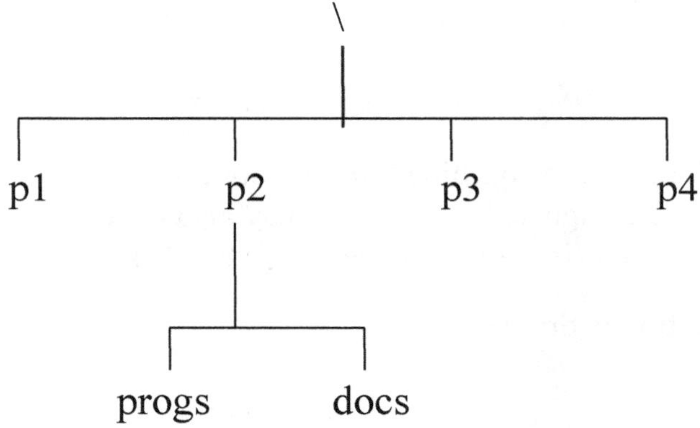

Fig 1-1 An MS-DOS directory

When you are naming directories there are two forms that you can use. There are **absolute** pathnames and **relative** pathnames.

An absolute pathname always starts with a \. For example the directory **\p2\progs** has been given an absolute pathname. If I just happened to be in the directory **\p2** I could refer to the same directory as **progs**. This is called a relative pathname.

To create a directory enter a command like this:

mkdir p1 or **mkdir \p1**

Now to move into this directory from you current directory you can type in

cd p1 if you are in the directory \ . (Relative pathname)

cd \p1 if you are anywhere else. (Absolute pathname)

1.2 Using the MS-DOS Editor

To create a file in this directory you could use the MS-DOS editor. This is a general-purpose editor that you could use for typing in programs, data files etc.

If you enter **EDIT** at the DOS prompt you will get a screen that looks like this:

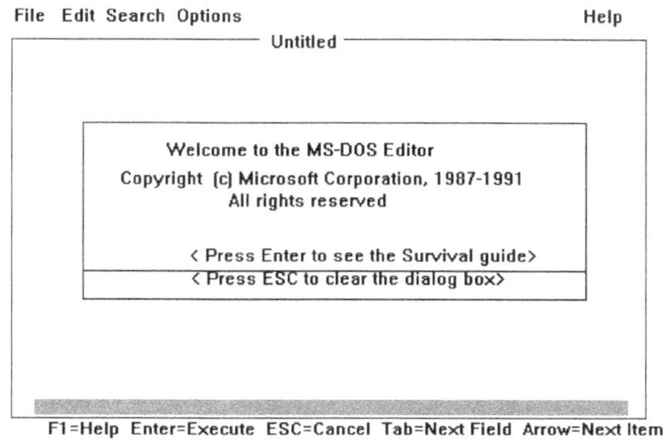

Fig 1-2 Entry Screen – MS-DOS Editor

If you now want to start editing press **Esc** and you will get a screen like this:

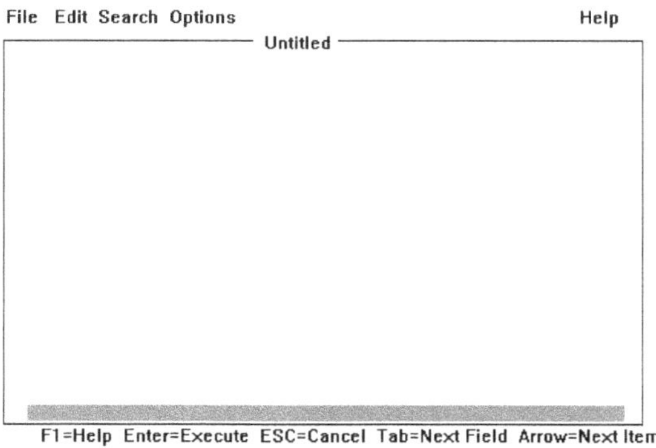

Fig 1-3 MS-DOS Menu Options

You are now ready to select an option from a menu at the top. To do so press **Alt** and the first letter of the option you require.

Most of the time you will just want to use the **File** and **Edit** options.

If you press **Alt F** you will get the file option and you will get a pop down menu underneath file. The screen should look like this the one in Fig 1-4.

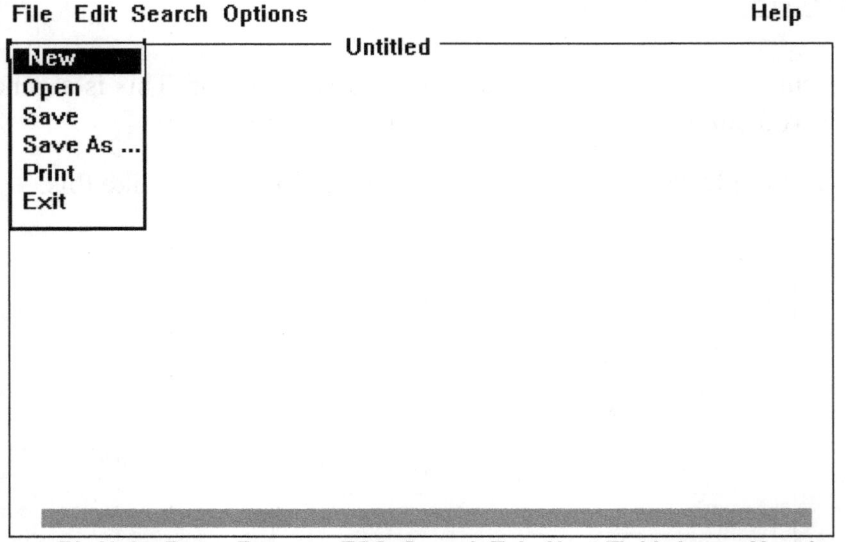

Fig 1-4 The File pop-down menu

You can select your option from the pop-down menu by using the up and down arrow keys (and ↓). The current option will be highlighted. To get the option now press return.

To create a new file, you will typically want to do the following from the **file** menu:

1. Select **New** to start a new file. Now all you have to do is some typing.
2. Choose **Save As**. You choose this option as the file doesn't have a name yet. You will then have to enter a file name before it is saved.
3. At regular periods in time (say every 10 minutes) save your file. This time you select the option **Save**. It will save your work with the current file name.
4. To exit from the editor choose the option **Exit**. If your work has been modified and not saved you will be asked if you want to save your work.

You may want to go back and add to the file that you were editing previously. To do this get back into the editor by typing **EDIT**. Then choose the **File** menu again.

5. To get your previous file loaded choose the option **Open**.You will get a screen that looks like Fig 1-5

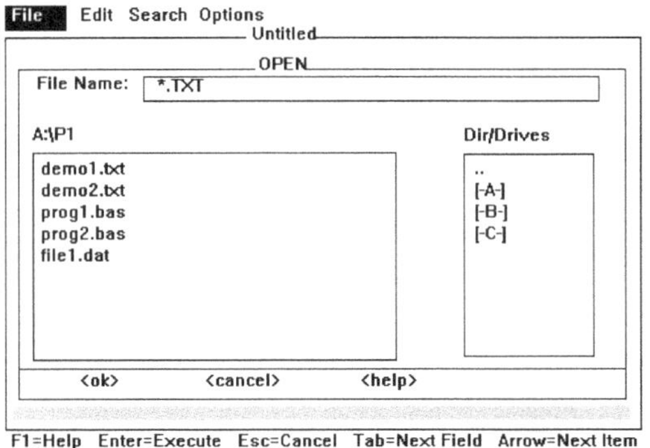

Fig 1-5 Loading a File

To enter the filename you can either:

1. Type name at the cursor in the box labelled **Filename**
2. Press **Alt F** and then highlight the file that you want by using the up and down arrow keys.

If the file that you want is on a different drive or in a different directory now is the time to press **Alt D**. You can now use the arrow keys to select the drive/directory that you require. This will now update the list of files displayed in the **Files** box.

If you want to take bits of text and move it somewhere else you can find the tools in the **Edit** menu.

You typically would use this to perform cut and paste operations.

If you press **Alt E** you get a pop-down menu that looks like this:

Cut	Shift + Del
Copy	Ctrl + Ins
Paste	Shift + Ins
Clear	Del

Fig 1-6 Edit pop-down menu

The instructions on the right-hand side indicate that you can perform these operations without having to use the menu at all.

A typical cut and paste operation goes like this:

1. Select the text you want to move. Press Shift + arrow keys

You should notice that all the text gets highlighted.

2. Now cut out the highlighted text. Press **Shift + Del.**

⇧ Delete

All the highlighted text gets deleted.

3. Move the cursor where you want the text to go. Use the up and down arrow keys.

4. Paste the text to this position on the screen. Press **Shift + Ins** .

⇧ Insert

You should find that the text now appears at this position.

1.3 Some more MS-DOS

So far we know something about directories, some commands such as DATE, TIME and DIR, and using the DOS Editor. It is now time to extend this knowledge.

You can list the files in your current directory by using the DIR command.

1.	dir	Ordinary directory listing
2.	dir/w	Wide listing.
3.	dir/p	Listing that pauses after each screen full.

You can copy files by using the COPY command in the following way.

1. You can copy a single file

   copy file.txt newfile.txt

2. You can copy a file to a different directory

Copy file.txt \p1\newfile.txt	here the copy of the file is a different name as well.
Copy file.txt \p1	If you just name the directory the file will have the same name

3. You can copy a group of files all in one go.

copy *.txt \p1	Here the character * is a wildcard. It matches any filename.

You can delete unwanted files:

1. Delete a single file.

    del file.txt

2. Delete a group of files

    del *.txt

3. You can delete all the files in your current directory

    del *.*

   You will now be prompted:

    All files in your directory will be deleted
    Are you sure (Y/N)?

   To which you reply **Y**.

Should you delete a file that you didn't really want to you can use the undelete command to bring it back again.

e.g. undelete file.txt

To examine the contents of the file you can use the TYPE command.

e.g. type file.txt

Finally it would be useful if you could copy an entire disk including directories. The command to do this is the **diskcopy** command. Beware it is a very dangerous command. Make sure you have write-protected you original disk by moving the plastic thing, so that there is a hole in the disk. Then if you put the wrong disk in first at least you won't wipe the contents of your disk.

The command to enter is

    diskcopy a: a:

You will be prompted what to do on the screen. First you have to put the **source** disk in and press a key. Then the **target** disk when you are told to.

Exercise 1-1

Try out the following on your system to acquaint yourself with DOS.

1. Format your disk and give it a label QBASIC.
2. Create directories called P1, P2, P3, P4, P5 and DOCS.
3. Move to the directory called P1.
4. Enter the DOS Editor and create a simple text file.
5. Save it and call it DEMO.TXT before quitting the editor.
6. Use the DIR command to find out the size in bytes of DEMO.TXT.
7. Create a copy of this in your \DOCS directory.

1.4 Getting to know the QBASIC Environment

It is important to know how to get into QBASIC and use the QBASIC environment.

Enter **qbasic** at the DOS prompt

and you get a screen that looks like this:

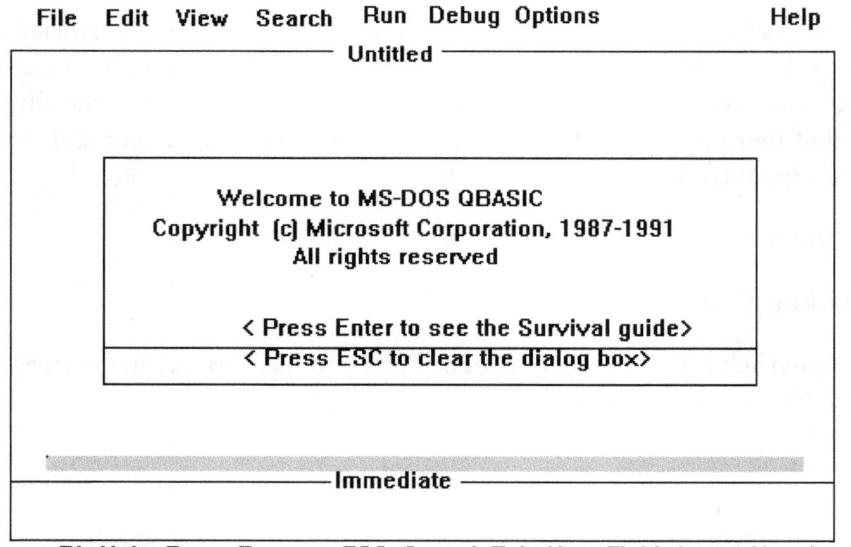

Fig 1-7 Q-BASIC Entry screen

You now really have two choices:

1. Press ENTER — if this is the first time. The survival guide is a simple help screen to get you started with the QBASIC Environment.

2. Press ESC — This is what you will want to do most of the time. It takes you into QBASIC proper. You will want to do this if you want to write a program, or run a program etc.

If you press **ESC**

you now get a screen that looks like this:

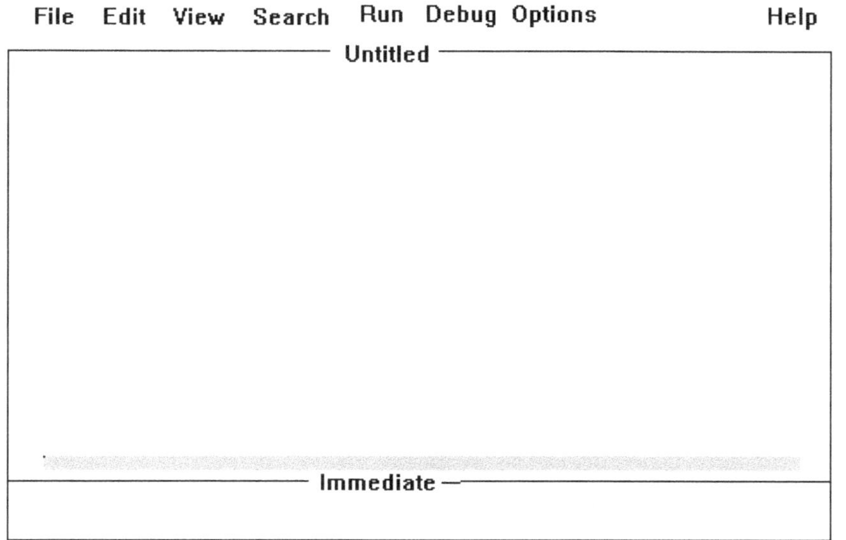

Fig 1-8 QBASIC Main Menus

You can now start typing in your program or you could choose a menu option in the same manner as using the DOS editor. That is press the **Alt** key and the first letter of the option you require.

If at any time you want to cancel a selection you can do this by pressing the **Esc** key.

If for example you press **Alt F** you will get a pop-down menu from File. The selection at the top is highlighted indicating the current selection. See Fig 1-9

If you want to create a NEW program simply press return

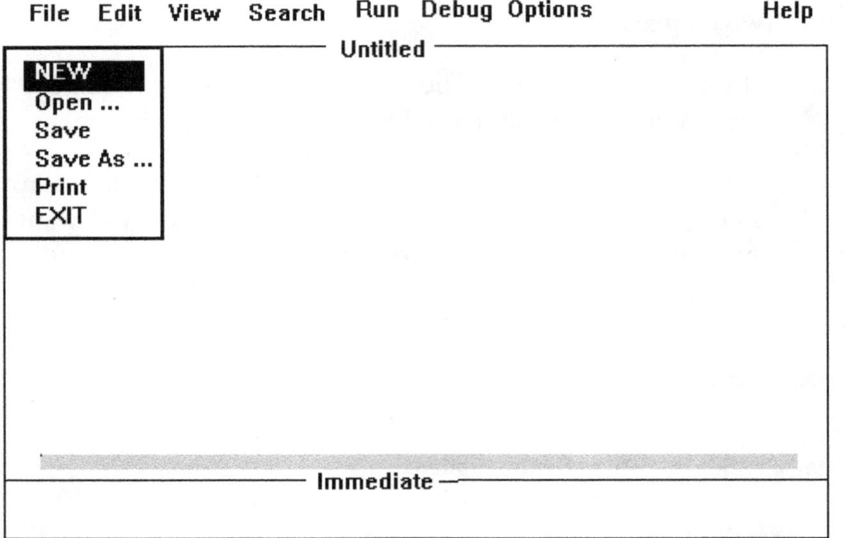

Fig 1-9 Choosing the File option

If you want to choose something else, use the up and down arrow keys (and ↓).

If you use the left and right arrow keys you can choose a different pop-down menu.

The most important features of these pop-down menus are now going to be discussed in the context of how you will need to use them.

1. To create a new file choose **New**, then type in your program.
2. To save your program choose **Save As**, then enter filename as for DOS editor. Note that the default type is .BAS for a QBASIC program.
3. You are advised to periodically save your program. This time choose the **Save** option as the system already knows the name of the file. Don't worry if you use the **Save As** option again. It will prompt you with the current filename anyway.
4. You can print the contents of your editing session at any time using the **Print** option.
5. The **Open** option is there for you to load another program into the QBASIC environment.
6. Finally when you have finished with QBASIC and want to quit use the **Exit** option. If you haven't saved your file you will be asked to do so.

The Edit menu is for providing editing functions, and also the capability of creating separate program modules such as SUB Programs (procedures) or FUNCTIONS.

Edit	
Cut	Shift+Del
Copy	Ctrl+Ins
Paste	Shift+Del
Clear	Del
New SUB ...	
New FUNCTION	

Fig 1-10 The Edit menu

1. Cut and paste operations are exactly the same as that for the DOS editor. If you have forgotten go back a few pages.

2. **New SUB ...** is there for you to create sub programs. You choose this option and press return. You are now given the opportunity to name the sub program. You are then given another window with the following in it:

   SUB subname

   END SUB

   It is now up to you to supply the contents.

3. **New FUNCTION** is similar. Here you are able to create your own functions in much the same way.

If you are going to create Functions or Sub Programs you will need a way to view them and also get back to the main program.

View
SUBs...
F2
Split
Output Screen
F4

Fig 1-11 The View menu

1. The most important of these is **SUBs...** as it enables you to choose which subprogram, function or main program you want to view.

Don't worry about this now as it will be discussed in more detail in chapter 8. (Using Sub programs and Functions)

When you get to the stage when you think you have finished your program and want to try it out you need to choose the **Run** option

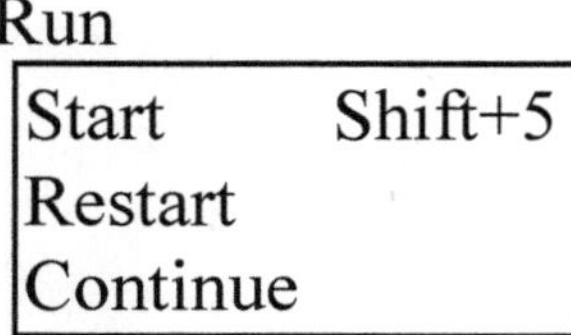

Fig 1-12 The Run menu

1. To run your program, choose the **Start** option.

2. If your program is interrupted and you want to continue where you left off use the **Continue** option.

The other menus are going to be left until later.

Exercise 1-2

1. Move to a directory called \p1

2. Get into QBASIC and enter the following program. Don't worry too much about lower or upper-case as QBASIC will sort it out for you.

```
INPUT "Enter name"; name$
FOR c = 1 TO 100
        PRINT name$
NEXT c
```

3. Save the program giving it the name first.bas.

4. Run your program.

5. If you need to make any corrections because it won't work properly make sure that you save it again.

6. Exit from QBASIC.

7. Examine the contents of the file called first.bas using the TYPE command.

2. A first attempt at programming

2.1 Introduction

A computer program can be thought to consist of 3 different components:

Input, Processing and Output

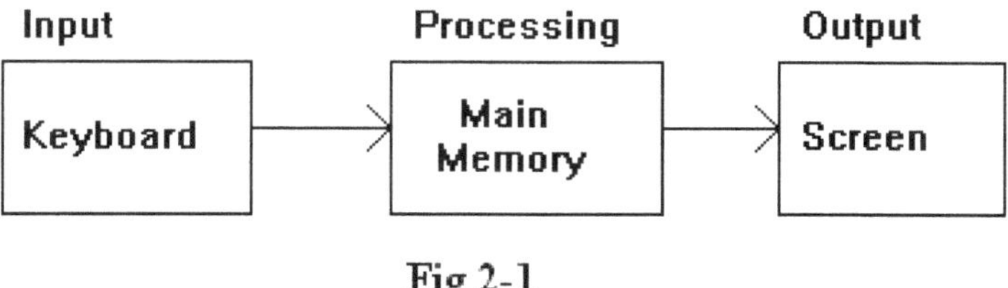

Fig 2-1

Input is the action of transferring data from an external device such as a keyboard or mouse to locations in main-memory.

Output is the action of transferring data from main-memory to an external device such as a screen or printer.

Processing is the term used here to describe the operations on data in main-memory.

Some or all of these components must be present in a program. Although it must be admitted that a program with no output would be rather pointless as it would be rather difficult to verify that it had in fact worked.

2.2 Arithmetic Expressions

When solving a simple problem in arithmetic using pen and paper we often write down an expression which summarises how the numbers are to be combined.

e.g. $\frac{5 \times 25}{9} + 32$

We can make this expression more general by using letters in place of one or more of the numbers. These letters are being used as variables and are there in our expression to represent any number we might choose to substitute.

The expression would now look like:

$\frac{5 \times C}{9} + 32$ and we could indicate we wish to make a substitution by writing let **C = 25**

In QBASIC we are also able write down expressions like this.

The two previous expressions would look like this:

5 * 25 / 9 + 32

and

5 * C / 9 + 32

Check out the table (fig 2-2) below to make sure that you know how QBASIC represents the arithmetic operators.

Going back to the original expression $\frac{5 \times C}{9} + 32$

We often want to write this as an equation giving a name to the result that we have just worked out. i.e.

$$F = \frac{5 \times C}{9} + 32$$

This is exactly what we do in our program.

F = 5 * C /9 + 32 This we interpret as multiply C by 5 then divide by 9, add 32 and store the result in F

What we have written down now is called a statement, as it will perform some defined action. Whereas an expression is to be thought of as part of a statement. This particular statement is called an **assignment** statement. The = character is the assignment operator. Below is a table containing a summary of the arithmetic operators.

Operation	Operator	Example	Result
Addition	+	3 + 5	8
Subtraction	-	12 - 9	3
Multiplication	*	3 * 7	21
Division	/	36 / 4	9
Raise to power	^	2 ^ 3	8
Negation	-	-1	-1
Integer Division	\	17 \ 3	5
Modulo Division	MOD	17 MOD 3	2

Fig 2-2 Arithmetic operators

Every one will already be familiar with the operators add (+), subtract(-), multiply (*), and divide (/). You may however have less familiarity with the other operators so I propose that we look at these in some more detail.

The exponential operator (^), also referred to as **raise to the power of** is used in situations where repeated multiplication takes place.

In mathematics $2 \times 2 \times 2 \times 2 \times 2 \times 2 \times 2$ can be written as 2^7 where the 7 (referred to as the power or index) is the number of times that 2 is multiplied by itself.

In QBASIC we could write this as 2*2*2*2*2*2*2 or as 2 ^ 7.

You can also use exponentials to represent square roots etc. For example consider the following :

$\sqrt{29}$ can be written as $29^{.5}$ or as $29^{½}$

in QBASIC this is represented as 29 ^ .5

Exponentials are also used in Mathematics to represent either very large numbers or very small numbers using what is called **standard form**.

31200000000 is written as 3.12×10^{10}

in QBASIC we would write 3.12 * 10 ^ 10

and 0.0000000067 or 6.7×10^{-9} is written as 6.7 * 10 ^ -9

The operators \ (integer division) and MOD could be employed as follows:

Suppose you had to convert 165 days into weeks and days remaining you would do the following:

165 \ 7	will divide 165 by 7 giving a whole number of weeks
165 MOD 7	will divide 165 by 7 giving the remainder (i.e. days remaining)

When the calculations get more complicated we need to worry about the order of evaluating the expression.

The order of working things out (Precedence) is as follows:

1.	Work out the contents of brackets first	( )
2.	Work out powers	^
3.	Unary operators	+, -
4.	Work out Multiply and divide	* , /, \
5.	Modulo division	MOD
6.	Lastly work out addition and subtraction	+, -

For example going back to the example c * 5 / 9 + 32 is interpreted as multiply c by 5, divide this by 9 and then add 32.

Using the table it is obvious why the multiplication and division is done before the addition. But why is the multiplication done before division?

That is because expressions in QBASIC are evaluated left-to-right and the multiplication operator is encountered first.

We could have rewritten this expression as 32 + 5 / 9 * c and it will still give us the same result. Multiplication and division is still done before addition because of the rules of precedence. This time however division is performed before multiplication. We could rewrite this example again as **(32 + 5) / 9 * c** but in this case we would get a different result. That is because the brackets, having a higher precedence, will force us to perform the addition first. This tells us that if we do need to perform operations of lower precedence first, we should enclose them between brackets.

Now consider the following expression:

$$\frac{n^2 - 1}{n - r}$$

A first attempt at coding this might look like this:

```
( n ^ 2 - 1 ) / n - r
```

Here we have remembered to put brackets around the top half of the expression to indicate that all of it is divided by n - r. We need to do the same with the bottom.

The correct version is:

```
( n ^ 2 - 1) / ( n - r )
```

A safe rule to employ is:

If in doubt, put brackets around it.

2.3 A first look at the storage

When working out the previous problem using pen and paper we write the final result and any intermediate workings on the paper. To do this in a QBASIC program we need to store the result in main memory or print it out.

Memory is organised as a large collection of units called words. The example below (fig 2-2) shows a chunk of memory split up into words to store numbers. When you store a number you are giving a name to the location as well as physically storing the number. This enables us to get back to the data we stored, simply by using the name we set up.

Variable name	Memory	address
c	0	1000
x	12.7	1004
min	0	1008
total	27.7	1012
		1016
		1020

The following statements (assignment statements) would set up the memory in fig 2-2

c = 0	Find some memory, call it c and store 0 in it.
x = 12.7	Store 12.7 in x.
min = c	Copy the contents of c to min
total = x + 15	Add 15 to the contents of x and store in total

Generally speaking the assignment statement is of the form:

variable = expression

Where **expression** can be an arithmetic expression, an expression involving strings or a logical expression. In every case the expression on the right-hand-side of the = sign is worked out or evaluated and the value is stored in the variable on the left-hand-side. Whatever type of expression is being used the assignment statement is a convenient way to store intermediate results.

Going back to the problem of performing a temperature conversion from Centigrade to Fahrenheit, we can now write:

```
C = 25              -- Store 25 in C

F = C * 5 / 9 + 32  -- Multiply the contents of C by 5
                       divide by 9 and add 32
                       then store the result in F
```

When you encounter problems involving more complicated expressions it is a good idea to break down the expression into several components. Then expressions corresponding to each of the components can be written. These components can then be combined to solve the problem as a whole. We will be examining this later in the chapter.

Exercise 2-1

1. Given the following QBASIC statements work out the values of all variables

```
x = 5
y = 3
z = 7 + x * y
a = (7 + x) * y
b = 10 + (z + x) / y
c = x * 5 ^2 + 10
```

2. Write assignment statements to work out the following:

(a) $V = 4\Pi r^2$ (b) $c = \sqrt{a^2 + b^2}$

(c) $S = \frac{a(r^n - 1)}{r - 1}$ (d) $c = 2t^3 + \frac{72}{t^2}$

2.4 Storing Characters

A string constant is a collection of characters enclosed by double quotes

"abcd", "QWERTY" , "1234" are all examples of string constants.

Individual characters or strings of characters can also be stored in memory by means of assignment statements. The variable for storing the string is designated as a string variable by the $ type tag which always appears at the end of the variable name.

name$ = "Tony"	Store the String constant "Tony" in name$.
myname$ = name$	copy the string in name$ into myname$.
n = name$	is an invalid assignment because n and name$ are of a different type.(Type mismatch.)
empty$ = ""	An empty string is represented by a pair of quotes and nothing between.

The only operator available for strings is +. This is called the **concatenation** operator and is used to join 2 strings.

word$ = "End" + "ing"	gives you the string "Ending" which is stored in word$.
fname$ = "Tony" lname$ = "Hawken" myname$ = fname$ + " " + lname$	myname$ has the string "Tony Hawken" stored in it.

2.5 The PRINT statement

So far we have looked at how to store data in memory, and in the case of numeric data we have manipulated the data to perform some calculation before storing the result in another variable in memory. Up till now we have no way of knowing what the result is, as we have not produced any output.

The PRINT statement is used for output to the screen.

You can use it for displaying String constants (Literal Strings)

```
PRINT "Print this string on the screen"
```

It can be used to print the contents of String variables

```
name$ = "Tony"
PRINT name$
```

It can be used to print a mixture of String constants and contents of variables.

```
name$ = "Tony"
PRINT "My name is "; name$          Note the use of ; and , as separators.
PRINT "My name is ", name$
```

Type in the above statements. Describe the difference between the first and second PRINT statement.

The PRINT statement can also be used to print out the results of arithmetic calculations.

PRINT 2 + 3	Print value of an arithmetic expression containing the sum of 2 constants.
x = 6 y = 10 PRINT x * y + 5	Print value of arithmetic expression involving variables.
PRINT	Print a blank line.
PRINT " Heading "	Print a literal string.
PRINT "The value of C is "; C	Print a literal string followed by the contents of a numeric variable.

A complete program might look like this:

```
PRINT "Program to compute Fahrenheit given Centigrade"
PRINT
C = 25
F = C * 5 / 9 + 32
PRINT
PRINT "The temperature "; C; "Centigrade is"; F; "degrees Fahrenheit"
```

2.6 Better looking output

A typical screen is 80 characters in width. For situations where you want to line up your output in columns you can use a TAB statement in preference to printing literal strings containing a fixed number of spaces. The TAB statement takes the form TAB(n) where n is the character position to start printing on. You would use this in conjunction with the print statement.

```
PRINT TAB(10); name$; TAB(30); tel$
```

The above example starts printing the value of name$ at character position 10 and then moves to character position 30 before printing the contents of tel$.

The output generated by several of these statements might look like this:

```
Fred Bloggs    345-4567
Andy Pandy     345-4321
Bill Benn      345-6543
```

An alternative to using the TAB function to specify which column position to start printing is to use the SPC function. SPC specifies the number of spaces to print next. For example SPC(10) means print 10 spaces.

For example we could have written

```
PRINT TAB(10); name$; TAB(30); tel$
```

as

```
PRINT TAB(10); name$; SPC(5); tel$
```

provided that the string name$ were the same length each time.

For interactive programs where a more user-friendly interface for data entry is required you can make use of the LOCATE statement. For text purposes the screen is typically divided into 25 lines or rows and 80 columns or character positions across the screen.

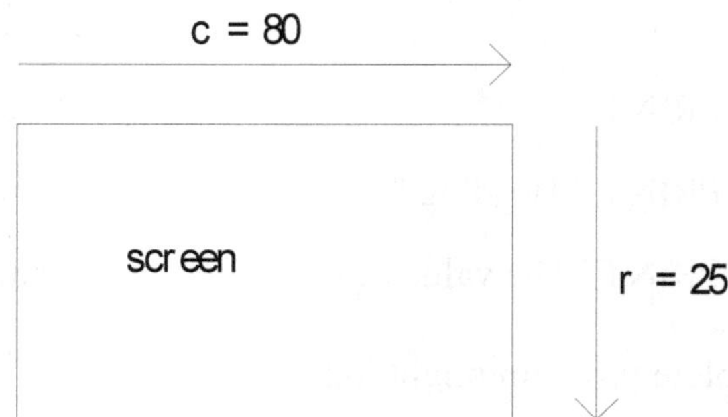

Fig 2-3 The dimensions of a screen in Text mode

The character position where you want to start printing can be identified by using the statement:

LOCATE r, c

Where r is the row (or lines down) and c is the column position (or characters across). The next PRINT statement will start printing at this position.

2.7 The INPUT statement

The input statement provides us with the means of getting input from the keyboard

```
INPUT C                          -- Accept keyboard input and store it in C
F = C * 5 / 9 + 32
PRINT F
```

When you run the program you get something like this:

```
?                                -- This is a prompt to enter data at the keyboard
                                    But what type of data is required ?
```

Lets redo this program so that we get a prompt to indicate the type of data required. We could use a PRINT statement to provide a prompt.

```
PRINT "Enter temperature in Centigrade"
INPUT C
```

or better still

```
PRINT "Enter temperature in Centigrade (0 - 100)"
INPUT C
```

Or you can just use an INPUT statement to get the same effect.

```
INPUT "Enter temperature in Centigrade "; C
```

As you can see it is important to provide an appropriate prompt when data has to be entered. This should indicate the type of data i.e. numeric or character data, and if possible, indicate a range of values that would be acceptable.

```
INPUT "Enter a temperature in Centigrade (0 - 100) "; C
```

It is just as important to document your programs, so that somebody who reads them gets a better understanding of how your program works. This is particularly the case when the programs become much longer and complicated.

The REM statement is a means of providing comments. It has no effect on the running of the program. It just provides a means of saying what the program does.

```
REM   Comment goes here.
REM   Any thing on the right-hand side of a REM is ignored
'     This is another form of comment equivalent to REM
```

A complete program using the above statements might look like this:

```
REM  -- Program to convert Centigrade to Fahrenheit
'
INPUT "Enter Temperature in Centigrade (0 - 100) : "; C
F = C * 5 / 9 + 32       ' Compute temperature in F
PRINT "The temperature "; C; "Centigrade is "; F; "degrees Fahrenheit"
```

Notice how you can place comments anywhere on a line; i.e. you don't have to put REM or ' at the beginning of a line to include a comment.

There are times when you want to enter many numbers from the keyboard. For example consider the problem of computing the average of 5 numbers.

```
INPUT a
INPUT b
INPUT c
INPUT d
INPUT e
average = (a + b + c + d + e) / 5
PRINT "Average of 5 numbers entered is "; average
```

This same program could be written as:

```
INPUT "Enter 5 numbers separated by commas ", a, b, c, d, e
average = (a + b + c + d + e ) / 5
PRINT "Average of 5 numbers entered is "; average
```

An attractive way to prompt the user for input, especially when a lot of data is to be entered is to use a combination of LOCATE, PRINT and INPUT statements. The following is an illustration.

```
LOCATE 5, 10
PRINT " Enter a number between 1 and 10"
LOCATE 7, 10
INPUT "Your number : ", num
```

If this were to be repeated you would obviously write over the top of the previous output, and that would look messy. One way round that is to execute the following code first:

```
SLEEP 2       ' Wait for 2 seconds
CLS           ' Clear the screen
```

Because the comma is always treated as a separator in the INPUT statement it is not possible to include a comma as part of the data. Consider the following:

```
INPUT "Enter address "; addr$
```

If you were to enter:

```
25a The High Street, Any Town, SE14 5HJ
```

You would get the following error message:

```
Redo from the start
```

You could get round this problem by using a LINE INPUT statement. LINE INPUT provides for the assignment of a string variable of an entire line (Including comma's and speech marks). The above statement should be rewritten as:

```
LINE INPUT "Enter address "; addr$
```

2.8 A Solved Problem

A quadratic equation is an equation of the form $ax^2 + bx + c = 0$

It can be solved with the formula

$$x = \frac{-b \pm \sqrt{b^2 - 4ac}}{2a}$$

This provides us with two solutions which can be coded as:

$$x_1 = \frac{-b + \sqrt{b^2 - 4ac}}{2a}$$

x1 = -b + (b * b - 4 * a * c) ^ .5 / (2 * a)

and

$$x_2 = \frac{-b - \sqrt{b^2 - 4ac}}{2a}$$

x2 = -b - (b * b - 4 * a * c) ^ .5 / (2 * a)

You will notice that **(b * b - 4 * a * c) ^ .5** is repeated in both assignment statements, and so to make the computation more efficient, it should be broken down into smaller components.

```
d = (b * b - 4 * a * c) ^ .5        ' only worked out once
x1 = (-b + d) / (2 * a)
x2 = (-b - d) / (2 * a)
```

The complete program will then end up like this:

```
REM -- Program to solve quadratic equations
INPUT "Enter coefficients a, b, c "; a, b, c
d = (b * b - 4 * a * c) ^ .5
x1 = (-b + d) / (2 * a)
x2 = (-b - d) / (2 * a)
PRINT "x is either "; x1 ; " or "; x2
```

Exercise 2.2

1. Write a program that will display the following on the screen :

```
********************************
*                              *
*      MERRY CHRISTMAS         *
*                              *
********************************
```

2. Write a program that will:

(a) allow a user to enter their Name, Address and Telephone number.

(b) print out the name, address and telephone number just entered.

3.

$$\text{Gas Mark} = \frac{F - 275}{25} + 1$$

gives an approximate conversion from degrees Fahrenheit to the British Gas mark on a cooker for temperatures between 275 and 1000 degrees F. Write a short program that will:

(a) allow a user to enter a temperature in Fahrenheit that is between 275 and 1000.

(b) compute the Gas mark and print out the result in an appropriate format.

(c) include appropriate comments to make the program readable.

4. (i) Write a program to display a menu such as:

```
                MENU
                -------

1.          Play Space Invaders
2.          Play PACMAN
3.          Play Super Mario
4.          Quit Menu
```

(ii) Extend the program so that it will accept user input. Make appropriate use of prompts and experiment with TAB and LOCATE.

2.9 Including data in a program

At times it is inconvenient to assign data to variables directly, or by means of using INPUT statements. This is particularly the case when you are running a program that requires a vast amount of data (especially if it is numerical data) because it is difficult to enter without making mistakes and also very time consuming.

An alternative approach is to store the data in the program using DATA statements, and then to use an appropriate number of READ statements to transfer this data into variables.

Consider the following:

```
READ name$, age                 '    Read first two pieces of data
                                '    into name$ and age respectively
PRINT "Name entered is "; name$
PRINT "Age is "; age
.
.
.
DATA "TONY", 38, "ADAM", 41, "JESSICA", 9
```

A subsequent READ statement of form READ name$, age will move on to the next two pieces of data and assign them to the variables name$ and age.

The RESTORE statement re-initialises the DATA pointer so that you can start reading the data again from the beginning.

The next program shows you how you can use READ and DATA to solve equations. Going back to a previous example that was to solve quadratic equations. Instead of using INPUT a, b, c or equivalent statements to enter the data we could use the following:

```
READ a, b, c
                        ' work out values of x1 and x2
                        ' print the solution

.                       ' read some more data for the next equation
.                       ' and so on
.

DATA 3, 6, 11           ' data for first equation
DATA 5, 7, 8            ' data for second equation
DATA 12.4, 23.3, 17.6   ' data for third equation
```

You can also use it to good effect when dealing with string data.

3. Selection -- Making a choice

3.1 Comparison and Logical Operators

When programming decisions and repetitions we often need the following operators:

Operator	Meaning
<	< **(less than)**
>	> **(greater than)**
<=	≤ **(less than or equal)**
>=	≥ **(greater than or equal)**
=	= **(equal to)**
<>	≠ **(not equal to)**
AND	**Logical and**
OR	**Logical or**
NOT	**not**

The operators <, >, ≤, ≥, =, ≠ are known as relational operators. They are used to form a comparison between 2 numbers or 2 strings.

A comparison such as :

a < b   will evaluate to 0 or -1

A value of 0 is to be interpreted as meaning **False** and a value of -1 as **True.** This is an example of a logical expression and its value can be printed like any other expression.

Should you have problems working out the truth values of logical expressions, you can always check by printing them out.

PRINT a < b   should display 0 or -1.

The unary operator NOT is used to negate an expression. That is an expression whose value is 0 will become -1 and vis versa.

This can be written as:

NOT a < b

or to make things clearer especially when the expressions become more complicated:

NOT (a < b)

The logical operators AND and OR are used to combine simple logical expressions to form more complex ones. Here is an example.

x > 5 AND x < 20

An expression formed with an AND operator like the one above will only evaluate true if both of the simpler conditions are true. In the example above we are testing whether the value of x is in the range 5 and 20.

i.e. **$5 < x < 20$**

The logical operator OR when used to combine two expressions will evaluate true if either or both of the expressions are true.

The expression **x > 5 OR y = 0** is interpreted as true if either of the expressions or both evaluate true.

When compound expressions get more complicated it is often necessary to include brackets to make the expression more readable, or possibly because you are unsure about the precedence.

The expression **(x > 5 AND x < 20) OR y = 0** is an example of this.

Here the brackets are unnecessary as AND has higher precedence than OR. It does however break the expression up and make it more readable

For your clarification I have included truth tables of the operators AND, OR and NOT.

AND

x	y	x AND y
F	F	F
T	F	F
F	T	F
T	T	T

OR

x	y	x OR y
F	F	F
T	F	T
F	T	T
T	T	T

NOT

x	NOT x
F	T
T	F

Fig 3-1 Truth tables

Exercise 3.1

1. Some examples of boolean (relational) expressions follow

(a) 5 = 7

(b) 9 <= 9

(c) 11 > 14 - 5

(d) (15 > 5) OR (7 = 0)

(e) (15 > 5) AND (7 = 0)

(f) NOT (15 > 5) OR NOT (7 = 0)

(g) NOT (15 > 5) AND (7 = 0)

(h) NOT ((15 > 5) AND (7 = 0))

For each of the 8 expressions above determine whether they evaluate true or false.

You can check your answers by running a QBASIC statement of the form:

PRINT < boolean expression >

Remember 0 = false

-1 = true

3.2 Conditional Statements

We often want the execution of a statement to depend on a condition. This is achieved using a conditional statement such as an IF statement.

In QBASIC the simplest format of the IF statement is:

IF <expression> THEN <statement>

This is to be interpreted as if the expression is true execute the statement, otherwise do nothing.

e.g. **IF num > 0 THEN PRINT "num is positive"**

This can be extended to provide an action if the expression evaluates false.

e.g. **IF num > 0 THEN PRINT "positive" ELSE PRINT "non-positive"**

Generally speaking the IF ... THEN ... ELSE construct as shown above has the following format:

IF <expression> THEN <statement 1> ELSE <statement 2>

which should be interpreted as:

Evaluate the expression. If it is true execute statement 1, otherwise execute statement 2.

This example can be taken a stage further. After all if we are going to classify numbers we might want to say they are Negative, Zero or Positive.

IF num < 0 THEN PRINT "negative" ELSEIF num > 0 THEN PRINT "positive" ELSE PRINT "ZERO"

The ELSEIF enables us to provide another test, and hence another statement to execute if the second expression evaluates true. If neither of the conditions is true then the final statement is executed. Unfortunately QBASIC is not a free-format language. You have to type all of this in on one line. This may be difficult especially if you have many conditions to test, and even possibly complicated expressions to evaluate as well.

Fortunately there is a second format for the IF statement which overcomes these problems. The above statement can be rewritten as:

```
IF num < 0 THEN
        PRINT "negative"
ELSEIF num > 0 THEN
        PRINT "positive"
ELSE
        PRINT "zero"
END IF
```

This also provides other benefits:

1. You can have as many ELSEIF clauses as you like

2. You can specify many statements to be executed for each condition

As an example I give you the following.

```
IF num < 0 THEN
        REM -- Negative action
        PRINT "Number is negative"
ELSEIF  num > 0 THEN
        REM -- Positive action
        PRINT "Number is positive"
ELSE
        ' Catch all condition -- if none of the above
        ' Number must be zero if is neither positive or negative
        PRINT "Number is zero"
END IF
```

This is the full format of the IF statement, often called a multiway statement. It is an implementation of a construct in Computer Science called the CASE structure. Later on in this chapter we will see that there is another statement which can be used in many situations where the IF statement could be used for multiway selection.

3.3 Example Program

(a) Write a program which will accept a given year. The program will then determine whether this year is a leap year and print an appropriate message. You may consider using the following rules for determining leap years.

- The year is divisible by 4 but not by 100
- The year is divisible by 4 and by 400

(b) Continue this program by allowing a user to enter a number that represents a month. Given this month and the fact that the year is a leap year, or not a leap year will work out how many days in the month.

Solution

(a)

```
INPUT "Enter year "; y
IF (y MOD 4 = 0 AND y MOD 100 <> 0) OR (y MOD 4=0 AND y MOD 400 = 0) THEN
    leapyear$ = "t"          ' flag to indicate leapyear
    PRINT "Year "; y; " is a leapyear"
ELSE
    leapyear$ = "f"
    PRINT "Year "; y; " is not a leapyear"
END IF
```

(b)

```
INPUT "Enter month (1 - 12) "; m
IF (m = 4) OR (m = 6) OR (m = 9) OR (m = 11) THEN
    days = 30
ELSEIF (m=1) OR (m=3) OR (m=5) OR (m=7) OR (m=8) OR (m=10) OR (m=12) THEN
    days = 31
ELSE                 ' Must be February
    IF leapyear$ = "f" THEN
        days = 28
    ELSE
        days = 29
    END IF
END IF
PRINT "There are "; days ; " in the month entered"
```

Try to figure out the logic of the last part of the program. What is the condition for 29 days to be returned?

3.4 The SELECT CASE statement.

Go back to the solution of the previous worked example. You will notice that the IF statements became rather complicated. We even had problems fitting the conditions on one line. What is more the test to see how many days to assign to February is a little confusing. Fortunately there is a much neater solution to this problem and others like it. Part (b) of the previous program could be written as follows.

```
INPUT "Enter month (number 1 - 12) "; m
SELECT CASE m
    CASE 4, 6, 9, 11
        days = 30
    CASE 1, 3, 5, 7, 8, 10, 12
        days = 31
    CASE 2
        IF leapyear$ = "n" THEN
            days = 28
```

```
        ELSE
            days = 89
        END IF
END SELECT
PRINT "There are "; days; "in the month entered"
```

In general the SELECT CASE statement starts with:

SELECT CASE expression

Where the expression evaluates either a numeric or a string value.

At the end the SELECT CASE statement is delimited by:

END SELECT

In between there are one or more CASE clauses. These CASE clauses are of the form:

CASE expression

Where expression can be:

a constant such as 4
a variable such as x
an arithmetic expression e.g. 2*n + 5
a relational expression (e.g.   IS > 0)
a list of constants (e.g. 4, 5, 8)
A range of values (e.g. 0 TO 10)

Each of these CASE clauses is providing a condition to test against the original SELECT CASE expression. If a match is provided there are statements to execute.

After these conditions, just before the END SELECT you could add the clause

CASE ELSE

followed by some other statements. This is a catch-all condition. It will only evaluate true if all the previous conditions evaluated false. The statements which follow it will only be executed if and only if all the other conditions evaluate false.

Exercise 3.2

1. (a) Write a program that will prompt a user to enter a number between 1 and 100

   (b) Test the number input to see if it is:

   (i) even
   (ii) odd
   (iii) greater than 50

   (c) Print appropriate responses for each of these tests.

2 Write a short program which will prompt a user for an exam mark in the range 1 - 100 and will respond by printing the mark and grade.

The rules for awarding grades are as follows:

mark	**grade**
79 - 100	A
67 - 78	B
54 - 66	C
40 - 54	D
< 40	F

3. A local company want to make a start at automating their payroll system. Currently the wage packets are made up individually. They get paid in cash and have a pay receipt that details hours worked, rate of pay, overtime and gross pay etc.

   (a) Assuming a basic week is 37.5 hours and any time over this is to be treated as overtime which is to be paid as 1.5 times the standard rate. Write a program that will accept input from the user for:

   Employee name, hours worked, rate of pay

   (b) Continue the program by working out:

   the overtime worked
   the basic salary (not including overtime)
   the overtime pay
   the gross pay (basic salary + overtime pay)

   (c) Extend this calculation by including the nett pay. Nett pay is calculated by deducting 25% tax from the taxable income. Assume that the first £60 of the weekly salary is non-taxable income.

   (d) Design a suitable pay-slip that will include all the information mentioned above. Amend your program so that it will print out a pay-slip corresponding to your design

3.5 Conditional statements and String comparison.

You can also use the relational operators for string comparisons. The order of two characters is determined by the relative value of their ASCII code. (See Appendix 2). Roughly speaking the purpose of performing String Comparison is to order strings according to alphabetical order. This of course will work provided that only alphabetic characters of the same case are used in the strings.

In the ASCII table we have :

		codes
Numeric characters	0 - 9	48 - 57
Uppercase characters	A - Z	65 - 90
Lowercase characters	a - z	97 - 122

As well as punctuation characters, various non-printing characters and also some graphics characters are present.

So we could write the following valid expressions:

"a" < "b"	Each of these can be verified by checking
"Z" < "a"	an ASCII table.
"4" < "6"	

Two strings are ordered by comparing their characters one at a time until there is a mismatch.

Consider the following:

"business" < "busy"

Which can be represented as:

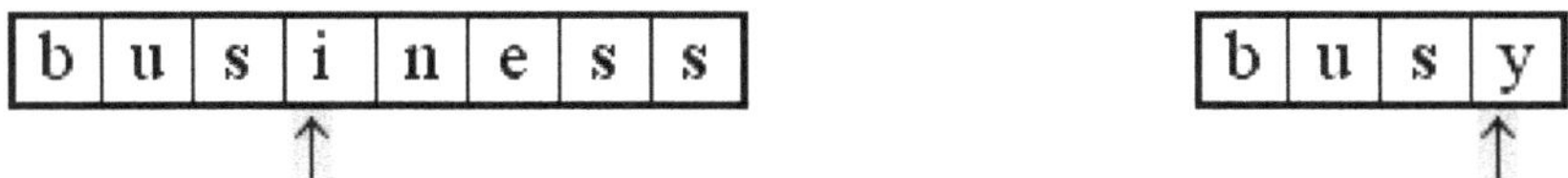

Here the first mismatch is at character position 4 indicating that "business" < "busy". In the same way if we consider the comparison of:

"word" < "words"

This would evaluate true because the first mismatch would be detected on the fifth character, making this expression true.

String expressions can be formed using all of the relational operators

<, <=, >, >=, =, <>, AND, OR, NOT

in exactly the same way that you can form expressions with numeric data. These expressions are then likely to be used to form part of a conditional statement.

3.6 Validation and Verification

Selection can be usefully employed to check input data. There are two main ways to check input data, Validation and Verification.

Validation is the process of the program checking that the data is input reasonable, and so likely to be correct. The following program fragment is used as an example.

```
INPUT "Enter a number between 1 and 10 "; num
'         validate data
IF (num >= 1) AND (num <= 10) THEN
          PRINT "Data correct"
ELSE
          PRINT "Invalid data"
END IF
```

This example uses a range check to see if the number entered is between 1 and 10 as requested.

Here is another.

```
INPUT "Enter name (10 characters) ", name$
IF LEN(name$) > 10 THEN
          PRINT "Name too long "
          PRINT " Truncation will occur"
'         name$ = LEFT$(name$, 10)
END IF
```

In this example a string function called LEN is used. This function computes the length of the string. Sometimes it is necessary for strings/fields in records to be a fixed length so it is necessary to truncate the string name$ so that it will fit in the record. The function LEFT$ is used in this case to extract the 10 left-most characters which are then stored in name$.

These and other string handling functions will appear in a later chapter. So don't worry too much about them yet.

Data can also be checked using a technique called verification. **Verification** is the process of getting the user to check the data. In practice this either means getting the user to enter the data again and the program checking that the data is exactly the same, or printing out all the data supplied, then ask the user if it is correct. These two techniques are illustrated below.

Input data entered twice

A common technique to check that a user has not mis-typed their password is to make them enter the same password twice. It can also be used in other situations where it is easy to make a mistake, such as typing in coded data.

```
INPUT "Enter new password "; pass1$
INPUT "verification -- please type again "; pass2$
IF pass1$ = pass2$ THEN
```

```
        pass$ = pass1$
ELSE
        PRINT "Verification Error -- Password unchanged"
END IF
```

User checks input data

Alternatively the program can display the data just entered, and request that the user checks to see if the data is correct.

```
INPUT "Enter Name : "; name$
INPUT "Enter Address : "; addr$
INPUT "Enter telephone number : "; tel$
CLS
PRINT " The details just entered are : "
PRINT
PRINT "Name : "; name$
PRINT "Address : "; addr$
PRINT "telephone number : "; tel$
PRINT
INPUT "Are these correct (y/n) ", ans$
IF ans$ = "Y" OR ans$ = "y" THEN
        ' process details
ELSE
        PRINT "Data ignored -- verification error"
END IF
```

3.7 Example program using String comparison.

1.(a) Write a program that prints a menu in the format and accepts input from a user to indicate their choice:

```
                MENU
                -------

1.      NAME        -- search for record by persons name

2.      ADDRESS     -- search for record by address

3.      TELEPHONE   -- search for record by telephone number

4.      QUIT        -- quit the menu

Enter your choice :
```

(b) The program will now print out the choice from the menu. At a later date the program will also include statements to perform the required action. For the moment leave comments indicating where this code will go. You should also check for invalid input.

Solution

```
REM   -- Example Menu program
CLS
PRINT "                                   MENU"
PRINT "                                   --------"
PRINT
PRINT " 1.            NAME          --  select record by persons name"
PRINT
PRINT " 2.            ADDRESS       --  select record by address"
PRINT
PRINT " 3.            TELEPHONE  --  select record by telephone number"
PRINT
PRINT " 4.            QUIT          --  quit the menu"
PRINT
INPUT " Enter your choice: "; choice$
'
SELECT CASE  choice$
        CASE  "NAME", "name"
                PRINT " select record by persons name "
                '       code for selecting record by name goes here
        CASE  "ADDRESS", "address"
                PRINT " select record by address "
                '       code for selecting record by address goes here
        CASE  "TELEPHONE", "telephone"
                PRINT " select record by telephone number"
                '       code for selecting record by telephone
                '       goes here
        CASE "QUIT", "quit"
                PRINT "quitting the menu"
        CASE ELSE
                PRINT " invalid choice entered"
END SELECT
```

Exercise 3.3

1. Write a short program that will prompt a user to enter 3 names. These names will then be printed back in alphabetical order.

2. (a) Write a program that will store information about local pubs in DATA statements. Each set of DATA statements corresponding to each pub should include the name, town, brewery and price of a pint.

   (b) The program should start off with a menu which will offer the following choices.

      1. Search by Name of Pub
      2. Search by Town
      3. Search by Brewery

   (c) After the user enters their choice, the program should perform a search for the required pubs. For each match all of the data should be printed out.

4. Repetition.

4.1 Looping a fixed number of times

A previous program that we looked at in chapter 2 involved the calculation of 5 numbers input at the keyboard. It looked like this:

```
INPUT a
INPUT b
INPUT c
INPUT d
INPUT e
average = (a + b + c + d + e)
PRINT average
```

This program does the job intended. But is is a bad example of programming as it is difficult to modify to satisfy similar problems. What do we do if we want a progam to calculate the average of 100, 1000 or more numbers?

You will notice in this form there is a pattern that is repeated 5 times. Each time we input a number. In QBASIC we can repeat statements a fixed number of times using a FOR statement. We could for instance write:

```
FOR c = 1 TO 100
        INPUT "Enter number"; num
NEXT c
```

The variable called **c** is called a control variable and is used to count how many times the statement(s) are to be repeated. In this example 100 times. The control variable **c** starts with a value of 1 (initial value), and each time the program loops a number is input and **c** is incremented by 1 until 100 is reached (final value).

We now have a problem in that every time we execute

INPUT"Enter number"; num

we lose the number previously entered. We need to adopt a slightly different strategy.

```
total = 0
FOR C = 1 TO 100
        INPUT "Enter number "; num
        total = total + num
NEXT C
```

We have included a variable called **total** so that we can get a running total each time we enter a number. Done this way it doesn't matter if **num** is overwritten. Notice how total is set to 0 initially. Why is this ? ...

The final program can now be written as:

```
total = 0
FOR c = 1 TO 100
        INPUT "Enter number "; num
        total = total + num
NEXT c
average = total / (c - 1)
PRINT " Average value is "; average
```

This version is a much better version and should we want a program to calculate the average of 1000 numbers it is an easy matter to change the program.

This program assumes that we know in advance how many numbers you are going to enter. If you are likely to have a different number of numbers to enter each time you run your program you could at least enter at the keyboard how many numbers you intend to process.

```
INPUT "How many numbers "; n
FOR c = 1 TO n
        '       process data
        '
NEXT c
```

Choosing a different problem, we can also make other uses of the control variable.

```
PRINT "         Multiplication Tables"
PRINT "          ---------------------"
INPUT "Enter number (table you want to practice) "; num
FOR c = 1 TO 10
        PRINT c; " * "; num; " = " ; c * num
NEXT c
```

In this example the control variable **c** is also used in the calculation **c * num** etc.

In general the for statement can be writtten as:

FOR counter = start TO end [STEP increment]
    statement(s)
NEXT [counter]

The **STEP increment** part enables us to change how much is to be added to the control variable each time. The default value is 1. This increment can be a whole number (say 10) , it can be a fraction (such as .1) or even a negative number.

```
FOR n = 100 TO 1 step -1
        PRINT n
NEXT n
```

The above piece of code illustrates how you can count backwards.

Exercise 4-1

1. Refer back to chapter 2 and look at the program to convert Fahrenheit to Centigrade. Modify this program so that the temperature in Centigrade is worked out for all temperatures 32 - 212F.

2. Write a program that will test for prime numbers.

   (a) A prime number has two divisors only (1 and iself). Start by testing all the numbers that divide into the given number.

   (b) You may want to use the MOD operator to test for a remainder on division, and the operator \ for integer division.

   (c) A nice extension would be to print a listing of all the factors in ascending order.

3. Refer back to section 2.7. Redo the problem of solving quadratic equations.

   (a) Your data for each coefficent should be stored in data statements.

   (b) There should be sufficient data to solve 10 quadratic equations.

   (c) The program should print out the solutions for all 10 equations.

4.2 Repeating an unknown number of times.

Suppose we want to work out the average of all numbers until there are no more numbers to enter. We now have the problem of telling the program there is no more data to enter. This can be achieved using a data terminator. That is we can choose a value which can't possibly be a valid data value for the problem in question and then test the value entered each time.

The following is a first attempt at calculating the total:

```
total = 0
DO
        INPUT "Enter number : "; num
        total = total + num
LOOP UNTIL num = -1
PRINT total
```

The above can be interpreted as meaning repeat the statements between **DO** and **LOOP** until num is set to -1.

There are two things wrong with it. We have no way of knowing how many numbers have been entered, and also the value of **total** is wrong. Somehow or other the data terminator -1 has been added to the total.

You could get round the problem as follows:

```
total = 0  :  c = 0
DO
        INPUT "Enter number : "; num
        IF num <> -1 THEN
                total = total + num        ' These statements don't get executed
                c = c + 1                  ' if the data terminator has been entered
        END IF
UNTIL num = -1
average = total / c                        ' We are now able to compute average
PRINT "Average is "; average
```

A more elegant solution would involve rearranging the statements.

```
total = 0  :  c = 0
INPUT "Enter number : "; num
DO
        total = total + num
        c = c + 1
        INPUT "Enter number : "; num
LOOP UNTIL num = -1
average = total / c
PRINT "Average is "; average
```

There are alternative but equivalent ways of using the **DO ... LOOP** construct. For completeness I have included them below:

1.
```
DO
        statement(s)
LOOP UNTIL num = -1
```

2.
```
DO UNTIL num = -1
        statement(s)
LOOP
```

3.
```
DO                                 ' In these examples you will notice
        statement(s)               ' that the condition has been negated
LOOP WHILE num <> -1
```

4.
```
DO WHILE num <> -1
        statement(s)
LOOP
```

And yet another way to do exactly the same thing is as follows:

5.
```
WHILE num <> -1
        statement(s)
WEND
```

In each case the condition is evaluated at the beginning of the loop. This means in theory that any of these looping constructs will repeat the statement(s) zero or more times.

4.3 Example programs

1. Write a program which will to obtain a number at random. It will then continue to prompt you to enter your guess until you get it right. It should also include refinements a display of the number of attempts taken.

```
REM -- Guess the number
CLS
PRINT "Guess the number ( 1 - 100 )"
PRINT
RANDOMIZE TIMER
num = INT(RND * 100) + 1
'
c = 1
INPUT "Enter your guess ", n
DO
        IF n = num THEN
                PRINT "Correct after "; c; " attempts"
        ELSE
                PRINT "Wrong number -- try again"
                IF n > num THEN
                        PRINT "Your guess is too big"
                ELSE
                        PRINT "your guess is too small"
                END IF
                PRINT " You have taken "; c; " attempts so far"
                SLEEP 4
                c = c + 1
                CLS
                INPUT "Enter your guess"; n
        END IF
LOOP UNTIL n = num
PRINT "You took "; c - 1; "attempts to guess the number"
```

The following statements you won't have seen yet.

```
RANDOMIZE TIMER          ' This will use the timer to generate a random
                         ' seed
num = INT(RND * 100) + 1 ' This will use the seed to generate a random
                         ' number between 0 and 1 which will be scaled
                         ' up to a number in the range 1 - 100
```

2. Write a program that will test the knowledge of capital cities. The data is to be stored using DATA statements and will terminate when a data terminator is detected.

```
REM -- Capital cities Quiz
CLS
WHILE country$ <> "ZZZZ"
        READ country$, capital$
        PRINT "The capital of "; country$; " is ";
        INPUT answer$
        IF answer$ = capital$ THEN
                PRINT "correct"
        ELSE
                PRINT "wrong answer"
                PRINT "The correct answer is "; capital$
        END IF
WEND
DATA "FRANCE","PARIS"
DATA "POLAND","WARSAW"
DATA "PORTUGAL","LISBON"
DATA "ITALY","ROME"
DATA "SPAIN","MADRID"
DATA "CHINA", "BEIJING"
DATA "ZZZZ","EOF"
```

3. Write a program to compute $\tan^{-1}x$ which is given by the series:

tan-1 x = $x - x^3/3 + x^5/5 - x^7/7 + ...$

```
REM -- compute arc tan
'
CLS
INPUT "Enter value of x: "; x
termx = x: sum = x
FOR n = 2 TO 100
        prod = termx * -x * x
        sum = sum + termx / (2 * n - 1)
NEXT n
PRINT "arc tan is "; sum
```

Here you will notice that each new term can be generalised as $(-x)^{2n-1}/(2n-1)$. But working out each term like this involves much computation. An easier method is to recognise that the power of -x can be calculated by multiplying the previous power of x by $-x^2$. Successive terms can then be obtained by dividing this by 2n-1.

Exercise 4-2

1. Refer back to question 3 in exercise 3-2. You are to continue this program so that it will produce a pay slip for each employee. In addition the program will:

   (a) Calculate the total salary and average salary of all employees as well as the total amount of tax paid by all employees.

   (b) Calculate the minimum and maximum salaries.

2. A travel agency specialising in European holidays needs a currency conversion program so that if a customer were to ask how much they could get for a certain amount of money, the agent can provide a quick reply.

Tourist rates

Country	rate	currency
Austria	17.00	Schillings
Belgium	49.75	Francs
Cyprus	0.74	Pounds
Denmark	9.50	Kroner
Finland	8.10	Marks
France	8.22	Francs
Germany	2.42	DM
Greece	363.00	Drachma
Holland	2.73	Guilders
Ireland	1.00	Punts
Italy	2360.00	Lira
Malta	0.56	Liri
Norway	10.53	Kroner
Portugal	253.00	Escudos
Spain	199.00	Pesetas
Sweden	11.57	Kroner
Switzerland	2.07	Francs
Turkey	47383.00	Lira

   (a) Write a program that will store this information in DATA statements

   (b) Include statements which will allow a user to enter the country they intend to visit and the amount of spending money they have.

   (c) The program will now search for the country they are going to visit, obtain the exchange rate and currency and perform the conversion.

   (d) Produce output in a suitable format with the amount of currency rounded to two decimal places.

4.4 Nested Loops

One of the earliest examples of repetition we looked at involved the production of multiplication tables. The simplest program to do this would look something like this:

```
INPUT "Enter a number (1-10) ", num
FOR n = 1 TO 10
        PRINT n * num
NEXT n
```

This would output a sequence of numbers which would be multiples of the number chosen. If you wanted the output on one line the body of the FOR loop could be replaced by the statement:

```
        PRINT n * num;
```

You may now want to modify this program to repeat this for all the numbers 1 - 10 rather than just 1. This could be achieved by having an additional control variable and repeating the code 10 times. You might start with the following:

```
FOR table = 1 TO 10
        FOR n = 1 TO 10
                PRINT table * n
        NEXT n
NEXT table
```

This will produce a stream of 100 numbers, 1 per line. What you probably wanted was a table made up of 10 lines, each line having 10 numbers. You will get yourself in an even worse mess if you just append a semi-colon to the end of the print statement. You also need to remember that you need to go on to a new line every 10 numbers.

If you take this into account and do something to tidy up the appearance of the output you will probably end up with something like this:

```
PRINT "Multiplication tables " : PRINT
FOR table = 1 TO 10
        PRINT table; "times table ";
        FOR n = 1 TO 10
                PRINT USING "###"; table * n;
        NEXT n
        PRINT           ' Need a new line after 10 numbers
NEXT table
```

What we have ended up with is a program that uses nested FOR loops. That is you have a FOR loop inside a FOR loop. The inner FOR loop is responsible for producing one line of output containing a label identifying which times table is being printed followed by 10 numbers. The outer loop repeats this operation 10 times, once for each line of output.

An extension of the PRINT statement (PRINT USING) is also being used to format the output. This ensures that the numbers in each column line up. In this example the number will occupy 3 character positions. This will be explained in more detail in the next chapter, but because it is such a useful feature for printing numbers I will continue to use it in the next examples.

Another application which uses the same technique is the printing of bar-charts. Given some input data, a simple bar chart or pictogram can be produced by a printing the same number characters as the data read. In this example an asterisk will be used and the data will be stored in DATA statements.

```
REM -- Produce bar chart for protein requirements
CLS
PRINT "Protein requirements (grams per day)"
PRINT
FOR c = 1 TO 9
        READ label$, amount
        PRINT USING "\                    \"; label$;
        FOR n = 1 TO amount
                '       Body of inner FOR loop for producing a bar of asterisks
                PRINT "*";
        NEXT n
        PRINT
NEXT c
'
DATA "Baby 3-6 months", 14,  "Child 7-9 years", 30,  "Boy 15-19", 50
DATA "Office worker", 45, "Manual Worker", 45, "Old man over 75", 38
DATA "Woman", 38, "Pregnant woman", 44, "Woman feeding baby", 55
```

And finally a more realistic example to produce a table. This time the table is the sort of thing a bank or building society might produce for its customers.

```
REM -- Print value of £1000 invested after adding compound interest
CLS
PRINT "Rate",
PRINT USING "##.#"; 3; SPC(8); 3.5; SPC(8); 4; SPC(8); 4.5; SPC(8); 5
FOR n = 1 TO 10
        PRINT "Period";
        PRINT USING "###"; n;
        FOR i = 3 TO 5 STEP 0.5
                PRINT USING "#########.##"; 1000 * (i / 100 + 1) ^ n;
        NEXT i
        PRINT
NEXT n
```

5. More Input and Output

5.1 Experimenting with colour

To make the output on the screen look more appealing you can introduce colour. In text mode there are 16 basic colours.

Number	Colour	Number	Colour
0	Black	8	Grey
1	Blue	9	Light Blue
2	Green	10	Light Green
3	Cyan	11	Light Cyan
4	Red	12	Light Red
5	Magenta	13	Light Magenta
6	Brown	14	Yellow
7	White	15	Intense White

Fig 5-1 Colours in Text Mode

The colours that you intend to use can be specified using the COLOR statement which has the format:

```
COLOR f, b
```

Where f is the foreground colour and b is the background colour.

Note : The background colour is not for the entire screen but for a small rectangle surrounding the character. Normally this would take the same colour as the rest of the screen.

The COLOR statement is used in conjunction with PRINT statements.

e.g.

```
COLOR 2, 0
PRINT "This line gets printed in Green"
COLOR 4, 0
PRINT "This line gets printed Red"
```

In all of these cases the background colour is black.

This use of colour can be particularly effective in situations where you need to emphasise text to make it more interesting to read. Another thing that you can do to get attention is to make the text blink. This can be achieved by adding 16 to the value of **f**, the foreground number.

e.g.

```
COLOR 18, 0
PRINT "Press a key to continue"
```

You can check out the effect of including background colours by typing in and running the following:

```
COLOR 4, 7
PRINT "Demo text"
```

And you will notice that the text is red, and the immediate background surrounding the string is white. This feature could be employed if you wanted to indicate the length of a string to be input.

```
e.g.        LOCATE 3, 8
            PRINT "Enter name:" ' Display prompt
            LOCATE  3, 20       ' Set up field marker
            COLOR 4, 7          ' "      "     "
            PRINT "          "  ' 10 spaces -- indicate string  is 10 characters
long
            LOCATE 3, 20        ' Position cursor over field
            INPUT name$
```

In all there are 64 different colours available to you but there are only 16 available at a time. The current set of 16 colours is called your palette of colours. You can however change any of the colours in your palette. They are physically implemented in QBASIC by putting aside 16 memory locations each of which store a number representing the colour. Think of these memory locations as being labelled 0 - 15 then they will have a number in them that represents the colours in fig 5-1. (See Fig 5-2).

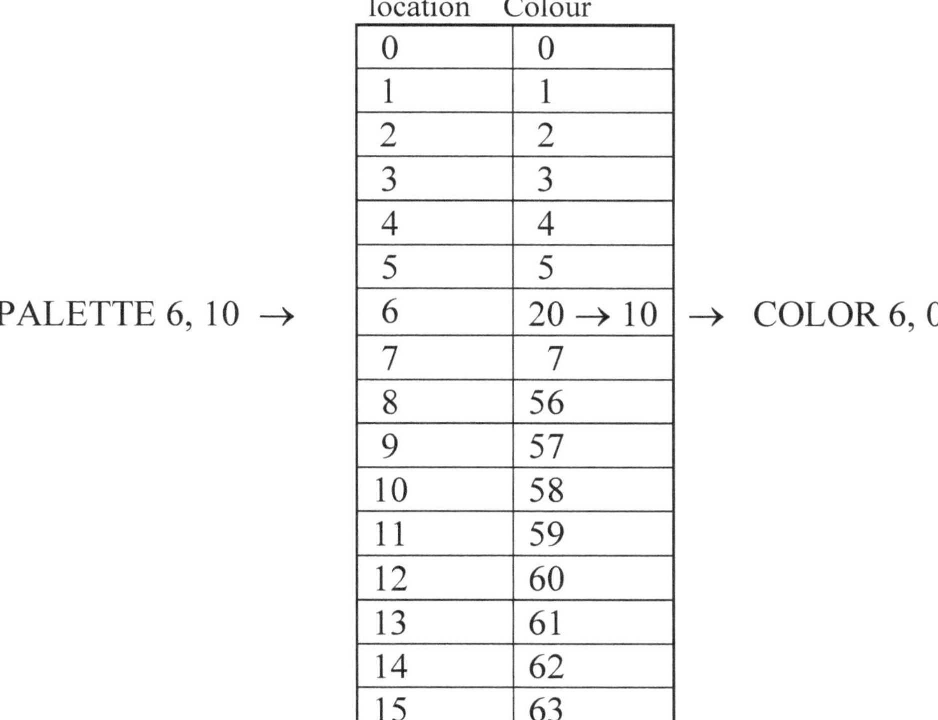

location	Colour
0	0
1	1
2	2
3	3
4	4
5	5
6	20 → 10
7	7
8	56
9	57
10	58
11	59
12	60
13	61
14	62
15	63

Fig 5-2 How the PALETTE statement updates the colour table.

The PALETTE statement is used to update the colour table. It has the form:

PALETTE m, c

Where **m** refers to the memory location and is a number in the range 0 - 15, and **c** is a number in the range 0 - 63 which represents the colour. It is to be interpreted as meaning update locate m with colour c.

You can now select your colour by using a COLOR statement:

COLOR f, b

which means locate the number in location f and change to the colour represented by this colour. Any statements which produce output on the screen , such as PRINT statements will be displayed in this colour.

Note if you change the colours in your palette by subsequent PALETTE statements then text already printed on the screen may mysteriously change colour. This can easily be demonstrated by trying out the program below:

```
REM - demonstrate effect of PALETTE command
CLS
LOCATE 5, 5
PRINT "colour"
COLOR 1, 0
LOCATE 5, 20
FOR c = 1 TO 10
        PRINT CHR$(219);
NEXT c
FOR n = 0 TO 63
        SLEEP 2
        PALETTE 1, n
NEXT n
```

5.2 PRINT USING ...

Numeric data can present problems when you want to display it in neat columns. Normally you want to print the numbers so that the are right justified like this:

Th	H	T	U
1	1	0	1
		2	3
	4	2	1
			9

This display can be produced by the following program:

```
PRINT "ThHTU"
FOR c = 1 TO 4
        READ num
        PRINT USING "#####"; num
NEXT c
DATA 1101, 23, 421, 9
```

The **format specifier** "#####" allocates a field 5 numeric characters in length. The PRINT USING statement takes the value of num and places it in the field so that num is right justified.

Other format specifiers allow you to format real numbers. Consider the following examples:

1. #### — Take an integer up to 4 characters in length.

   If a real number is entered it will be rounded to the nearest whole number.

2. ####.## — Allocate a field 7 characters in length including decimal point. Up to 4 characters to the left and up to 2 on the right of the decimal point.

   If a real number containing more than 2 decimal places is entered it will be rounded to 2 decimal places. Less than 2 decimal places the number will be filled with trailing zeros.

3. ###,###,###.## — Large numbers can be grouped into groups of 3 digits.

4. +####.## — Numbers can be signed. In this case positive numbers will always have a + sign in front, negative numbers a -.

   ####.##+ — Using this variation the sign will appear last.

5. ####.##- A minus sign will appear if negative, a space otherwise.

6. £#####.## Currency sign such as £ or $ can be printed in front for representing numbers as money.

7. *#####.## Will place an asterisk at the beginning.

8. **#####.## or **£#####.## Will replace all leading spaces by asterisks. This is a very useful facility when printing cheques as it stops people altering the amount on the cheque.

When dealing with very large numbers you need to be able to print the number in an exponential format.

1. #.##^^^^ Used for displaying numbers in exponential format.

The number 12340000 using "#.##^^^^" is displayed as 0.12E+08. If you want it displayed in standard form you will need to use the format specifier "##.##^^^^". Now you will get 1.23E+07.

Note if ever you enter a number where the number of digits on the left-hand-side exceeds the size in the field you get an indication of overflow.

Consider the following program segment:

```
num = 123456.789
PRINT USING "#####.##"
```

will give %123456.79 (The % indicates overflow -- an indication that you need to change your format specifier).

PRINT USING can also be used to format Strings. You can use the following:

1. "&" used if you want to include the entire string.

   e.g.
   ```
   name$ = "Tony Hawken"
   PRINT USING "&"; name$
   ```

   or a more likely specifier would include literal text such as in the following

   ```
   PRINT USING "My name is & . How are you ?"; name$
   ```

2. "!" will extract the first character from any string.

3. \ \ Will extract a specified number of characters from the beginning of the string. That is the number of characters taken up by the format specifier.

You can even store the format specifier in a string variable. Now we can write the following:

```
f$ = "My name is \  \"
name$ = "Tony Hawken"
PRINT USING f$; name$
```

giving the output:

```
My name is Tony
```

This gives us a lot more flexibility especially when we want to write complex format specifiers which include several strings or numbers to be formatted.

The following illustrate this:

```
t1$ = "The number"
t2$ = "can be written as "
t3$ = "to 2 decimal places"
num = 12.2345
PRINT USING "&  ##.#### & ##.## &"; t1$, num, t2$, num, t3$
```

or can go even further by writing:

```
f$ = "& ##.#### & ##.## &"
PRINT USING f$; t1$, num, t2$, num, t3$
```

5.3 Output to a printer.

So far the only output we have considered has involved output to a screen. There are many applications where a printout is required as well. Consider the previous problem of producing a payroll for a small company. This is an obvious candidate for producing printed output.

The LPRINT statement can be used in same way as the PRINT statement, but this time the output is directed to a printer.

```
LPRINT "name: "; name$
                                is essentially the same as
PRINT "name: "; name$
```

except that output is sent to a printer in the case of LPRINT statements. The use of ; to suppress carriage return, and , and TAB to format into print-zones is also the same.

One major problem with using LPRINT is performing form-feeds. At the end of your printed page you need to include:

```
LPRINT CHR$(12)          ' perform a form-feed
```

Without this you may find that the last page of your printout gets stuck in the printer. Should you forget and you want to fix the situation you can do the following:

1. Exit to DOS

2. Create an empty file. (Could use the DOS editor)

3. PRINT empty.txt (where empty.txt is an empty file).

Another problem is the width of the line on a printed page. Usually you want no more than 80 characters and should more be required you will want the text to be wrapped around to the next line.

This can be achieved with the statement:

```
WIDTH n              ' if your output is directed to the screen
```

or

```
WIDTH "LPT1"; n      ' if output is directed to the printer
```

Where n specifies the maximum number of characters before a linefeed takes place.

And finally if you want formatted output, in place of PRINT USING ... you can use LPRINT USING ... statements.

A very common situation in interactive programs is the use of both PRINT and LPRINT statements. The PRINT statements are there for the user of the program and the LPRINT statements are intended for the desired output.

e.g.

```
INPUT "Enter name: "; name$
INPUT "Enter address: "; addr$
PRINT " These are the details input"
PRINT
PRINT name$; addr$
INPUT "Are they correct (y/n) "; ans$
IF ans$ = "y" OR ans$ = "Y" THEN LPRINT name$, addr$
.
.
LPRINT CHR$(12)     ' Print a form-feed at the end
```

Exercise 5-1

1. Write a program that will:

   (a) Store 10 numbers in DATA statements.

   (b) Input the user for a format string.

   (c) Read the 10 numbers and print them out using the format string.

   Extend the program so that it will continue to loop until you indicate that you have had enough.

2. Modify the previous program to read strings and will output them using input format strings.

3. Go back to exercise 4-2 Q1. Modify this program so that it can now produce printed payslips.

4. Write a program that will allow a form teacher to record the end-of-year marks for Mathematics, English and Science for each member of their form.

   (a) The program should allow the teacher to enter the name and marks for up to 20 students.

   (b) Each mark entered should be a number representing a percentage.

   (c) The output of the program should be in the following format:

	Student Name	Maths	English	Science	Average
1	Tony Hawken	92	62	73	75.67
2					
3					
4					
.					
.					
.					
n					
	Class Average	--	--	--	--.--

5.4 Using String Functions

In most applications it is extremely important to manipulate text such as sentences, words and characters. Up until now our string manipulation has been rather limited. Only concatenation and use of format strings with the PRINT using ... statement.

To put this right we will now look at some string functions. See fig 5-3.

The first thing that we are going to do is to extract substrings. In QBASIC this is done using the LEFT$, RIGHT$ and MID$ functions.

LEFT$("Encylopaedia", 7) returns the 7 left-most characters in the string.
i.e. "Encyclo".

RIGHT$("Encyclopaedia", 6) returns the 6 right-most characters in the string.
i.e. "paedia".

MID$("Encyclopaedia", 3, 5) returns the 5 character substring starting at character position 3. i.e. "cyclo".

In each case we can either store the return value or print it out.

e.g. sub$ = LEFT$("Encyclopaedia", 7)

e.g. PRINT LEFT$("Encyclopaedia", 7)

Another useful function is the LEN function. This returns the number of characters in a string. It can be used to validate strings to check that they are not too long etc. The following program is used to demonstrate this.

```
INPUT "Enter filename 1-8 characters "; file$
IF LEN(file$) > 8 THEN
        PRINT "Filename too long"
        PRINT "truncated to first 8 characters"
        file$ = LEFT$(file$, 8)
END IF
file$ = file$ + ".dat"
```

In other situations you may want to search for a particular substring. The INSTR function returns the position of a given substring.

```
name$ = "Hawken, Tony"
l = LEN(name$)
cpos = INSTR(name$, ",")
PRINT RIGHT$(name$, l - cpos); " "; LEFT$(name$, cpos - 1)
```

In this example we are using INSTR to locate the position of a comma so that we can reverse the forename and lastname.

Operation	Name of Function	Example	Result
Length	LEN	LEN$("Words")	**5**
Find location of substring	INSTR	INSTR("Word","r") a$ = "Encyclopaedia" b$ = "lop" INSTR(a$, b$)	**3** **6**
Extract left part of string	LEFT$	LEFT$("Words", 3)	**"Wor"**
Extract right part of string	RIGHT$	RIGHT$("Words", 3)	**"rds"**
Extract middle part of string	MID$	MID$("Words", 3, 1)	**"r"**
Convert string to number	VAL	VAL("1994")	**1994**
Convert number to string	STR$	STR$(1994)	**"1994"**
Change to lowercase	LCASE$	LCASE$("Words")	**"words"**
Change to uppercase	UCASE$	UCASE$("Words")	**"WORDS"**
Current date	DATE$	DATE$	**"18-06-1994"**
Current time	TIME$	TIME$	**"09-37-10"**
Remove leading spaces	LTRIM$	LTRIM$(" Words")	**"Words"**
Remove trailing spaces	RTRIM$	RTRIM$("Words ")	**"Words"**
Add spaces	SPACE$	SPACE$(5)	" "

Fig 5-3 Built in String Functions.

When you want to compare strings using the relational operators <, <=, >, >=, =, <> it is important to make sure that the characters you are comparing are the same case. To ensure that this is so you can either convert everything to uppercase or lowercase using the functions LCASE$ and UCASE$ respectively. Here is an example:

```
sentence$ = "This is the example text to search"
INPUT "Enter word to search for"; word$
wpos = INSTR(sentence$, LCASE$(word$));
PRINT "Word searched for found at position "; wpos
```

It is useful to be able to convert from numeric data to string and vis versa. This is because certain operations that you might want to perform on string data are not possible. We can use the VAL function to convert a string to a number and the STR$ function to convert a number to a string.

example 1

```
INPUT "Enter year"; yr
year$ = STR$(yr)
PRINT "Date is "; "June " + year$
```

example 2

```
INPUT "Enter year "; yr$
yr = VAL(yr$)
PRINT "Next year is ", yr + 1
```

And finally if you want to use the current date in your program, you can obtain the system date by using the function DATE$.

```
dat = DATE$
day = LEFT$(dat, 2)
month = MID$(dat, 3, 2)
year = RIGHT$(dat, 2)
PRINT "Day is "; day
PRINT "Month is "; month
PRINT "Year is "; year
```

5.5 Character Input

The keyboard input we have seen so far has involved use of INPUT statements. Whenever data is entered it must be terminated with a carriage return. Consider the following program fragment:

```
PRINT "                    Menu"
PRINT "                    -----"
PRINT
PRINT " 1.    NAME         -- Search for record by persons name"
PRINT " 2.    ADDRESS      -- Search for record by address"
PRINT " 3.    TELEPHONE    -- Search for record by telephone number"
PRINT " 4.    QUIT         -- Quit the Menu"
PRINT
INPUT "Enter your choice: "; choice
SELECT CASE choice
       CASE 1
              '       process by NAME
       CASE 2
              '       process by ADDRESS
       CASE 3
              '       process by TELEPHONE
       CASE 4
              '       QUIT
END SELECT
```

It would be nice if we could respond by pressing a single key. This can be achieved using an INPUT$ statement. The above INPUT statement could be rewritten as:

```
PRINT "Enter your choice (1 - 4) ";
choice$ = INPUT$(1)
```

The INPUT$ statement above will pause until a key is pressed and will then assign the character pressed to choice$. INPUT$ will only return strings. If you want a number you will have to convert it using the VAL function.

i.e. choice = VAL(choice$)

Similar to the VAL and STR$ functions are the character handling functions ASC and CHR$. The ASC function takes as an argument a character and returns a number (the ASCII code). The CHR$ function is the inverse of ASC. It takes as an argument an ASCII code and returns a character. These two functions in conjunction with INPUT$ provide an even more flexible approach to character I/O.

If we are to use CHR$ with INPUT$ it means we can use other keys besides such as the function keys etc. You can usually find the ASCII code of any key on your keyboard by inspecting a table of ASCII codes or alternatively you could write a simple program to display the ASCII code of keys pressed. Such a program might look like this:

```
ch$ = INPUT$(1)
PRINT "the ASCII code is "; ASC(ch$)
```

A common key used to quit whatever you are doing is the **Esc** key. This key has an ASCII code 27. With this knowledge you might want to extend the above program fragment so that you can experiment further with ASCII codes.

```
DO UNTIL a$ = CHR$(27)
        a$ = INPUT$(1)
        PRINT "Key just pressed has an ASCII code "; ASC(a$)
LOOP
```

Another use of INPUT$ is illustrated in the following program. Here it is the intention to use the keys d, u, l and r to move the cursor down, up, left and right.

```
REM -- Demonstration of INPUT$ to position the cursor -- version 1
CLS
r = 1 : c = 1
DO UNTIL a$ = CHR$(27)
        a$ = INPUT$(1)
        SELECT CASE a$
                CASE "d", "D"
                        '       Move cursor down
                        r = r + 1
                CASE "u", "U"
                        '       Move cursor up
                        r = r - 1
                CASE "l", "L"
                        '       Move cursor left
                        c = c - 1
                CASE "r", "R"
                        '       Move cursor right
                        c = c + 1
                CASE " "
                        '       Plot character
                        LOCATE r,c
                        PRINT CHR$(176)
        END SELECT
LOOP
```

In this example program pressing the spacebar is used to plot the character ░. This program however is very poor in that no check is made to see if the cursor has moved off the screen. You will recall that a standard text screen has 25 lines with 80 characters on each line. so each time a key is pressed to move the cursor a simple check should be made to test the current value of **r** and **c**.

An improved version of the program might look like this:

```
REM -- illustration of INPUT$  to move the cursor -- version 2
CLS
r = 1 : c = 1
DO UNTIL a$ = CHR$(27)
        a$ = INPUT$(1)
        SELECT CASE a$
                CASE "d" , "D"
                        '       Move cursor down
                        IF r < 25 THEN
                                r = r + 1
                        ELSE
                                PRINT CHR$(7)           ' Beep
                        END IF
                CASE "u" , "U"
                        '       Move cursor up
                        IF r  > 1 THEN
                                r = r - 1
                        ELSE
                                PRINT CHR$(7)
                        END IF
                CASE "l" , "L"
                        '       Move cursor left
                        IF c > 1 THEN
                                c = c - 1
                        ELSE
                                PRINT CHR$(7)
                        END IF
                CASE "r" , "R"
                        '       Move cursor right
                        IF c < 80 THEN
                                c = c + 1
                        ELSE
                                PRINT CHR$(7)
                        END IF
                CASE " "
                        '       Plot character
                        LOCATE r, c
                        PRINT CHR$(176)
        END SELECT
LOOP
```

A furthur improvement would be to use the arrow keys instead of **u**, **d**, **l** and **r**.
A first attempt might assume the following ASCII codes:

↓	↑	←	→
28	29	30	31

But unfortunately it is not quite as simple as that. We can't get away with the following:

```
SELECT CASE ASC(a$)
        CASE 28
                r = r + 1
        CASE 29
                r = r - 1
        CASE 30
                c = c - 1
        CASE 31
                c = c + 1
        CASE 32
                PRINT CHR$(176)
END SELECT
```

The reason for this is that most computers use two characters to represent certain keys on the keyboard. The arrow keys in particular are some of the keys to be represented in this manner. So if you are going to write programs that are going to to use such keys you must make sure you are familiar with the way in which they are represented. So some keys are represented by one character, and others by two. This would indicate that we wouldn't be able to use INPUT$ as we need to know how many characters are going to be returned in advance. Fortunately we can use an INKEY$ statement. The statement:

```
ch$ = INKEY$
```

returns the characters if any waiting in the keyboard buffer. Unlike INPUT$ the program does not pause until you have typed something in.

If a key is pressed the character codes for that key are stored in ch$. If ch$ is one character long then ch$ contains just the ASCII code. If it is 2 characters in length the key is represented by a scan code and an ASCII code. To find out what the codes are try out the following program. You will then be in a position to rewrite the programs to move the cursor around the screen.

```
DO
        ch$ = INKEY$
        IF LEN(ch$) = 1 THEN
                PRINT "ASCII code is "; ASC(ch$)
        ELSE
                PRINT "Scan code is "; ASC(LEFT$(ch$, 1))
                PRINT "ASCII code is "; ASC(RIGHT$(ch$, 1))
        END IF
LOOP WHILE ch$ <> CHR$(27)
```

Exercise 5-2

1. In certain old books the date printed is displayed using Roman numerals. As a reminder the Roman numerals have the following values:

I	1
V	5
X	10
L	50
C	100
D	500
M	1000

   Write a program which will accept a Roman Numeral and will then convert it to an ordinary decimal number before printing it out.

2. Write a program that will draw boxes such that:

(a) The size of the box can be determined by a given length and height

(b) The location can be determined by the co-ordinates of the top left-hand corner
(c) You use the characters below:

Code	Character	Code	Character	Code	Character
201	╔	187	╗	205	═
200	╚	188	╝	186	║

Fig 5-4 Extended ASCII characters

(d) Experiment with inserting Text in such a box.

3. Write a program that will:

(a) Move a cursor around the screen by pressing the arrow keys

(b) Print CHR$(176) every time the space-bar is pressed

(c) If the space-bar is pressed and the current character has ASCII code 176 will overwrite this with a space (rub out the character).

   Hint.. You can check the ASCII code of the current screen position by using the statement:

   code = SCREEN(r,c)

   This will assign the ASCII value of the character on line r, column c to code.

6. Time for an Assignment

6.1 Introduction

At some time in your course you will need to hand in an assignment, which as well as the printout of your program will include other documentation. How much and in what form you present your write up very much depends on the course you are following. Typically you may well have to include some or all of the following.

1. **A statement of the problem** (or specification).

   In simple terms you need to know what the project is about. If you choose your own assignment, it is up to you to provide the specification.

2. **An Analysis.**

   This is your interpretation of the problem. You are supposed to explain the problem in such a way, to show that you understand what is required, and suggest how it could be attempted. An analysis often involves research. You could look for similar problems and discuss how they relate to the problem that you have to solve.

3. **Design.**

   A design is a plan of how you are going to solve the problem. In this particular case, how you are going to write a QBASIC program.

   It is typically made up of a number of components such as:

   - Design of Input. e.g. Screen layout and data entry
   - Design of Output e.g. Output to screen and /or printer
   - Data Storage
   - Design of the program

4. **Implementation**

   This means writing the program and getting it to work. Proof of this stage is often satisfied by providing a listing of the program, and some of the output from the program.

5. **Testing**

   The first criteria for testing a program is to ensure that it produces the correct results in all situations. This often involves providing test data to see if you get the results that you would expect to get. Another thing to consider is the ease of use to a user.

6. Evaluation of the System

Here you have to discuss your solution.

As this is an early stage of your course you can't be expected to include all of these features. I am going to concentrate on producing the program using techniques that have been discussed in the previous 5 chapters. Also you probably haven't been taught any formal design techniques. For that reason I am going to use techniques that appeal to common sense rather than use any formal design methods.

6.2 The Problem

A company that currently sells Computer Consumables by mail order, wants to replace the printed catalogue by a Computerised Ordering System. In very simple terms they want a program that will list the items for sale, allow the customer to enter the quantities they wish to order before printing out the Order Form. The program should also make provision for collecting the customer details.

This program is to be distributed on a 3½" inch floppy disk. The customer runs the program, after entering the details obtains a printed order form. The customer then sends the order form with a cheque for the computed total to obtain the required goods.

To satisfy the company that you are able to write such a program, you are invited to write a smaller version of the program for ordering floppy disks.

You are expected to use the following information:

Floppy Disk type	Disks	Unit price per-box	Qty
Maxell Disks	3.5 DS DD	10	4.49
	3.5 DS HD	10	6.49
	5.25 DS DD	10	2.99
	5.25 DS HD	10	4.79
TDK Disks	3.5 DS DD	10	4.79
	3.5 DS HD	10	6.99
	3.5 DS HD (coloured)	20	14.99

The order form must also contain the following customer details:

Name , Address line 1, Address line 2, Town, Postcode, Country, Postcode and Telephone number.

6.3 Getting Started

It is probably best to start with screen layout. Try reproducing the information in the catalogue on the screen. It is important that you keep the screen layout simple and tidy. Make sure that the columns of letters and figures always line up.

For those of you who find this difficult, you may want to start by writing out the text on graph paper. You will now be able to decide where each column should start.

At this stage you can type you program in to make sure that the text appears how you intend it to. Remember to use TAB statements to start at a particular column position. The difficult part is getting the decimal point of numbers to line up. PRINT USING and a suitable format string will solve this problem.

If you want a pleasing 'User-friendly' screen it is important to be able to position the cursor next to a meaningful prompt. It is also useful if you indicate the maximum number of characters that you can enter, and the sort of data that is valid. A simple technique is to print a string such as "------" which the user can type over when they enter their data.

Having done this you may already have encountered some problems, and had to change your mind. Take notes as you go along. This is useful if at some point you can't get the program to work. It is also useful when you want to write some documentation.

6.4 Design

Most teachers tell you to complete your design before attempting to use the computer. This is all very well if are an experienced programmer and know what you are doing. I would advise that at first you try out some ideas for small parts of the program, and experiment. All the time taking notes.

Then when you feel you have some idea of what you are doing you are ready for design. Designing a program is the process of piecing the bits together. You may however as part of the design process have to rebuild some of the bits. The thing to remember is 'There are many ways to write a program, All of them correct'.

A program design usually starts with the programmer considering screen layout for input and output. The programming itself is usually very easy when you know where things are to appear on the screen. Plan it on paper first. Then write a few test programs to try out the layout. Do this for each of the screen layouts you intend to have in your program. Keep your screen designs and the program fragments that can generate such screens. We will be using them later.

We are now in a position to start designing the program proper.

One method of designing a program is called 'Top down Design' using a technique called 'Stepwise Refinement'. The idea is to start with a very general description of the program. This description typically only has a few components. Then take each of these components in turn and provide more detail (add refinement). This often means that the components themselves get broken into smaller components, until such a time that the components are detailed enough that they can be translated into QBASIC code.

This design method can be represented using either **pseudo-code** or a more graphical means such as **structure-charts**. I intend to use both and leave it up to you which you prefer to use.

A first design could look like this:

pseudo-code

```
Order program
    Order Disks
    Do calculations
    Print Order Form
```

Structure Chart

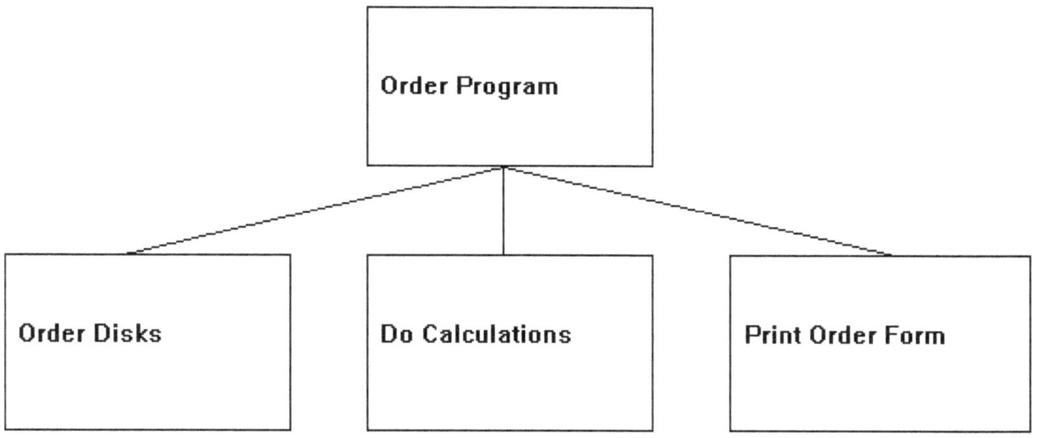

Fig 6-1 A first Design

Your first comment might be. "That is far too vague. How do I do that?"

The answer to this is simple. You need to expand each of the components that are still to vague. That is break them down into smaller components until it is possible to work out how to write the program.

A good design not only helps you to produce a program that is more likely to work without errors, but is itself a useful part of the documentation. It makes it easier for some one else to understand your program

With refinement the design may look like this:

```
Order Program
        Order Disks
                Produce Data Entry Screen
                Enter Quantity of Disks to order
                Enter Customer Details
        Do Calculations
                Calculate subtotal for each type of disk ordered
                Calculate postage
                Calculate total order value
        Print Order Form
                Print Customer Details
                Print Main Heading (Indicate the columns)
                For each Type of Disk ordered
                        Print sub-heading (Brand of Disk)
                        Print details of each disk, including subtotal (value of
                        disks)
                Print cost of postage
                Print total value of order
```

Fig 6.2 A design with refinement

I have deliberately left out the structure-chart representation. Perhaps you would like to do that yourself as an exercise.

At this stage you probably have enough detail to write the program. You may well have arrived at this design because you have already written some of the code using this algorithm.

6.5 Implementation

You program implementation or coding should be guided by your final design. Try small chunks at a time and run the program to test it. A reasonable task to attempt would be to produce a program to produce an order form to order disks. Referring back to the design we know that to order disks we need to do the following:

```
Order disks
        Produce data entry screen
        Enter quantity of disks to order
        Enter customer details
```

The first of these (Produce data entry screen) should have already been designed, and possibly coded when you designed the screen layout. To implement the second component (Enter quantity of disks to order) requires you to allow the user enter a number for each type of disk. Finally the customer details may well go on a separate screen. How to code this should be obvious from the screen design.

It is a good idea to work like this implementing and testing a small part of the program at a time. If you do have any errors it is easier to locate where things are going wrong.

Finally when you have a complete program that appears to work correctly, remember to tidy up the appearance and insert appropriate comments to describe each part of the program

A program listing of the complete program is as follows:

```
REM -- Disk Order Form
'
' Disk types
d1$ = "3.5 DS DD": d2$ = "3.5 DS HD"
d3$ = "5.25 DS DD": d4$ = "5.25 DS HD"
d5$ = "3.5 DS HD Multi-coloured"

' Unit Prices for Floppy Disks
a = 4.49: b = 6.49: c = 2.99: d = 4.79: e = 4.79: f = 6.99: g = 14.99
'
' Produce Data Entry Screen
'
CLS
PRINT TAB(20); "Floppy Disk Order Form"; TAB(40);
PRINT
PRINT "MAXELL Disks"; TAB(30); "unit"; TAB(40); "Price"; TAB(50); "Qty"
PRINT
PRINT d1$; TAB(30); "10"; TAB(40); a; TAB(50); ".."
PRINT d2$; TAB(30); "10"; TAB(40); b; TAB(50); ".."
PRINT d3$; TAB(30); "10"; TAB(40); c; TAB(50); ".."
PRINT d4$; TAB(30); "10"; TAB(40); d; TAB(50); ".."
PRINT
PRINT "TDK Disks"; TAB(30); "unit"; TAB(40); "Price"; TAB(50); "Qty"
PRINT
PRINT d1$; TAB(30); "10"; TAB(40); e; TAB(50); ".."
PRINT d2$; TAB(30); "10"; TAB(40); f; TAB(50); ".."
PRINT d5$; TAB(30); "20"; TAB(40); g; TAB(50); ".."
PRINT : PRINT
PRINT "type of postage required (UK, Europe, World)    ......"


'
```

```
' Enter quantity of disks to order
'
LOCATE 5, 50: LINE INPUT a$: a1 = VAL(a$)
LOCATE 6, 50: LINE INPUT b$: b1 = VAL(b$)
LOCATE 7, 50: LINE INPUT c$: c1 = VAL(c$)
LOCATE 8, 50: LINE INPUT d$: d1 = VAL(d$)
LOCATE 12, 50: LINE INPUT e$: e1 = VAL(e$)
LOCATE 13, 50: LINE INPUT f$: f1 = VAL(f$)
LOCATE 14, 50: LINE INPUT g$: g1 = VAL(g$)
LOCATE 17, 50: LINE INPUT p$
'
SELECT CASE UCASE$(p$)
        CASE "UK"
                postage = 1.25
        CASE "EUROPE"
                postage = 1.95
        CASE "WORLD"
                postage = 3.5
END SELECT
'
SLEEP 2: CLS
'
'    Enter Customer Details
CLS
PRINT TAB(20); "Customer Details"
PRINT
PRINT "Name:"; TAB(20); "....................."
PRINT "Address1:"; TAB(20); "..............................."
PRINT "Address2:"; TAB(20); "..............................."
PRINT "Town:"; TAB(20); "...................."
PRINT "Postcode:"; TAB(20); ".........."
PRINT "Country:"; TAB(20); "...................."
PRINT "Telephone:"; TAB(20); "................"
'
LOCATE 3, 20: LINE INPUT name$
LOCATE 4, 20: LINE INPUT ad1$
LOCATE 5, 20: LINE INPUT ad2$
LOCATE 6, 20: LINE INPUT town$
LOCATE 7, 20: LINE INPUT post$
LOCATE 8, 20: LINE INPUT country$
LOCATE 9, 20: LINE INPUT tel$
'
SLEEP 2: CLS
'
' Print out Order Form
'
LOCATE 10, 10: PRINT "Printing Order Form"
LPRINT name$
```

```
LPRINT ad1$
LPRINT ad2$
LPRINT town$
LPRINT post$
LPRINT country$
LPRINT "tel: " + tel$
'
FOR c = 1 TO 5
        LPRINT
NEXT c
'
' Print Main Heading
LPRINT "Disk Type"; TAB(30); "unit"; TAB(40); "Unit"; TAB(50); "Qty"; TAB(60);
"Subtotal"
LPRINT TAB(40); "Price"
LPRINT
'
IF (a1 <> 0) OR (b1 <> 0) OR (c1 <> 0) OR (d1 <> 0) THEN
        ' Print Subheading
        LPRINT : LPRINT "Maxell Disks": LPRINT
END IF

' Print Maxell disks ordered
IF a1 <> 0 THEN
        LPRINT d1$; TAB(30); "10"; TAB(40); a; TAB(50); a1; TAB(60); a * a1
END IF
IF b1 <> 0 THEN
        LPRINT d2$; TAB(30); "10"; TAB(40); b; TAB(50); b1; TAB(60); b * b1
END IF
IF c1 <> 0 THEN
        LPRINT d3$; TAB(30); "10"; TAB(40); c; TAB(50); c1; TAB(60); c * c1
END IF
IF d1 <> 0 THEN
        LPRINT d4$; TAB(30); "10"; TAB(40); d; TAB(50); d1; TAB(60); d * d1
END IF
'
IF (e1 <> 0) OR (f1 <> 0) OR (g1 <> 0) THEN
        ' Print Subheading
        LPRINT : LPRINT "TDK Disks": LPRINT
END IF
'
' Print TDK disks ordered
IF e1 <> 0 THEN
        LPRINT d1$; TAB(30); "10"; TAB(40); e; TAB(50); e1; TAB(60); e * e1
END IF
IF f1 <> 0 THEN
      LPRINT d2$; TAB(30); "10"; TAB(40); f; TAB(50); e1; TAB(60); f * f1
END IF
IF g1 <> 0 THEN
```

```
    LPRINT d5$; TAB(30); "20"; TAB(40); g; TAB(50); g1; TAB(60); g * g1
END IF
LPRINT : LPRINT
'
' Print out totals
disktotal = a * a1 + b * b1 + c * c1 + d * d1 + e * e1 + f * f1 + g * g1
LPRINT "Total cost of Disks = "; TAB(25); "£";
LPRINT USING "####.##"; disktotal
LPRINT "Cost of postage = "; TAB(25); "£";
LPRINT USING "####.##"; postage
total = disktotal + postage
LPRINT "Total cost = "; TAB(25); "£";
LPRINT USING "####.##"; total
LPRINT CHR$(12)
```

6.6 Testing

I am not going to spend much time telling you how to test your program at this stage.

There are some things that you need to bear in mind even for the most simple of assignments.

1. The program must work giving correct results.

   Check the results using a calculator and compare the results with those obtained using your program.

2. The Input part of the program must be easy to use

   Add additional prompts if necessary. But don't make them too complicated by including too much information.

3. The Output

   Must be neat, easy to read and convey the correct information. This is often called acceptance testing. i.e. it must be acceptable to the customer who intends to use your program.

At a later stage you will need to look at ways of making your program more robust. This involves including :

Verification - User can indicate if they are satisfied with data they have entered

Validation - The program will check to see if the data entered is reasonable
Error Checking - Program will anticipate different types of error situation and should they occur take appropriate action.

Validation and verification have been mentioned in previous chapters. If you are so inclined you may want to think about how you could use both these features and error handling to enhance the program. Wait until chapter 11, where these issues will be treated in more detail.

6.7 Evaluation

The purpose of the evaluation is to provide a realistic appraisal of your assignment. It should reveal the weak-points as well as the areas where the program fulfils the user requirements. For each of the weak-points try and suggest where and how improvements could be made.

The method used to implement an ordering system for a small part of the catalogue as asked for is adequate to tackle the task. The data entry for both disks and customer details is done in such a clear and simple way, that there is very little chance of the user entering wrong details. If this should happen there is no way of correcting the incorrect data. Also there is no validation to check whether the data entered is reasonable.

This program would also be difficult to modify to become part of a larger system. For a larger range of products it is essential to have a menu to choose the types of products to order. To make this effective it is necessary to be able to break down the code into reusable modules, such as procedures and Functions. (See chapter 8)

Functions provide a good means of validating input data. These can be added at any time. You could for instance write a module to carry out some well-define procedure only to find that it doesn't work very well with invalid data. To overcome this problem you decide to write a validation procedure. Now all you have to do is to insert a function call prior to the data being used.

There will be large amounts of data to be stored. It is not practical to use such methods as storing in variables, or using data statements. For large amounts of data it is necessary to use files. (See chapters 12, 13 and 14)

Most of the calculations to produce sub-totals for each of the products ordered are much the same. This duplication of effort could be avoided if we were able to use table structures such as arrays. (See Chapter 7)

7. Arrays

7.1 Introducing Arrays

So far we have given each variable its own name. In a program that involves much repetition this is both impractical an unnecessary. Instead give the entire collection of data items a name and identify individual elements by a number called an index.

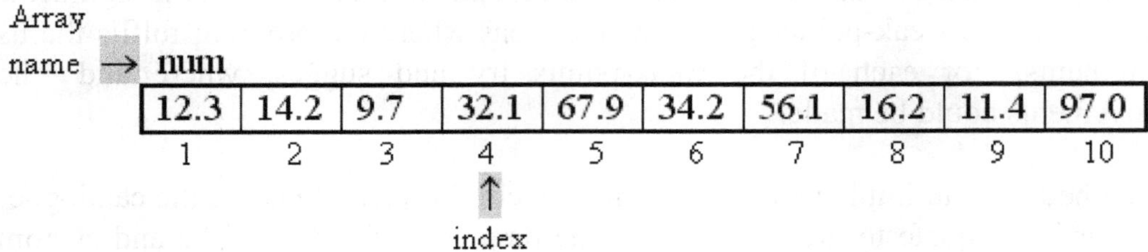

Fig 7-1 An array of numbers

Such a collection of like data items is called an array. An array is merely a chunk of allocated memory big enough to store the like data items.

An array of numbers can be created using the following statement:

```
DIM num(10)
```

In this example an array called num is created which can hold 10 numbers. The default indexing however will be in the range 0 - 9. If you want to reference the array from 1 to 10 you will need to change this to:

```
DIM num(1 TO 10)
```

In a similar way you can create arrays containing elements of other data types such as strings.

e.g. `DIM line$(25) ' will create an array of 25 strings.`

At this point we now need to investigate how such an array as num can be accessed. Numbers can be entered into an array element in any of the following methods:

```
num(4) = 2.9                        ' Assignment

INPUT "Enter number"; num(5)        ' Keyboard input

READ num(6)                         ' Reading from data statements
DATA  34.2
```

And once the data is stored it can be accessed at a later date as follows:

```
x = num(5)                    ' Assignment to extract data item

PRINT num(6)                  ' Output to screen or printer
```

In many programming languages it is necessary to store a value in an array location before you can access it. If this is not done the value is said to be undefined and will often result in an error message. To ensure this doesn't happen it is customary to initialise an array before any attempt is made to use it. An obvious way to do this is to use a FOR loop as we do at least know how many elements there are in the array.

```
FOR i = 1 TO 10
        num(i) = 0
NEXT i
```

In this example **i** the control variable is being used as an index to store zero in each element of the array num. Should you forget this while using QBASIC you needn't worry as it is done for you automatically when the DIM statement is executed. In a similar way if you create an array of strings it will automatically be initialised to spaces.

Quite often when you are using arrays you will have to access the entire array.

```
REM -- Print contents of an array -- Ex 1
FOR  i = 1 TO last_element
        PRINT num(i)
NEXT i

REM -- Sum an array of numbers -- Ex 2
sum = 0
FOR i = 1 TO last_element
        sum = sum + num(i)
NEXT i
PRINT "Total is "; sum

REM -- Smallest element -- Ex 3
min = num(1) :  p = 1
FOR i = 2 TO last_element
        IF min > num(i) THEN
                min = num(i)
                p = i    ' Record index of smallest element
        END IF
NEXT i
PRINT "The smallest element is num("; p; ") and has a value "; min
```

All of these examples assume that either the array is full or we know in advance exactly how many elements we have in the array. We obviously need some way of recording the number of elements stored or to include a data terminator at the end.

num1 records the largest index used
num2 uses a data terminator

	num1
1	12.5
2	34.6
3	27.9
4	52.8
5	78.9
p → 6	45.8
7	0
8	0
9	0
10	0

	num2
1	12.5
2	34.6
3	27.9
4	52.8
5	78.9
6	45.8
7	-1
8	0
9	0
10	0

Fig 7-2 Marking the end of an array

Supposing we want to compute the average value of the stored data items. What we don't want to do is to involve any array elements that are not valid data. In the first case we have a variable p which contains the index of the last element to be processed. So to compute an average is much the same as before except we go no further than element p.

```
sum = 0
For i = 1 TO p
        sum = sum + num1(i)
NEXT i
average = sum / p
```

In the second example using a data terminator we can't use a FOR loop as we don't know how many elements need to be processed. Instead we have to test for the data terminator and maintain our own counter.

```
terminator = -1
i = 1 : sum = 0
DO
        i = i + 1
        IF num2(i) <> terminator THEN sum = sum + num2(i)
LOOP UNTIL num2(i) = terminator
average = sum / (i - 1)
```

Should you make a mistake in the logic of your program and you try to access an array element where the index is not in the range 1 to 10 you will get the message:

Subscript out of range

' indicating that QBASIC does **boundary checking** before accessing the array'.

7.2 Arrays of Strings and Things

An array of strings can be implemented in much the same way as an array of numbers. The statement:

```
DIM name$(10)
```

will set up an array that will store up to 10 strings which will be indexed from 0 to 9.

The names stored can now be accessed as before. To be useful we would want to attach some information to this name. For instance our application might be to record the examination marks for Maths, English and Science for all the names in our list. This could be achieved by creating an array for each subject to record the marks.

	name$		maths		english		science
0	Colmerauer, A	0	92	0	37	0	65
1	Hopper, G	1	73	1	56	1	45
2	Kemeny, J	2	78	2	67	2	76
3	Kernighan, B	3	56	3	59	3	83
4	Ritchie, D	4	60	4	78	4	89
5	Stroustrup, B	5	49	5	64	5	76
6	Wirth, N	6	87	6	74	6	82
7		7	0	7	0	7	0
8		8	0	8	0	8	0
9		9	0	9	0	9	0

Fig 7-3 Arrays needed to store exam marks for each student

Clearly if we have to find out the various exam marks for an individual we will need to read all the arrays using the same index. For instance how would you determine the individual with the highest total mark?

You might do something like this:

```
maxtotal = maths(0) + english(0) + science(0)
maxindex = 0
for c = 1 to 6
        IF maxtotal < maths(c) + english(c) + science(c) THEN
                maxtotal = maths(c) + english(c) + science(c)
                maxindex = c
        END IF
NEXT c
PRINT "The individual with the highest total mark is "; name$(maxindex)
PRINT "The highest total mark is "; maxtotal
```

For this example this method of storing information in a number of records appears to be adequate, but later on you will see that this representation is rather cumbersome.

Another approach would be to create a record structure containing the name and maths, science and english marks for an individual. Such a record structure might look like this:

name	maths	english	science
Kemeny, J	78	67	76

Fig 7-4 A record structure to hold exam marks

In languages such as Pascal or C it would be possible to create an array of records. This is also possible in QBASIC but before we can do this I need to stop and talk about simple data types in QBASIC. So far I have told you there are strings and numbers. Now is the time to be more accurate.

There are 4 types of numbers in QBASIC:

1. INTEGER denoted by varname% (16 bit whole number)
2. LONG denoted by varname& (32 bit whole number)
3. SINGLE denoted by varname! (Single precision real number)
4. DOUBLE denoted by varname# (Double precision real number)

The default number type which we have restricted ourselves to so far is SINGLE. Because it is the default you don't need to use the tag ! after the variable name.

And we have variable length strings denoted by varname$.

We cannot use variable length data types in record structures. For that reason we need another way of declaring strings. This we can do as follows:

```
DIM sname AS STRING * 20          ' Create a string 20 characters in length
```

In a similar way we can declare all the other data types without the need for using tags.

e.g.

```
DIM num AS SINGLE
```

The next problem is how do we group these variables to form a record structure. This can be achieved by using the TYPE statement which effectively enables us to create new data types.

For example we could create a new data type which has the structure of the record in Fig 7-4.

```
TYPE studentmarks
        sname AS STRING * 20
        maths AS SINGLE
        eng AS SINGLE
        sci AS SINGLE
END TYPE
```

Now that we have a new data type we can create variables that have this structure.

```
DIM studentrec AS studentmarks
```

will create a variable containing 4 fields (sname, maths, eng, sci).

```
DIM smarks(10) AS studentmarks
```

will create an array of 10 elements. Each element having this record structure.

You can access individual fields in a variable by referencing the field name.

e.g.

```
studentrec.sname = "Hopper, G"      ' Store "Hopper, G" in field sname
                                      of variable studentrec
studentrec.maths = 73

smarks(4).sname = "Ritchie, D"      ' Store "Ritchie, D" in array element with
                                      index 4 and field sname.
```

A larger program fragment to show the use of arrays of records follows:

```
FOR c = 1 TO 5
        READ smarks(c).sname, smarks(c).maths, smarks(c).eng, smarks(c).sci
        NEXT c
        DATA "Colmerauer, A", 92, 37, 65
        DATA "Hopper, G", 73, 56, 45
        DATA "Kemeny, J", 78, 67, 76
        DATA "Kernighan, B", 56, 59, 83
        DATA "Ritchie, D", 60, 78, 89
        '    Print out contents of array
        FOR c = 1 TO 5
                PRINT smarks(c).sname, smarks(c).maths, smarks(c).sci, smarks(c).sci
        NEXT c
```

In this example an array of records is populated and then printed out. You will be pleasantly surprised by the output as it is nicely formatted in columns. The reason for this is obvious. Fixed length fields are being used so you won't need to use PRINT USING statements.

Exercise 7.1

1. Write a program that will:

   (a) input up to 100 numbers from the keyboard and record the index of the last number stored.

   (b) work out the current minimum, maximum and total every time a number is read from the array and display it in the following format.

```
Index        minimum      maximum     total
---------------------------------------------------------
  1            34           34          34
  2            25           34          59
  .             .            .           .
  .             .            .           .
```

2. Write a program that will create an array of student records like the one illustrated in fig 7-4.

   (a) Populate the array by entering data at the keyboard

   (b) Access the entire array and workout the lowest, highest and average score.

   (c) Obtain the names of all the students who have marks less than 50 in Maths.

3. Write a program that will print labels suitable for sticking on floppy disks.

   (a) There should be 15 labels printed per A4 page of paper.

   (b) Each label should be contained in a box like that of fig 7-5 and should measure approximately 7cm by 5cm.. Refer back to exercise 5-2 Q2 to remind yourself how to do this.

   (c) Allow the user to enter up to 5 short lines of text, that can be inserted into each of the 15 labels.

```
A course in
Programming
with QBASIC
(sample programs)
Tony Hawken 1995
```

Fig 7-5 A label for floppy disks

7.3 An introduction to Searching and Sorting

In this section we are going to look at some more advanced applications of arrays. This will give you an introduction to the topic of searching and sorting data.

The simplest type of searching technique is called a **Linear Search**. In simple terms this means starting at the beginning of an array and scanning the array one element at a time until the required item is found. The main loop to access the array might look like this:

```
i = 1
DO WHILE ( i <= 10 ) AND ( num(i) <> x)
        i = i + 1          ' Skip past unwanted items
LOOP
```

We now need to test which of the two conditions terminated the loop.

```
IF num(i) = x THEN
        PRINT "Item found at location "; i
ELSE
        PRINT "Item not found"
END IF
```

This is an effective method to search for items in an array if the array is very small. But for large arrays it would be very slow as the number of comparisons and hence the time taken is proportional to the number of elements in the array.

A faster method to search for an item in an array is called a Bisection Search. For this to work the items in the array must be sorted. The algorithm goes like this:

Set l = first element, set u = last element.

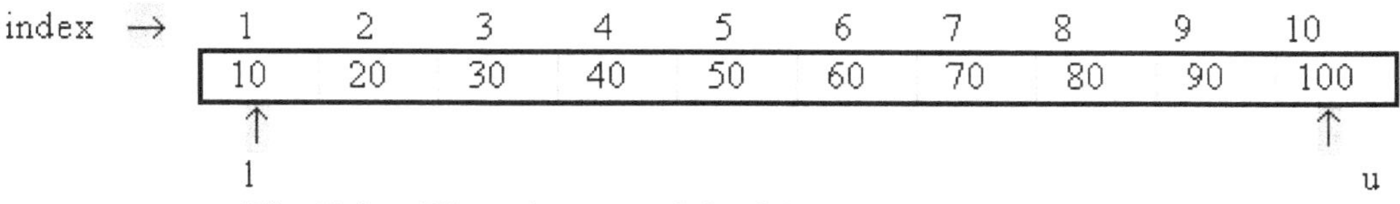

Fig 7-6 Bisection search looking for the number 30

Guess where the number is by selecting the middle element. The midpoint can be determined by **midpt = (l + u) \ 2** . If we perform an integer division it doesn't matter whether we start with an even number or odd number of elements. In this case our initial mid-point will be element 5. We now have 3 possibilities:

1. number = num(midpt) ' Element is found.

2. number < num(midpt) ' Search left sublist

3. number > num(midpt) ' Search right sublist

In this case condition 2 applies so we want to search the left sublist.

To do this set **u = midpt - 1**

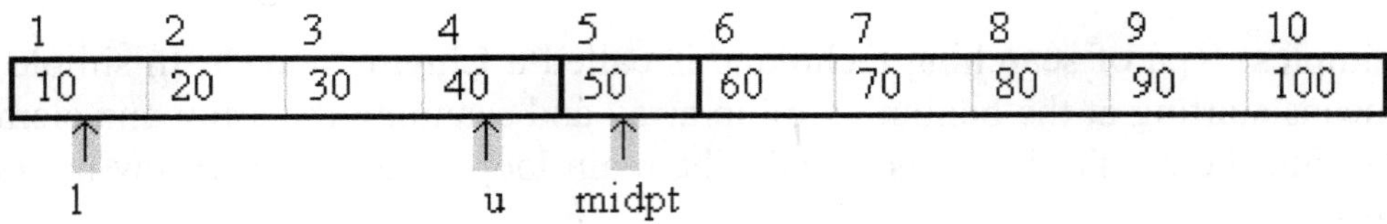

Fig 7-7 Bisection search after initial comparison.

The new mid point can now be calculated with the expression (l + u) \ 2 which gives us the value 2. A comparison of num(midpt) is made to see whether the element is found etc. This is repeated until either the desired data item is found or u > l. A complete program follows:

```
REM -- Demonstration of bisection search
CLS
DIM num1(1 TO 10)
true = 1        'Symbolic constant
false = 0
'
Populate the array with test data
FOR C = 1 TO 10
READ num1(C)
NEXT C
DATA 10,20,30,40,50,60,70,80,90,100
'
INPUT "Number to search for "; number
l = 1: u = 10:   ' Set lower and upper bounds
found = false
DO UNTIL l > u OR found = true
        midpt = (l + u) \ 2
        PRINT "midpoint is "; midpt
        IF number = num1(midpt) THEN
                found = true
        ELSEIF number < num1(midpt) THEN
                u = midpt - 1
        ELSE
                l = midpt + 1
        END IF
LOOP
'
IF found = true THEN
        PRINT number; " found at location "; midpt
ELSE
        PRINT number; " not found"
END IF
```

Sorting is much more complicated than searching and involves many more comparisons. For this reason we will look at the simplest of sorts and leave a more detailed analysis until later. The simplest sort is the **bubble sort**. It contains two components , comparison and interchange. Adjacent elements of an array are compared to see if they are in the correct relative position. If not they must be swapped round. A strategy for doing that is as follows:

```
IF a(j) < a(j-1) THEN
        ' Swap elements
        temp = a(j)     ' Temp is needed because a(j) will be overwritten
        a(j) = a(j-1)
        a(j-1) = temp
END IF
```

Draw a diagram and test the above program fragment to make sure you understand what is going on.

Now a systematic means of ensuring that all elements are compared. A bubble sort compares adjacent elements for the entire array, swapping elements that are out of place 1 at a time.

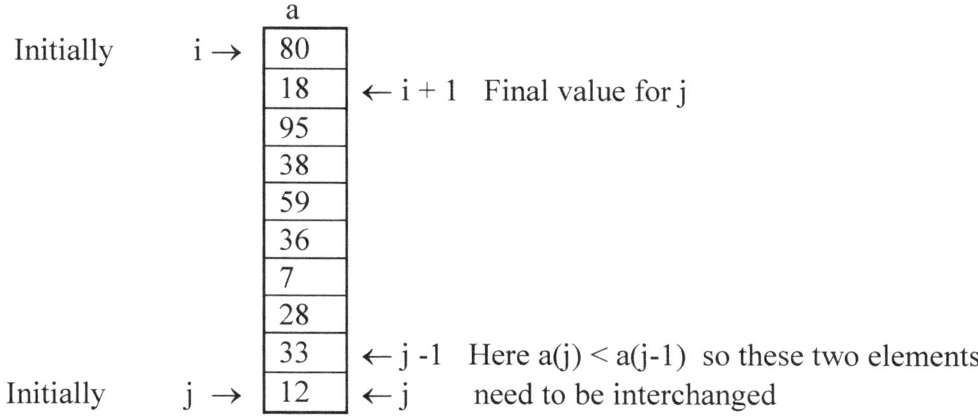

Fig 7-8 Start of a bubble sort

Looking at fig 7-8 You will see for the first iteration j points to the last element and i to the first. two elements a(j) and a(j-1) will be compared to see if they are in the correct place. The index j will continually be decremented until it takes a value i+1. Each time adjacent elements will get compared and will be swapped if they are in the wrong order. The complete program goes like this:

```
FOR i = 1 TO size -1  ' where size is the number of elements
        FOR j = size TO i + 1 STEP -1
                IF a(j) < a (j - 1) THEN
                        ' Swap elements
                        temp = a(j)
                        a(j) = a(j - 1)
                        a(j -1) = temp
                END IF
        NEXT j
NEXT i
```

7.4 Multi-dimensional arrays

So far we have used one-dimensional arrays only. These are often called lists. Now is the time to look at arrays of higher dimensions. You can in fact create arrays with up to 60 dimensions in QBASIC, but I am going to limit the number of dimensions to 2 and 3.

A 2 dimensional array is called a table. It is a very common structure in every-day life. Objects like chess-boards, the screen of your monitor made up of pixels, a map all have a tabular structure and hence can be represented as two dimensional arrays. We are now going to look at some simple uses of tables. The simplest is possibly a multiplication table.

col ↓

×	1	2	3	4	5	6	7	8	9	10
row →1	1	2	3	4	5	6	7	8	9	10
2	2	4	6	8	10	12	14	16	18	20
3	3	6	9	12	15	18	21	24	27	30
4	4	8	12	16	20	24	28	32	36	40
5	5	10	15	20	25	30	35	40	45	50
6	6	12	18	24	30	36	42	48	54	60
7	7	14	21	28	35	42	49	56	63	70
8	8	16	24	32	40	48	56	64	72	80
9	9	18	27	36	45	54	63	72	81	90
10	10	20	30	40	50	60	70	80	90	100

Fig 7-9 A multiplication table

This can be set up as follows:

```
REM -- Multiplication tables
CLS
DIM table(1 TO 10, 1 TO 10)
FOR row = 1 TO 10
        FOR col = 1 TO 10
                table(row, col) = row * col
        NEXT col
NEXT row
'       Print table
FOR row = 1 TO 10
        FOR col = 1 TO 10
                PRINT USING "####"; row * col;
        NEXT col
        PRINT
NEXT row
```

This is a particularly easy problem because the value of each element is obtained by multiplying row * col. Printing the table out is a little more difficult because you have to work out when to start printing on the next line. A little thought would tell you that you need to execute a PRINT statement when you have finished each row.

A rather more difficult application of 2 dimensional arrays is the production of calendars. For the moment lets look at just one month.

M	**T**	**W**	**Th**	**F**	**S**	**Su**
					1	2
3	4	5	6	7	8	9
10	11	12	13	14	15	16
17	18	19	20	21	22	23
24	25	26	27	28	29	30
30						

Fig 7-10 The month Jan 1994

This is much more difficult because there is no obvious rule by which we can compute the value of an array element given the row and col indexes. Lets backtrack and look at a similar but much simpler problem. Create a grid with the following numbers in it.

day ↓

week →

1	2	3	4	5	6	7
8	9	10	11	12	13	14
15	16	17	18	19	20	21
22	23	24	25	26	27	28
29	30	31				

Fig 7-11 A simpler problem

A first attempt at creating an array with these values might be:

```
DIM cal(1 TO 6, 1 TO 7)        ' cal(week, day)
'
c = 1
FOR week = 1 TO 6
        FOR day= 1 TO 7
                cal(week, day) = c
                c = c + 1
        NEXT day
NEXT week
```

But this will give us the days 1 - 42. We want to stop at 31.
This could be achieved by checking the number of days:

```
IF c <= 31 THEN cal(week, day) = c
```

An finally we want to start printing day 1 on Saturday. i.e. the 6th element in our table. This could be achieved by skipping the first 5 elements.

```
REM -- calendar -- attempt 1
CLS
DIM cal(1 TO 6, 1 TO 7)
'
c = 0: offset = 5: n = 1
FOR week = 1 TO 6
        FOR day = 1 TO 7
                IF n > offset THEN
                        c = c + 1
                        cal(week, day) = c
                END IF
                n = n + 1
        NEXT day
NEXT week
'       Print out calendar
FOR week = 1 TO 6
        FOR day = 1 TO 7
                PRINT USING "###"; cal(week, day);
        NEXT day
        PRINT
NEXT week
```

This will produce output looking like this:

```
  0   0   0   0   0   1   2
  3   4   5   6   7   8   9
 10  11  12  13  14  15  16
 17  18  19  20  21  22  23
 24  25  26  27  28  29  30
 31  32  33  34  35  36  37
```

Fig 7-12 Output from calendar program -- first attempt

There are two things wrong with this.

1. The days of the month go up to 37 instead of stopping at 31.

2. Numeric arrays are initialised with zero's so any element not assigned a number will be printed out as zero.

The first problem can be put right by including a test to stop storing numbers in the array once the day number reaches 31. To solve the second problem you need to modify the print routine so that if a zero is detected spaces will be printed instead. And finally it would be nice to have the days of the week printed above the table. The final program appears below.

```
REM -- calendar -- attempt 2
CLS
DIM cal(1 TO 6, 1 TO 7)
'
c = 0: offset = 5: n = 1
FOR week = 1 TO 6
        FOR day = 1 TO 7
                IF (n > offset) AND (c < 31) THEN
                        c = c + 1
                        cal(week, day) = c
                END IF
                n = n + 1
        NEXT day
NEXT week
'
PRINT "M  T  W  Th F  S  SU"        ' Print header (days of week)
FOR week = 1 TO 6
        FOR day = 1 TO 7
                IF cal(week, day) = 0 THEN
                        PRINT "   ";              ' Replace zero's with spaces
                ELSE
                        PRINT USING "###"; cal(week, day);
                END IF
        NEXT day
        PRINT
NEXT week
```

Exercise 7.2

1. Write a program that will create an array called list capable of holding 100 numbers. Now extend this program so that it will:

   (a) Populate the array with numbers at random. Note the following expression will create a number in the range 1 - 100.

   RND*100 + 1

   (b) Use a bubble sort to sort the array.

   (c) Count the number of comparisons being performed.

   (d) Count how many swaps take place.

   (e) will check that the final data is sorted.

2. Extend program 1 by allowing a user to enter a number they want to search for. The program should:

   (a) use a bisection search

   (b) evaluate the number of comparisons taken to find the number

   (c) be run many times to compute the average number of times taken to find a particular number.

3. Repeat programs 1 and 2 except this time use a record structure such as the one in fig 7-4. The records should be sorted on the name field and subsequent searches should also be on the name field.

4. Type in the calendar program on the previous page and then modify the program so that it will now:

   (a) Input a number in the range 1 - 12 for the month required.

   (b) Print the name of the month followed by the calendar for that month with the appropriate number of days.

8. Using Functions and Procedures

8.1 Introduction

As programs get larger it is important to be able to split the program into smaller components. Most programming languages achieve this by providing constructs such as functions or procedures which break the program up into a number of self-contained modules that communicate with each other. Each of these modules should be able to perform a useful task and should be available for use anywhere in the program. Such a facility makes a program easier to develop, easier to debug and improves the readability of the program.

In very simple terms:

1. A **function** is a block of code containing statements that perform a calculation and returns an answer called the **return value**.

2. A **procedure** is a block of code containing statements that when executed perform some **actions** that satisfy a certain task.

You have probably met functions already in the mathematics classroom.

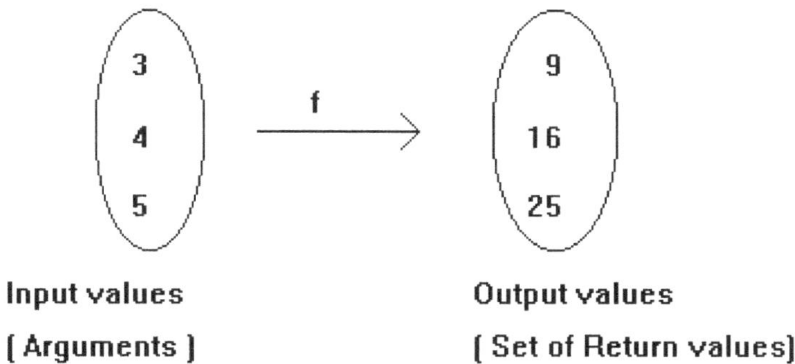

Fig 8-1 A simple function

Using the above example in fig 8-1 we could write the following:

```
f(3) = 9
y = f(4)          ' In this example f(4) returns 16 which is assigned to y
```

QBASIC has a number of built in functions which can be used like this. For example there are a number of Mathematical functions such as SQR, SIN, COS, TAN and ATN etc. The following code demonstrates the use of a predefined function:

```
n = 8
PRINT "The Return value is "; SQR(n+1)
```

In this example the parameter passed to the function SQR is evaluated giving 9. The function now works out the square root of 9 giving a return value of 3 which is printed out. In other situations it may be practical to assign the result to a variable especially if this result is an intermediate value.

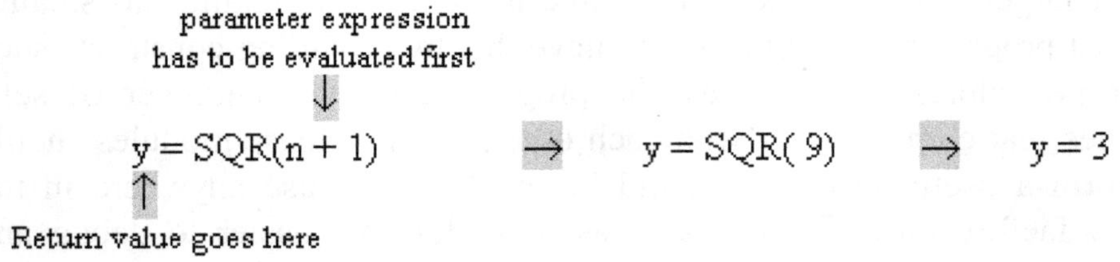

```
        parameter expression
       has to be evaluated first
                  ↓
   y = SQR(n + 1)        →   y = SQR( 9)    →    y = 3
   ↑
Return value goes here
```

QBASIC also has standard string handling functions such as LEFT$, RIGHT$ and MID$ etc. These can be used in exactly the same way. The only thing you have to remember is that in most cases the return value is a string. The following shows this.

```
word$ = "Encyclopedia"
first5$ = LEFT$(word$, 5)
PRINT "The first 5 characters of "; word$; " are "; first5$
```

8.2 FN functions

Standard BASIC provides user-defined functions as a means of creating your own functions. But as you will soon see this method is rather limited.

A user-defined function or FN function must always begin with the letters FN followed by a name and possibly one or more parameters.

e.g DEF FNcube (x) = x * x * x

creates a definition of a function called FNcube. It has one parameter called x and returns the value x*x*x.

To use this function you need to execute a function call such as:

```
y = FNcube(3)
```

or

```
x = 5
PRINT "Value returned is "; FNcube(x + 1)
```

FN functions can also be used to process strings. It would be useful if the return value were itself a string.

```
                    return value is a string
                              ↓
e.g.    DEF FNfirst3chars$ (a$) = LEFT$(a$, 3)
                              ↑
                    parameter is a string
```

In this example we have to indicate that the return value is a string. This is done by placing a $ tag at the end of the function name.

You can create a function that returns true or false.

e.g   DEF FNislower(ch$) = (chr$ >= "a") AND (ch$ <= "z")

In this example a number **-1** or **0** is returned which can be interpreted as **true** or **false**. We can now use such functions in a slightly different manner.

e.g.   IF FNislower(ch$) THEN ...

Now suppose you want to write a function that will compute the maximum of two numbers.

i.e.   DEF FNmax(x, y) = ...

The format of the FN function that we have seen so far is not powerful enough to cope with this problem. There is however an extended syntax which permits blocks of statements as well as an expression within the function body. To illustrate this I will implement a function to compute the minimum of two numbers.

```
DEF FNmin (x, y)
    IF x < y THEN
        FNmin = x
    ELSE
        FNmin = y
    END IF
END DEF
```

8.3 Function Procedures

QBASIC offers a much more powerful alternative to FN functions called the Function Procedure. A function procedure is typically defined in a separate window and unless you are in that window the definition will be hidden from you.

To create a Function Procedure definition:

1. choose the **Edit** menu by pressing **Alt E**.

2. Select the **New FUNCTION** option by using the arrow keys.

3. You will be prompted for a function name. Type it in and press return.

Name: | max |

4. You will now enter a new window with an empty function template:

```
                parameters go here
                        ↓
FUNCTION max
                             ← Body of function goes here
END FUNCTION
```

5. Type in the rest of the function.

```
FUNCTION max (x, y)
    IF x > y THEN
        max = x
    ELSE
        max = y
    END IF
END FUNCTION
```

To test out the function:

1. Return to the main program window. This is achieve by selecting the **View** menu.

   Press **Alt V**

   You will now get a pop-down menu. Choose the option **SUBs**. You will now be given a list of functions like this:

   ```
   main.bas
       max
   ```

2. Choose main.bas to get back to the main program. Use the arrow keys.

3. In the main program you can test out your function by typing in some simple function calls. This is the time to test out your function fully to makes sure it works properly before you incorporate it into the program for real.

```
REM -- Test function max
'
PRINT max ( 4, 6)
```

4. To get a feel of how things are implemented you might want to check the contents of the file main.bas. To do this exit QBASIC and at the DOS prompt enter:

```
TYPE main.bas
```

5. You should see something like this:

```
DECLARE max! (x!, y!)
REM -- Test function max
'
PRINT max ( 4, 6)


FUNCTION max (x, y)
        IF x > y THEN
                max = x
        ELSE
                max = y
        END IF
END FUNCTION
```

You should note that for each function defined there is a declaration at the beginning of the program prior to the function call. And should there be more than one function, the function definitions will be maintained in alphabetical order.

To give you a feel of what you can do with function procedures a few simple examples follow.

1. Return a random number in the range 1 - 100

```
FUNCTION randomnum
        ' A function that requires no parameters
        RANDOMIZE TIMER
        ' and returns a number in the range 1 - 100
        randomnum = (RND * 100 + 1) \ 1
END FUNCTION
```

2. Convert Centigrade to Fahrenheit

```
FUNCTION converttof (c)
    ' A function that takes 1 parameter (SINGLE)
    ' And returns a SINGLE
    concerttof = 9 / 5 * c + 32
END FUNCTION
```

3. Given a number 1 to 7 return the day of the week

```
FUNCTION day$( n%)
    SELECT CASE n%
        CASE 1
            day$ = "Monday"
        CASE 2
            day$ = "Tuesday"
        CASE 3
            day$ = "Wednesday"
        CASE 4
            day$ = "Thursday"
        CASE 5
            day$ = "Friday"
        CASE 6
            day$ = "Saturday"
        CASE 7
            day$ = "Sunday"
    END SELECT
END FUNCTION
```

4. A function that counts the number of occurrences of a letter in a string.

```
FUNCTION lettercnt%( str$, l$)
    cnt% = 0
    ' Truncate l$ if it is more than one character
    IF LEN(l$) > 1 THEN l$ = LEFT$(l$, 1)
    FOR c% = 1 TO LEN(str$)
        IF MID$(str$, c%, 1) = l$ THEN cnt% = cnt% + 1
    NEXT c%
    lettercnt% = cnt%
END FUNCTION
```

8.4 A longer example

Most books have an ISBN that uses a modulo 11 check digit system for validation purposes. The following are examples of valid ISBN's:

1-85805-080-4
0 521 29101 1

You will notice that the number is punctuated by either hyphens or spaces. It doesn't matter where the hyphens or spaces are. The digit furthest on the right is called the check digit The rule for obtaining the check digit is as follows:

1. Each of the digits except the checksum is given a weight. Starting at the right the weight is 2, the next on the left is 3 and so on.

2. Each of the digits is multiplied by its weight and all of these products are summed.

3. the sum is divided by 11 and the remainder is kept.

4. Calculate the checksum by subtracting the remainder from 11

The following program enforces these rules. It also takes into account that an ISBN can have hyphens or spaces in it.

```
DECLARE FUNCTION validisbn! (a$)
DECLARE FUNCTION remhyphens$ (a$)
'
'       Test program
FOR c = 1 to 10
        READ isbn$
        PRINT remhyphens$(isbn$)
        '
        IF validisbn(isbn$) THEN
                PRINT "Correct ISBN"
        ELSE
                PRINT "Incorrect ISBN"
        END IF
NEXT C
'
'       Test data
DATA "0-13-663022-7", "0 853 12423 X"
DATA
DATA
DATA
DATA
```

```
'       Functions
'

FUNCTION remhyphens$ (a$)
        b$ = ""
        FOR c% = 1 TO LEN(a$)
                ch$ = MID$(a$, c%, 1)
                IF ch$ <> "-" AND ch$ <> " " THEN
                        b$ = b$ + ch$
                END IF
        NEXT c%
        remhyphens$ = b$
END FUNCTION

FUNCTION validisbn (a$)
        true = -1: false = 0
        b$ = remhyphens$(a$)
        IF LEN(b$) = 10 THEN
                sum = 0
                IF RIGHT$(b$, 1) = "X" OR RIGHT$(b$, 1) = "x" THEN
                        checksum = 10
                ELSE
                        checksum = VAL(RIGHT$(b$, 1))
                END IF
                weight = 2
                FOR c% = 9 TO 1 STEP -1
                        digit = VAL(MID$(b$, c%, 1))
                        sum = sum + digit * weight
                        weight = weight + 1
                NEXT c%
                sum = sum MOD 11
                IF checksum = 11 - sum THEN
                        validisbn = true
                ELSE
                        validisbn = false
                END IF
        ELSE
                validisbn = false
        END IF
END FUNCTION
```

Exercise 8-1

1. Write a FN function to compute the hypotenuse of a right-angled triangle given the other two sides. Test it out by printing the 3 sides of the triangle.

2. Write a program to perform temperature conversion for values 1^0 C - 100^0C. The program should have a function to perform the conversion and will print out both temperatures in Centigrade and Fahrenheit in a neat table to 2 decimal places.

3. Write a function with the heading:

   FUNCTION sumsquares(n%)

   whose value is the sum of the squares of the integers 1 to n%.

4. Write a program that will input the name of a file of format:

   filename.type

   The program should include a function that will truncate the filename to 8 characters and the filetype to 3 characters before returning the modified filename.

5. Type in the validation program in the previous section. Document the program by including comments in appropriate places in the program. Now get a printout.

6. Write a Program that will:

   (a) Contain the following functions.

   (i) A function to validate date strings. Given a date stored in a string of the following format:

   "mm-dd-yyyy"

   The function must check that dd is 2 numeric digits in the range 1 -31, mm is 2 numeric digits in the range 1-12, and yyyy is 4 numeric digits in the range 1950 - 1990. If valid -1 should be returned, 0 otherwise.

   (ii) A function which when given a valid date string will return the days in the date.

   (iii) A function which when given a valid date string will return the month.

   (iv) A function which when given a valid date string will return the year.

   (b) Write a test program that reads in a list of names and dates of birth from data statements and will test all of these functions by validating the date, and if valid will provide the day, month an year they were born. Make sure that some of your test data will fail the validation test.

   (c) Go back to your validation function. Modify it so that now it returns -1 if the date is valid and an error code if it is invalid.

(d) Write another function that will take an errorcode as an argument and will return an appropriate error message. Modify your main program to use this function so that if an invalid date is detected an appropriate error message will be printed out.

(e) Modify your main program so that it will now use these functions to work out the age of everyone from their date of birth. You may have to use the DATE$ function to get the current date. You will be glad to know that DATE$ returns a date in the format "mm-dd-yyyy".

8.5 Creating Procedures (Sub programs)

A portion of code which is likely to be used in several places in the program is better written as a procedure or subprogram. A subprogram has its own data (local variables) and typically if it needs to share data from the calling program it will do so in the form of parameters. The creating of subprograms is much the same as for functions. They can be created in a separate window allowing QBASIC to hide information that you don't need to see.

Consider the problem of writing a program to automate a payroll as in Ex 3-2 Q3. In this case it is obvious that for each employee a payslip will be required. The code needed for this task can become the body of the sub program. For each employee the sub program will need to know their name, hours worked and rate of pay. This information can be passed using parameters. Such a procedure could be created as follows:

1. Select the **Edit** menu.

   press **Alt E**

2. Choose the **NEW SUB ...** option.

3. You will now get prompted for a Sub Program name. Type it in and press return.

   Name: **payslip**

4. You will now enter a new window with an empty sub program template in it.

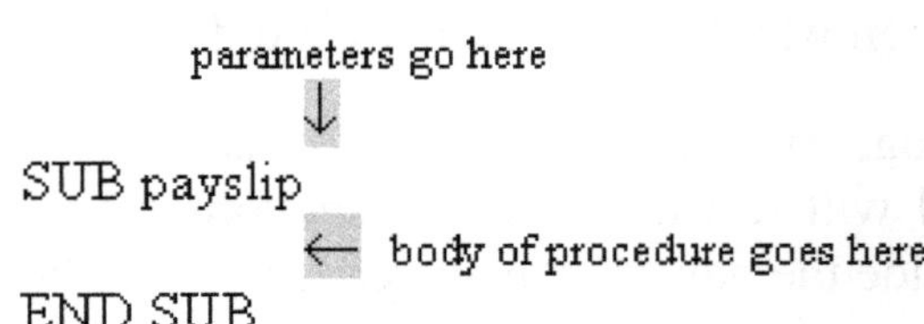
parameters go here
SUB payslip
body of procedure goes here
END SUB

5. Type in the body of the procedure first.

```
SUB payslip
    IF hours > 37 THEN
        overtime = hours - 37
        basicpay = 37 * rate
        overtimepay = overtime * rate * 1.5
        grosspay = basicpay + overtimepay
    ELSE
        basicpay = hours * rate
        overtimepay = 0
        grosspay = basicpay
    END IF
    PRINT USING " \         \"; name$;
    PRINT "    ";
    PRINT USING " £###.## "; basicpay, overtimepay, grosspay
END SUB
```

6. Now type in the parameters.

```
SUB payslip (name$, hours, rate)
    IF hours > 37 THEN
        overtime = hours - 37
        basicpay = 37 * rate
        overtimepay = overtime * rate * 1.5
        grosspay = basicpay + overtimepay
    ELSE
        basicpay = hours * rate
        overtimepay = 0
        grosspay = basicpay
    END IF
    PRINT USING "\         \"; name$;
    PRINT "    ";
    PRINT USING " £###.## "; basicpay, overtimepay, grosspay
END SUB
```

To test out the function you will need to get back to the window with the main program in it and write some procedure calls with some test data.

To get back to the main program:

1. Press **Alt V** to choose the View option.

2. You will now get a pop-down menu with the following in it:

```
main.bas
    payslip
```

3. Choose main.bas to get back to the main program.

In this window you can write some statements to test the sub program.

1. You might start with the following

```
'        Test Sub Program
INPUT " Enter name: ", name$
INPUT " Enter hours worked: "; hours
INPUT " Enter rate per hour: "; rate
'
CALL payslip (name$, hours, rate)
```

2. In the context of a payroll program you are now likely to modify this and end up with something like this:

```
'       First attempt at payroll
'
PRINT "Name          basic   o/v   gross"
PRINT
DO
        READ name$, rate
        PRINT "Enter hours worked for "; name$
        INPUT "Hours worked "; hours
        CALL payslip ( name$, hours, rate)
LOOP  UNTIL name$ = "Eof"
'
DATA "Fred Bloggs", 6.50
DATA "Andy Pandy"; 5.65
DATA .
```

8.6 Communication between Program Modules

So far we have seen that we can pass data to both functions and procedures by means of parameters. Now is the time to look in detail at how parameter passing works and to look at other alternatives.

QBASIC is unlike most other programming languages in that the parameter passing method is determined by the procedure call, not the procedure definition. This gives greater flexibility as you can write a procedure or function that can pass parameters "by value" or "by reference".

The mechanism that will be described first is "CALL BY VALUE". This means that literal values only are passed to the procedure. "Call by value" is indicated in the procedure call by making the actual parameters expressions that have to be evaluated rather than just variable names. For the procedure call:

CALL payslip (n$ + "", h + 0, r + 0) ' All parameters are **call by value**

because all parameters need to be evaluated. See Fig 8-2.

Main Program

```
n$ = "Tony"
h=45
r= 15.45
CALL payslip( n$ + "", h + 0, r + 0)
```

		n$	h	r
	Actual parameters	"Tony"	47	15.45
payslip		↓	↓	↓
		name$	**hours**	**rate**
	Formal parameters	"Tony"	47	15.45

LOCAL variables

overtime	10	← hours - 37
basicpay	571.65	← 37 * rate
overtimepay	154.50	← overtime * rate * 1.5
grosspay	726.15	← basicpay + overtimepay

Fig 8-2 Demonstration of Parameter passing (Call by value)

A procedure call of the form:

CALL payslip(n$ + "",h + 0, r + 0)

involves the following steps:

1. The value of the actual parameters are evaluated.

2. All variables used inside the procedure are created as local variables which are lost when you exit the procedure. A special set of local variables are created corresponding to the formal parameters.

3. The values of the actual parameters are copied to the corresponding formal parameters of the procedure.

   i.e. name$ ← value of n$
   hours ← value of h
   rate ← value of r

4. The statements that constitute the procedure body are executed.

5. Exit from the procedure. Control goes back to the part of the program where the procedure call took place. All local variables of the procedure disappear.

An alternative to passing data through parameters is to use global variables. This can be achieved by using the keyword SHARED.

```
SUB payslip
        SHARED name$, hours, rate
        .
        .
        .
END SUB
```

Declaring variables SHARED effectively states that the variables are global, are already created outside the procedure and are available for the procedure to use.

This however is a practice that is frowned apon by most programmers. Having global data in programs gives the procedure the opportunity to modify the data in a way the programmer had not intended. It just happens that the procedure payslip doesn't modify name$, hours and rate. In any case the designers of QBASIC have tried to make this practice difficult by making variables inside procedues LOCAL by default.

The "Call by Value" parameter passing mechanism can only pass literal values such as the value of a string, a number, an array element which is a string or a number.

In situations where you need to process an entire structure such as an array "Call by value" is of no use at all. There are two alternatives:

1. Make the array global

   e.g.
   ```
   SUB subname
           SHARED num( )
           .
           .
   END SUB
   ```

2. pass the array name by reference

   e.g. `CALL subname( num( ) )`

   using the procedure:

   ```
   SUB subname ( n( ) )
           ' Process array n( )
           .
           .
   END SUB
   ```

In the second example the array name **num** is substituted for **n**. Any reference to the array **n** is treated as meaning the array **num**. This name substitution enables you to use this procedure on any array you choose.

In this section we have made most reference to procedures. Most of what has been said about procedures applies equally to functions. Where a function differs is that a function produces a return value when you exit the function.

To illustrate this point there follows some examples to compute grosspay:

example 1

```
' A function using no parameters and global variables

FUNCTION grosspay
        SHARED  hours, rate
        IF hours > 37 THEN
                overtime = hours - 37
                basicpay = 37 * rate
                overtimepay = overtime * rate * 1.5
                grosspay = basicpay + overtimepay
        ELSE
                grosspay = hours * rate
        END IF
END FUNCTION
```

example 2

```
' A function using parameters

FUNCTION grosspay ( hours, overtime)
        IF hours > 37 THEN
                overtime = hours - 37
                basicpay = 37 * rate
                overtimepay = overtime * rate * 1.5
                grosspay = basicpay + overtimepay
        ELSE
                grosspay = hours * rate
        END IF
END FUNCTION
```

2a.

```
' An example of Call by Value

INPUT "Enter hours, rate "; h, r
PRINT "Gross pay is "; grosspay(h + 0, r + 0)
```

2b.

```
' An example of Call by reference

INPUT "Enter hours, rate "; h, r
PRINT "Gross pay is "; grosspay(h, r)
```

And finally we finish this section with an introduction to STATIC variables. A static variable is similar to a local variable except that it keeps its value. It is not re-initialised every time the function is called. To demonstrate why they are useful we will be looking at the problem of generating pseudo-random numbers.

A first attempt may use a global variable called seed:

```
REM -- First attempt
'
seed = 0
FOR c = 1 to 10
        PRINT c, rand1
NEXT C

FUNCTION rand1
        SHARED seed
        seed = (25173 * seed + 13849) MOD 65536
        rand1 = seed
END FUNCTION
```

This will work perfectly well unless some other part of the program uses the variable seed. It is no use making the variable seed LOCAL as this will be re-initialised to 0 each time the function is called resulting in the same random number being generated each time. You could pass the value seed as a parameter as in the following:

```
REM -- Second attempt
'
seed = 0
FOR c = 1 TO 10
        seed = rand2(seed)
        PRINT c, seed
NEXT c

FUNCTION rand2 (seed)
        seed = (25173 * seed + 13849) MOD 65536
        rand2 = seed
END FUNCTION
```

But by far the neatest approach is to use static variables as in the following:

```
REM -- Third attempt
'
FOR c = 1 TO 10
        PRINT c, rand3
NEXT c

FUNCTION rand3
        STATIC seed
        seed = (25173 * seed + 13849) MOD 65536
        rand3 = seed
END FUNCTION
```

In this case the first time the function rand3 is called seed will be set to 0. On leaving the function the value of seed will be retained so that it will return a different number for each function call. It effectively produces the same results as using global variables but is much safer.

Exercise 8-2

1. Given that the distance between two points (x1, y1) and (x2, y2) is given by the expression:

   $$(x2 - x1)^2 + (y2 - y1)^2$$

   Write a function that will return the distance such that:

   (a) In your first version the function has no parameters.

   (b) In your second version your program will use 4 parameters and pass the parameters 'by Value'

   (c) In your third you will use the same function as before but pass the parameters 'by Reference'.

   Make sure that these functions are tested with 10 pairs of points stored in data statements.

2. Refer back to exercise 3-2 Q3. Rewrite the program so that it will:

   (a) Have a procedure that will produce a suitable menu which will convey the following information and allow a user to enter their choice.

   Menu
   ------

   1. Produce a payslip
   2. Print table of Employees and Job position
   3. Display minimum, maximum and average rate of pay
   4. Quit Menu

   Enter your choice 1 - 4

   (b) Store the following information about each employee in data statements:

   name, Job position, rate of pay

   (c) Have functions to compute minimum, maximum, and average rate of pay.

   (d) A procedure that will prompt for name and hours worked and will produce a payslip that will include the following:

   name, job position, hours worked, overtime, basic pay, overtime pay, gross pay, tax paid and nett pay.

   (f) A procedure that will display a table of all the employees, which will include name, Job position and rate of pay.

8.7 Processing Arrays

Structures like arrays cannot be passed as a whole to a procedure or function. They can either be declared to be global or they can be passed by reference. To consider the advantages of the two methods there follows two example programs to populate an array with random numbers.

example1

```
REM -- Example using a global array
DIM num1(1 TO 100), num2(1 TO 200)
'
CALL populate (100)

SUB populate (n%)
        SHARED num1( )
        FOR c% = 1 TO n%
                num1(c%) = (100 * RND + 1) \ 1
        NEXT c%
END SUB
```

This example is very inflexible as the procedure populate will only work with arrays called num1, wheras if we were to pass the array name 'by reference' we could use the procedure to process many different arrays of numbers.

example 2

```
REM -- Example demonstrating 'Call by reference'
DIM num1(1 TO 100), num2(1 TO 200)
'
CALL populate (num1( ), 100)        ' Process all elements of num1
CALL populate (num2( ), 200)        ' Process all elements of num2


SUB populate ( a( ), n%)
        FOR c% = 1 TO n%
                a(c%) = (100 * RND + 1) \ 1
        NEXT c%
END SUB
```

This version is much better as we can use the same procedure to process any array of numbers. This is because the 'Call by Reference' mechanism substitutes any array name we choose to pass for a( ).

The same is true for functions. If we wanted to write a function to compute the average value of all elements in an array we would still use the 'Call by Reference' mechanism.

The function following will suffice to demonstrate this:

```
FUNCTION ave( a( ), n%)
        sum = 0
        FOR c% = 1 TO n%
                sum = sum + a(c%)
        NEXT c%
        ave = sum / n%
END FUNCTION
```

The above function could then be used in the following manner:

```
REM -- Compute average value of elements
'
DIM av(1 TO 3)
DIM num(1 TO 10), numlist(1 TO 100), largelist(1 TO 1000)
'
' Store results of function calls in array called av
av(1) = ave( num( ), 10)
av(2) = ave( numlist( ), 100)
av(3) = ave( largelist( ), 1000)
'
' Print out results
FOR c = 1 TO 3
        PRINT USING "###   #####.##"; c, av(c)
NEXT c
```

8.8 Producing a Calendar

In the last chapter we looked at 2-dimensional arrays and how we could use them to store the months for a calendar.We are now going to look at the problem of working out a complete calendar for any given year after 1994.

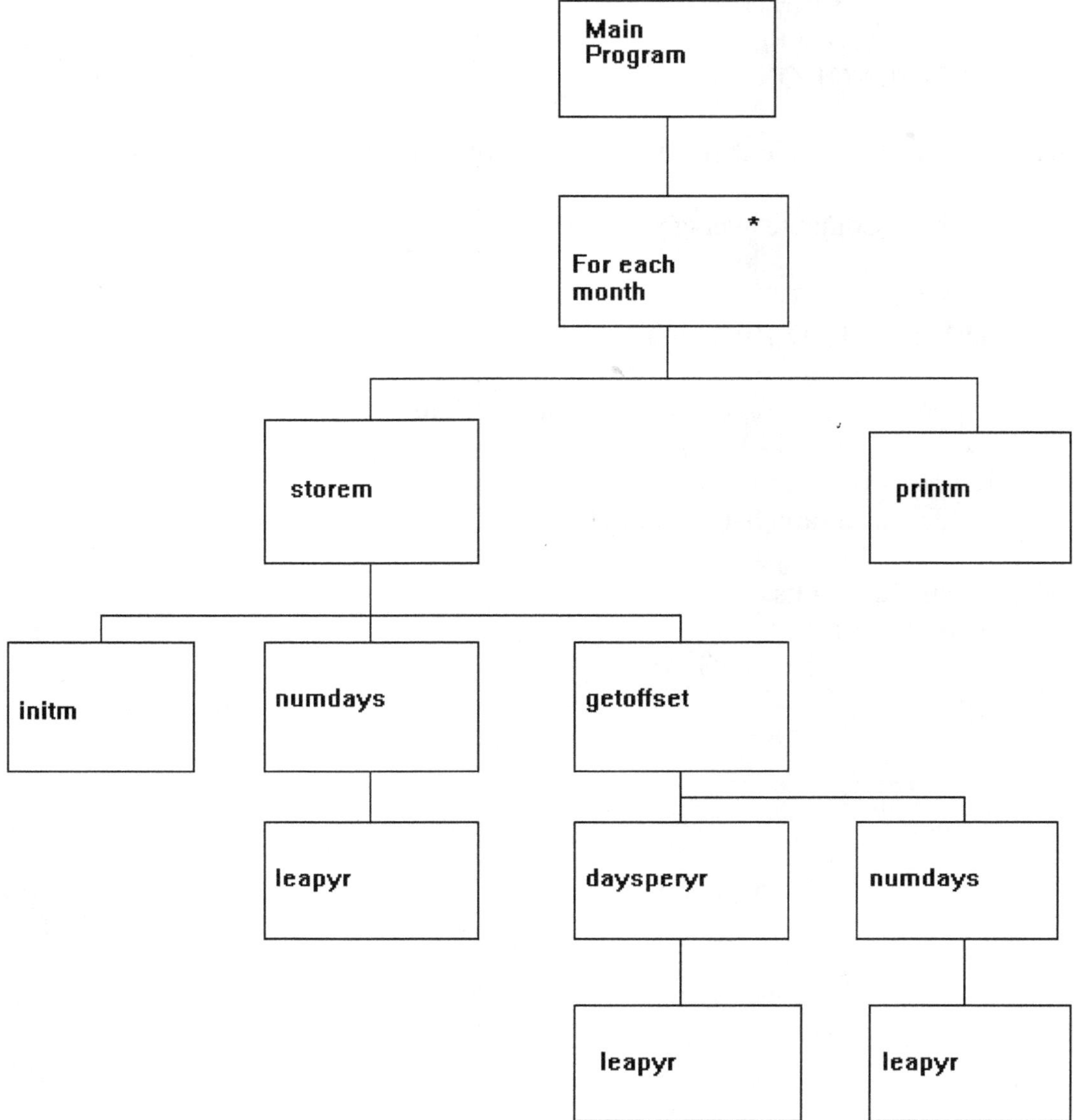

Fig 8.3 Hierarchy chart for the calendar program

It is proposed that we continue where we left off in chapter 7. We know how to represent a month. What we need to be able to do is to compute the number of days in each month and the offset for storing the days in the array. That is we need to know on what day the first of the month falls. The method used here is to have January 1st 1994 as the starting point for all the calculations. January 1st 1994 just happens to be a saturday. So if the week starts on a monday that will give us an offset or starting position of 6. The offset of each month is calculated by counting the number of days in all the previous months and dividing by 7 to get an offset.

To help us do this we have the following functions:

Function	Purpose
numdays	returns the number of days given a number 1-12 for the month. This is not so easy as we need to know whether the current year is a leapyear to work out February.
leapyr	Return -1 if leapyear, 0 otherwise
dayspery r	Returns number of days in year.
getoffset	Returns the position of first of month in the array

The actual actions are performed by procedures. Because only one array is used we need to constantly initialise it before storing the next month. This is achieved by calling **initm** . That leaves **storem** to store the current month in m( ), and **printm** to print it out.

The full program listing now follows:

```
DECLARE FUNCTION dayspery r! (yr!)
DECLARE SUB initm (m!( ))
DECLARE FUNCTION leapyr! (yr)
DECLARE FUNCTION numdays! (month!, year!)
DECLARE FUNCTION getoffset! (month!, yr)
DECLARE SUB storem (m!( ), mnth, yr)
DECLARE SUB printm (m$, m!( ), r, c)
'
REM -- Display Calendar in two halves
'
DIM m(1 TO 6, 1 TO 7)
CLS
jan1994 = 6
INPUT "Enter year "; y
SLEEP 2
'
'       Process first 6 months
CLS
CALL storem(m( ), 1, y)
CALL printm("Jan", m( ), 1, 1)
CALL storem(m( ), 2, y)
CALL printm("Feb", m( ), 1, 40)
CALL storem(m( ), 3, y)
CALL printm("Mar", m( ), 9, 1)
CALL storem(m( ), 4, y)
CALL printm("Apr", m( ), 9, 40)
CALL storem(m( ), 5, y)
CALL printm("May", m( ), 16, 1)
```

```
CALL storem(m( ), 6, y)
CALL printm("Jun", m( ), 16, 40)
'
a$ = INPUT$(1)
'     Process next 6 months
'
CLS
CALL storem(m( ), 7, y)
CALL printm("Jul", m( ), 1, 1)
CALL storem(m( ), 8, y)
CALL printm("Aug", m( ), 1, 40)
CALL storem(m( ), 9, y)
CALL printm("Sep", m( ), 9, 1)
CALL storem(m( ), 10, y)
CALL printm("Oct", m( ), 9, 40)
CALL storem(m( ), 11, y)
CALL printm("Nov", m( ), 16, 1)
CALL storem(m( ), 12, y)
CALL printm("Dec", m( ), 16, 40)
'
'        Functions and Procedures

FUNCTION daysperyr (yr)
    IF leapyr(yr) = -1 THEN
        daysperyr = 366
    ELSE
        daysperyr = 365
    END IF
END FUNCTION

FUNCTION getoffset (month, yr)
    SHARED jan1994
    offset = jan1994
    FOR y = 1994 TO yr - 1
        offset = offset + daysperyr(y)
    NEXT y
    offset = offset MOD 7
    IF m = 1 THEN
        getoffset = offset
    ELSE
        FOR m = 2 TO month
            offset = offset + numdays(m - 1, yr)
        NEXT m
        getoffset = offset MOD 7
    END IF
END FUNCTION
```

```
SUB initm (m( ))
    FOR w = 1 TO 6
        FOR d = 1 TO 7
            m(w, d) = 0
        NEXT d
    NEXT w
END SUB

FUNCTION leapyr (y)
    true = -1: false = 0
   IF (y MOD 4 = 0 AND y MOD 100 <> 0) OR (y MOD 4 = 0 AND y MOD 400 = 0) THEN
        leapyr = true
   ELSE
        leapyr = false
   END IF
END FUNCTION

FUNCTION numdays (month, yr)
    SELECT CASE month
        CASE 1, 3, 5, 7, 8, 10, 12
            numdays = 31
        CASE 4, 6, 9, 11
            numdays = 30
        CASE 2
            IF leapyr(yr) = -1 THEN
                numdays = 29
            ELSE
                numdays = 28
            END IF
    END SELECT
END FUNCTION

SUB printm (m$, m( ), r, c)
    LOCATE r, c
    PRINT "          "; m$
    LOCATE r + 1, c
    PRINT "   M   T   W   Th  F   S   Su"
    FOR week = 1 TO 6
        r = r + 1
        LOCATE r + 1, c
        FOR day = 1 TO 7
            IF m(week, day) = 0 THEN
                PRINT "    ";
            ELSE
                PRINT USING "####"; m(week, day);
            END IF
        NEXT day
        PRINT
    NEXT week
END SUB
```

```
SUB storem (m( ), mnth, yr)
    c = 0: n = 1
    CALL initm(m( ))
    maxdays = numdays(mnth, yr)
    offset = getoffset(mnth, yr)
    IF offset = 0 THEN offset = 7
    FOR week = 1 TO 6
        FOR day = 1 TO 7
            IF (n > offset - 1) AND (c < maxdays) THEN
                c = c + 1
                m(week, day) = c
            END IF
            n = n + 1
        NEXT day
    NEXT week
END SUB
```

8.9 Recursion

Recursion is the technique of describing something in terms of itself. So a recursive procedure or function is said to be self-referential. Recursion is an alternative method to iterative algorithms.

The simplest example that appears in many books dealing with the topic of recursion is factorials. One way of describing a factorial is to give an example like the following and then generalise it.

$5! = 5 \times 4 \times 3 \times 2 \times 1$ (where ! is a short-hand for factorial)

More generally we could say:

$n! = n \times (n-1) \times (n-2) \times \ldots\ldots \times 3 \times 2 \times 1$

To be more accurate we would also have to state that 0! = 1.

We could implement this non-recursively using the following function:

```
FUNCTION fac# (n%)
    prod# = 1
    IF n% = 0 THEN
        fac# = 1
    ELSE
        FOR c% = n% TO 1 step -1
            prod = prod * c%
        NEXT c%
        fac# = prod
    END IF
END FUNCTION
```

But if you look at the first definition again you will notice that it can easily be expanded as follows:

$$n! = n \times (n-1) \times (n-2) \times \ldots\ldots\ldots\ldots \times 3 \times 2 \times 1$$

$$\begin{aligned} \Rightarrow \quad n! &= n \times (n-1)! \\ (n-1)! &= (n-1) \times (n-2)! \\ (n-2)! &= (n-2) \times (n-3)! \\ &. \\ &. \\ &. \\ 3! &= 3 \times 2! \\ 2! &= 2 \times 1! \\ 1! &= 1 \times 0! \end{aligned}$$

and we know what 0! is. 0! = 1 by definition.

These expressions are called recurrence relations. If we take the most general expression which is:

$$n! = n \times (n-1)!$$

and the terminating condition 0! = 1, we can easily write a recursive function to do the same thing. Such a recursive function may look like this:

```
FUNCTION fac# (n%)
        IF n% = 1 THEN
                fac# = 1
        ELSE
                fac# = n% * fac#( n% - 1)
        END IF
END FUNCTION
```

This is in many respects simpler and more elegant than the previous function definition but there is a price to pay. If you were to try out the recursive function with the following function call:

```
PRINT fac#(100)
```

It would result in the following error message:

```
Out of Stack Space
```

This can be resolved by adding the statement

```
CLEAR ,, 20000
```

at the beginning of the program. This particular statement clears 20000 bytes of stack space.

Now is the time to explain how recursion works.

		Stack		Stack	
	0!	1		1	**Pop items off stack**
	1!	1 × 0!		1 × 1	↓
	2!	2 × 1!	→	2 × 1	
	3!	3 × 2!		3 × 2	
↑	4!	4 × 3!		4 × 6	
push items on stack	5!	5 × 4!		5 × 24	

Fig 8-4 Recursive evaluation of 5!

Each time a recursive call is made it is stored on the stack ready to be used at a later time. When a termination condition arises (0! = 1) this stops. The first item is popped off the stack and the value substituted into the expression below. This continues until the last item on the stack is removed. By this time 5! has been evaluated. See fig 8-4.

The next example is a look at printing recursively. Suppose we had to print out the characters of a string until a terminator "\" is detected this could easily be done iteratively as follows:

```
SUB printchar (a$)
        c = 1
        WHILE ch$ <> "\"
                ch$ = MID$(a$, c, 1)
                IF ch$ <> "\" THEN PRINT ch$
                c = c + 1
        WEND
END SUB
```

To do this recursively you could use a function or a procedure as follows:

```
FUNCTION putc$ (a$, n)
        IF MID$ (a$, n, 1) = "\" THEN
                putc$ = CHR$(7)        ' terminate with a beep
        ELSE
                putc$ = MID$ (a$, n, 1) + putc$ (a$, n + 1)
        END IF
END FUNCTION

SUB printc (a$, n)
        IF MID$(a$, n, 1) = "\" THEN
                PRINT CHR$(7)
        ELSE
                PRINT MID$(a$, n, 1); printc(a$, n + 1)
        END IF
END SUB
```

Exercise 8-3

1. (a) Write a program to maintain a sorted list of up to 100 records with the following record structure:

```
TYPE employee
        name AS STRING * 20
        jobpos AS STRING * 10
        rateofpay AS SINGLE
END TYPE
```

   (b) The program should have a procedure which will produce a menu with the following options:

   1. Search for a record
   2. Insert a record
   3. Delete a record
   4. Display a list of employees
   5. Quit the menu

   (c) Write procedures/functions to implement all the options in the menu.

2. Write a program to print a string 1 character at a time with a 1 second pause between characters.

   (a) The first version should use a non-recursive procedure

   (b) The second version should use a recursive function

   (c) The third a recursive procedure.

3. Fibonacci numbers can be defined by the recurrence relations:

$$F_1 = 1 \ , \ F_2 = 1 \ , \ F_n = F_{n-1} + F_{n-2}$$

   (a) Write a non-recursive function to compute Fibonacci numbers.

   (b) Write a recursive function to do the same thing.

9. Simple Graphics and Sound

9.1 Plotting in Text Mode

In the early days of computer graphics, students at university used to write Fortran programs that would produce pictures made up of normal characters. The trick was to choose appropriate characters that produced the right amount of shading.

The advantage of this type of graphics is that it can be produced on any computer and whatever appears on the screen can be reproduced on any printer. The main disadvantage is the very low resolution and complete lack of graphics commands.

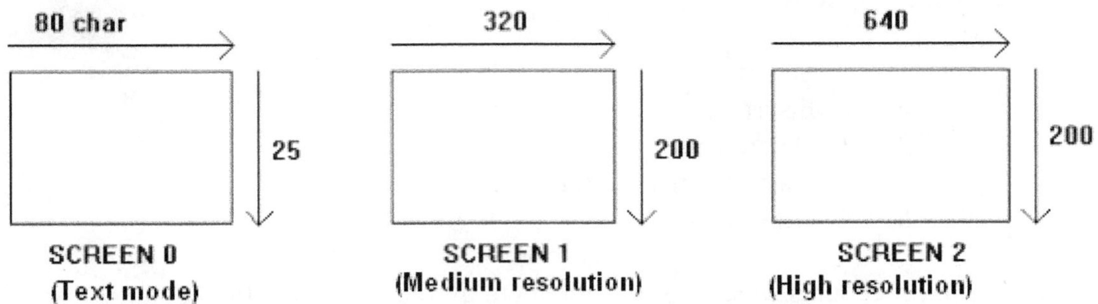

Fig 9-1 Resolution for Graphics screens

In text mode the resolution of the screen is 80 characters per line × 25 lines per screen. We have already used LOCATE and PRINT statements to position characters on a screen. If you were to take a grid of transparent graph paper 80×25 or 80×50 you could create an impressionist picture by colouring individual squares. These can then be reproduced by using PRINT CHR$(219) on the screen. Don't forget about the COLOR statement if you want to work in colour.

As an example of the range of colours you can get try out the following program. In this program the colour of each character position is determined at random.

```
FOR lines = 1 to 25
        FOR  columns = 1 to 80
                LOCATE (lines, columns)
                        c = (16 * RND ) \ 1
                        COLOR c
                        PRINT CHR$(219);
        NEXT columns
NEXT lines
```

Plotting your own picture is somewhat more tedious. Back to the graph paper again before you start programming. A slightly more sophisticated approach would be to create 5×5 picture elements which can be slotted in place.

As an example we will look at designing large letters that can be printed on the screen. A reasonable likeness can be achieved using a 10×8 grid. You might want to start using graph paper for the initial representation. But how do you store this information in the computer ? You could for instance:

1. Use a 10×8 array which will store 0's and 1's.

2. Use a one-dimensional array containing 10 strings, each of 8 characters.

Fig 9-2 The number 3

Rather than type in the information at a keyboard it is preferable to use DATA statements. The two methods of representation are illustrated below:

```
REM -- Method 1
DIM a1(1 TO 8, 1 TO 10)
FOR row = 1 TO 10
        FOR col = 1 TO 8
                READ x
                a1(row, col) = x
        NEXT col
NEXT row
'
DATA 0,1,1,1,1,1,1,0,1,1,1,1,1,1,1,1,1,1,0,0,0,0,1,1 ...
DATA ...
```

```
REM -- Method 2
DIM a2$(1 TO 10)
FOR row = 1 TO 10
        read x$
        a2$(row) = x$
NEXT row
'
DATA "01111110","11111111","11000011","00000011","00011110"
DATA "00011110","00000011",11000011","11111111", "01111110"
```

Once the characters are stored in arrays as suggested you will need a procedure to print the character using their contents. Using the second method as an example of this the procedure will need to:

```
For each string in the array
        For each character in the string
                If character is a "1" print CHR$(219)
                otherwise print a space
```

A workable version follows. You will note that it is also important to be able to position this character. Hence the parameters **row** and **col**.

```
SUB printnum (num$( ), row, col)
        FOR c = 1 TO 10
                LOCATE row , col
                FOR ch = 1 TO 8
                        IF MID$(num$( c) , 1, 1) = "1" THEN
                                PRINT CHR$(219);
                        ELSE
                                PRINT " ";
                        END IF
                NEXT ch
                PRINT
                row = row + 1 ' Move  to next line
        NEXT c
END SUB
```

9.2 Creating a Digital Clock

Using the representation for storing large characters discussed in the last section we are going to look at a simple application. Creating a digital clock.

A first design might go something like this:

```
For all the numbers 0 - 9
        Load the characters into arrays
Continue until an Esc is pressed
        Print out time in large letters
```

The design can then be expanded. In particular we need to know how the time is going to be printed out:

```
Print out time in large letters
        Obtain time (t$ = TIMER$)
        Extract hours, minutes and seconds from time
        For each of hours, minutes, seconds
                Print character corresponding to left digit and right digit
                ( separated by colon as a separator)
```

The entire program follows. As an exercise you may consider constructing a structure chart to show the relationship between the various procedures and functions.

```
REM -- digital clock program
DECLARE SUB loadnumbers ( )
DECLARE FUNCTION hours$ (t$)
DECLARE FUNCTION minutes$ (t$)
DECLARE FUNCTION seconds$ (t$)
DECLARE SUB selectnum (d$, r!, c!)
DECLARE SUB printtime ( )
DECLARE SUB loadnum (num$( ))
DECLARE SUB printnum (num$( ), r!, c!)
'     Declare character arrays
DIM zero$(1 TO 10), one$(1 TO 10), two$(1 TO 10)
DIM three$(1 TO 10), four$(1 TO 10), five$(1 TO 10)
DIM six$(1 TO 10), seven$(1 TO 10), eight$(1 TO 10)
DIM nine$(1 TO 10), pt$(1 TO 10)
'
CLS
'
CALL loadnumbers
'
DO UNTIL a$ = CHR$(27)
        a$ = INKEY$
        CALL printtime
```

```
LOOP
'    Data for character arrays
REM -- zero
DATA "01111110", "11111111", "11000011", "11000011", "11000011"
DATA "11000011", "11000011", "11000011", "11111111", "01111110"
REM -- one
DATA "00011000", "00111000", "00011000", "00011000", "00011000"
DATA "00011000", "00011000", "00011000", "00011000", "00111100"
REM -- two
DATA "01111110","11000011", "10000001", "00000011", "00000111"
DATA "00001100", "00011000", "00110000", "01100000", "11111111"
REM -- three
DATA "01111110", "11111111", "11000011", "00000011", "00011110"
DATA "00011110", "00000011", "11000011", "11111111", "01111110"
REM -- four
DATA "00001000", "00011000", "00111000", "01101000", "11001000"
DATA "11111111", "00001000", "00001000", "00001000", "00001000"
REM -- five
DATA "11111111", "10000000", "10000000", "10000000", "11111110"
DATA "00000011", "00000001", "10000001", "11000011", "01111110"
REM -- six
DATA "00111100", "01000010", "10000001", "10000000", "10000000"
DATA "10111110", "11000011", "11000011", "11000011", "01111110"
REM -- seven
DATA "11111111", "11111111", "00000011", "00000110", "00001100"
DATA "00011000", "00110000", "01100000", "11000000", "11000000"
REM -- eight
DATA "01111110", "11000011", "11000011", "11000011", "01111110"
DATA "01111110", "11000011", "11000011", "11000011", "01111110"
REM -- nine
DATA "01111111", "11000011", "11000011", "11000011", "01111111"
DATA "00000011", "00000011", "00000011", "00000011", "00000011"
REM -- pt
DATA "00000000", "00000000", "00011000", "00000000", "00000000"
DATA "00000000", "00011000", "00000000", "00000000", "00000000"

'    Functions and Procedures

FUNCTION hours$ (t$)
        hours$ = LEFT$(t$, 2)
END FUNCTION

SUB loadnum (num$( ))
        FOR c = 1 TO 10
                READ b$
                num$(c) = b$
        NEXT c
END SUB
```

```
SUB loadnumbers
        SHARED zero$( ), one$( ), two$( ), three$( ), four$( ), five$( )
        SHARED six$( ), seven$( ), eight$( ), nine$( ), pt$( )
        CALL loadnum(zero$( ))
        CALL loadnum(one$( ))
        CALL loadnum(two$( ))
        CALL loadnum(three$( ))
        CALL loadnum(four$( ))
        CALL loadnum(five$( ))
        CALL loadnum(six$( ))
        CALL loadnum(seven$( ))
        CALL loadnum(eight$( ))
        CALL loadnum(nine$( ))
        CALL loadnum(pt$( ))
END SUB

FUNCTION minutes$ (t$)
        minutes$ = MID$(t$, 4, 2)
END FUNCTION

SUB printnum (num$( ), row, col)
        FOR c = 1 TO 10
                LOCATE row, col
                FOR l = 1 TO 8
                                IF MID$(num$(c), l, 1) = "1" THEN
                                        PRINT CHR$(219);
                                ELSE
                                        PRINT " ";
                                END IF
                NEXT l
                PRINT
                row = row + 1
        NEXT c
END SUB

SUB printtime
        SHARED pt$( )
        t$ = TIME$
        ldigit$ = LEFT$(hours$(t$), 1)
        rdigit$ = RIGHT$(hours$(t$), 1)
        CALL selectnum(ldigit$, 1, 1)
        CALL selectnum(rdigit$, 1, 11)
        '
        CALL printnum(pt$( ), 1, 21)
        '
        ldigit$ = LEFT$(minutes$(t$), 1)
        rdigit$ = RIGHT$(minutes$(t$), 1)
        LOCATE 20, 1
        CALL selectnum(ldigit$, 1, 31)
```

```
        CALL selectnum(rdigit$, 1, 41)
        '
        CALL printnum(pt$( ), 1, 51)
        ldigit$ = LEFT$(seconds$(t$), 1)
        rdigit$ = RIGHT$(seconds$(t$), 1)
        CALL selectnum(ldigit$, 1, 61)
        CALL selectnum(rdigit$, 1, 71)
END SUB

FUNCTION seconds$ (t$)
        seconds$ = RIGHT$(t$, 2)
END FUNCTION

SUB selectnum (d$, r, c)
        SHARED zero$( ), one$( ), two$( ), three$( ), four$( )
        SHARED five$( ), six$( ), seven$( ), eight$( ), nine$( )
        SELECT CASE d$
                CASE "0"
                                CALL printnum(zero$( ), r, c)
                CASE "1"
                                CALL printnum(one$( ), r, c)
                CASE "2"
                                CALL printnum(two$( ), r, c)
                CASE "3"
                                CALL printnum(three$( ), r, c)
                CASE "4"
                                CALL printnum(four$( ), r, c)
                CASE "5"
                                CALL printnum(five$( ), r, c)
                CASE "6"
                                CALL printnum(six$( ), r, c)
                CASE "7"
                                CALL printnum(seven$( ), r, c)
                CASE "8"
                                CALL printnum(eight$( ), r, c)
                CASE "9"
                                CALL printnum(nine$( ), r, c)
        END SELECT
END SUB
```

Exercise 9.1

1. A floor robot can travel in one of 4 directions, North, East , South and West. Under certain conditions however the robot malfunctions and the path it will follow is unpredictable.

   Write a program that will trace the robots path. You are to assume that:

   (a) The robot is represented by CHR$(219) and starts at the middle of the screen.

   (b) Each of the directions is assigned a number (1 - 4). The direction taken will be determined by generating a random number in the range 1 - 4.

   If you haven't done any boundary checking you may get the error message:

   Illegal Function call

   indicating that you have attempted to plot a character off the edge of the screen.

   Modify your program so that:

   (c) The robot will stop when it reaches the edge of the screen.

   (d) The number of steps taken to reach the edge of the screen is printed out.

9.3 Lines Points and Circles

In graphics mode the screen is made up of thousands of picture elements (pixels). In the case of medium resolution graphics (SCREEN 1) there are 320×200 pixels and for high resolution there are 640×200 pixels. See Fig 9.1

These pixels are either switched on or off. If you want to plot a point you switch on the pixel nearest to that point by using the command:

```
PSET (x, y)
```

If you want to switch it off i.e. rub out the point you enter:

```
PRESET (x,y)
```

So in the same manner that we printed characters in Text mode, we can plot or rub out points in one of the graphics modes.

In addition to these there are many other graphics primitives such as LINE which can be used to:

1. Plot lines

   ```
   LINE (x1, y1)-(x2, y2)
   ```

   draws a line between the points (x1, y1) and (x2, y2).

2. Draw rectangles

   ```
   LINE (x1, y1)-(x2, y2), , B
   ```

   Draws a rectangle with bottom-left corner (x1, y1) and top-right corner (x2, y2).

3. Draw filled rectangle

   ```
   LINE (x1, y1)-(x2, y2), , BF
   ```

   Draws the same rectangle as above but filled in.

When drawing lines the LINE statement can be abbreviated to:

```
LINE-(x1, y1)
```

This format is used if you want to draw a line between the point (x1, y1) and the point last referenced. This is often used in conjunction with the PSET statement as follows:

```
PSET 20, 40
LINE-(100, 130)
```

and is equivalent in effect to the single statement:

```
LINE (20, 40)-(100, 130)
```

These ideas will now be explored further by tackling a simple problem. You are now required to think about how you can draw a cube.

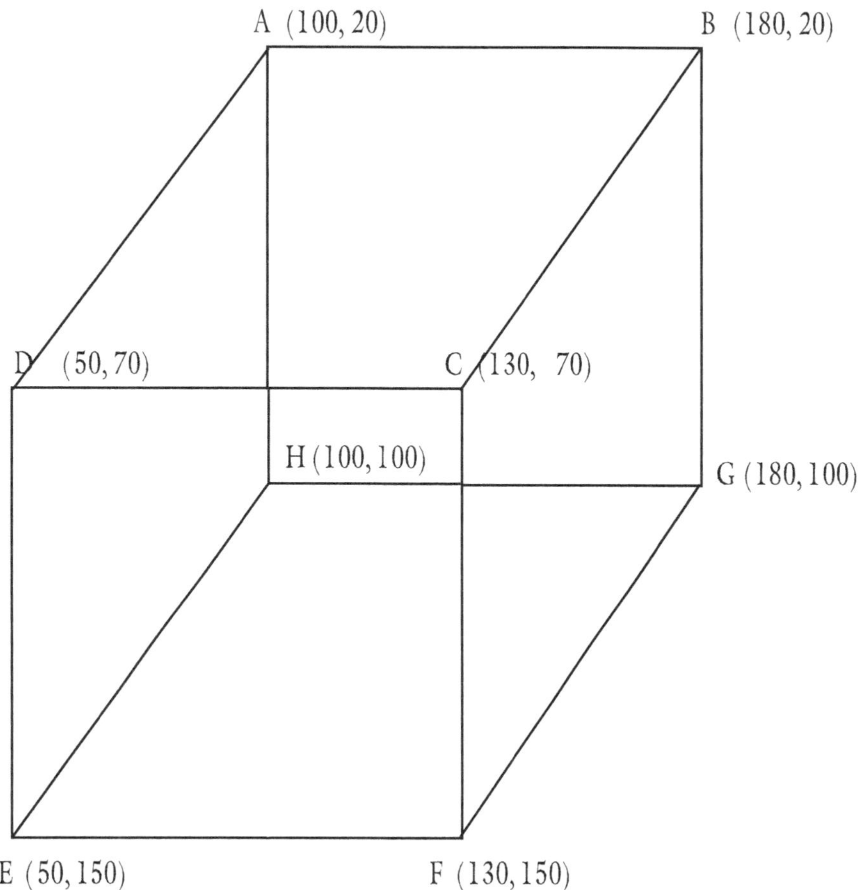

Fig 9-3 Drawing a cube in medium resolution

There are several strategies that you could try out.

1. Work out the lines you need to draw by making a list such as:

   Lines AB, BC, CD, DA, EH, HG, GF, FE, ED, HA, BG, FC

   and write a program which has an appropriate LINE statement for each line in your list.

   ```
   REM -- Version 1
   SCREEN 1
   LINE (100, 20)-(180, 20)      ' etc.
   ```

2. Work out a path that will pass along every line of the cube such as:

   Path A →B→C→D→A→H→E→F→G→H→E→D→C→F→G→B

   Use PSET to plot point A and follow this with statements of form LINE-(x,y) to connect up the list of points. This is probably the best method if you are going to store your points in DATA statements.

   ```
   REM -- Version 2
   SCREEN 1
   PSET (100,20)
   LINE -(180, 20)        ' etc.
   ```

3. And lastly you will notice that the cube is made up of two squares and four other lines. So it could be constructed using:

   ```
   REM -- Version 3
   SCREEN 1
   LINE (100, 100)-(180,120), , B
   LINE (50, 150)-(130, 70), , B
   LINE (50, 70)-(100, 20)
   LINE (130, 70)-(180, 20)
   LINE (50, 150)-(100,100)
   LINE (130, 150)-(180, 100)
   ```

The circle statement can be used to draw a circle. It has the format:

```
CIRCLE (x, y), r
```

where (x, y) is the centre of the circle and r the radius.

An arc of a circle can be drawn using the extended syntax of the CIRCLE statement. For instance the statement:

```
CIRCLE (100, 100), 80, 0, 3.14159 / 2
                       ▲      ▲
                     start   end
```

will create an arc of a circle with an inside angle of 90^0 between the ends. It has two other parameters a start angle and an end angle, both of which are to be expressed in radians. For those of us used to thinking in terms of degrees:

360 degrees = $2\times\pi$ Radians (π is taken as 3.14159)

Regions can be filled in or painted using the PAINT statement. The idea is you choose a point inside the region you want to fill. Then use a command such as:

```
PAINT (x, y)  ' (x, y) is any point inside the enclosed region
```

An example of the PAINT statement follows. Here it is being used to colour in a circle.

```
CIRCLE (100, 50), 20
PAINT (100, 50)        ' (100, 50) is a point inside the circle
```

9.4 Using Colour

Colour can be introduced into both medium resolution graphics and high resolution graphics by use of the COLOR statement. It has a general format:

```
COLOR b, p
```

Where b denotes the background colour, and p the palette number (0 -1).

Number	Colour	Number	Colour
0	Black	8	Grey
1	Blue	9	Light Blue
2	Green	10	Light Green
3	Cyan	11	Light Cyan
4	Red	12	Light Red
5	Magenta	13	Light Magenta
6	Brown	14	Yellow
7	White	15	Intense White

Fig 9-4 The standard colours

The background can be any of the colours in Fig 9-4. However when it comes to drawing lines and plotting points etc the range of colours is limited to four colours (whatever is in palette 0 or palette 1)

m	Palette 0	Palette 1
0	background colour	background colour
1	green	cyan
2	red	magenta
3	brown	white

Fig 9-5 Contents of palettes 0, 1

The following statement:

```
COLOR 8, 1
```

Will select a grey background and palette 1. Any subsequent statement will now by default draw in white (colour 3 of palette 1)

The following illustrates this:

```
SCREEN 1
COLOR 8, 1                      ' Set background colour to grey and palette = 1
PSET (100, 100)                 ' Plot a white point (Colour 3 of current palette is
                                ' default)
LINE-(150, 100)                      ' Draw a white line
LINE (120, 20)-(170,50), , BF        ' A white filled in rectangle
CIRCLE (50, 50), 30                  ' A white circle
PAINT (50,50)                        ' Fill in the white circle
```

You can override the default colour by adding the colour to any of the above by including a number m for the colour in the graphics command.

i.e.
```
PSET (x, y), m
LINE-(x1, y1), m
LINE (x1, y1)-(x2, y2), m
LINE (x1, y1)-(x2, y2),m , B
LINE  (x1, y1)-(x2, y2),m , BF
CIRCLE (x, y), r, m
PAINT (x, y), m
```

and in the case of the PAINT statement there is yet another format:

```
PAINT (x, y), m, b
```

where b is the colour of the boundary to be filled. With this version you can specify the colour of the boundary of the shape you want to fill in. This is necessary if you want to paint it a different colour.

To illustrate these ideas further lets look at the problem of creating a simulation using traffic lights. The following program fragment could be used as a starting point to produce a picture of a set of traffic lights:

```
SCREEN 1
COLOR 8, 0
green = 1 : red = 2 : amber = 3 ' Note colour 3 which is stated as brown
'                                 is a bit like amber.
LINE (75, 155)-(125, 25), , B
CIRCLE (100, 50), 20, red
PAINT (100, 50), red            ' The colour for PAINT must be the same as
'                                 the boundary
```

An alternative to using this is to specify the colour of the boundary to be painted as in the following:

```
CIRCLE (100, 50), 20' Take default colour which is brown
PAINT (100, 50), red, 3      ' Now need to specify what colour the boundary
'                              is or disaster will befall you
```

9.5 User-defined co-ordinate systems

One of the problems of using the screen to produce graphics is that the co-ordinate system provided goes in the same direction as text mode. This is fine if we are concerned with displaying lines of text, but very confusing if we are used to co-ordinate systems that start with (0,0) at the bottom left-hand corner etc. We can get round this problem by using the WINDOW command. For any serious graphics work you need to be able to do this.

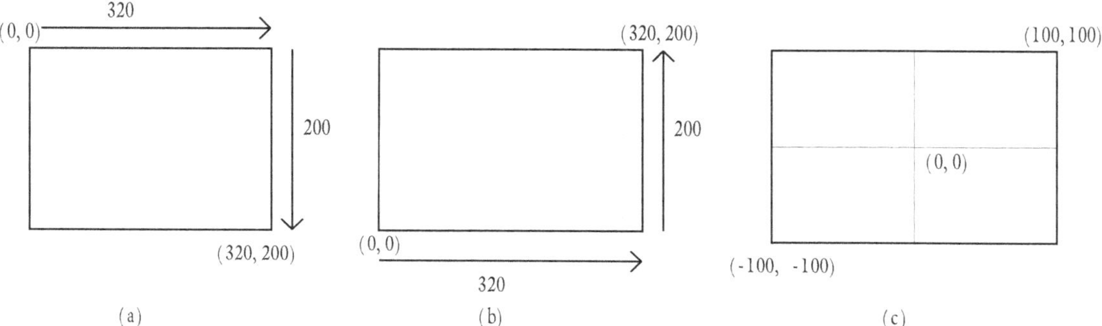

Fig 9-6 Effect of using the WINDOW command

If you refer to Fig 9-6 you will see that there are 3 example screens.

(a) Is the default medium resolution screen. It could however be created with the command:

```
WINDOW SCREEN (0, 0)-(320, 200)
```

The key word SCREEN indicates that the co-ordinates will go in the same direction as text mode.

(b) A much more useful version for graphics work, with the co-ordinates going in the correct direction. It is produced with:

```
WINDOW (0, 0)-(320, 200)
```

(c) You can customise your screen co-ordinates in any way you like. This one however is produced using:

```
WINDOW (-100, -100)-(100, 100)
```

Exercise 9-2

1. (a) Write a program to simulate the operation of a set of traffic lights such as the following:

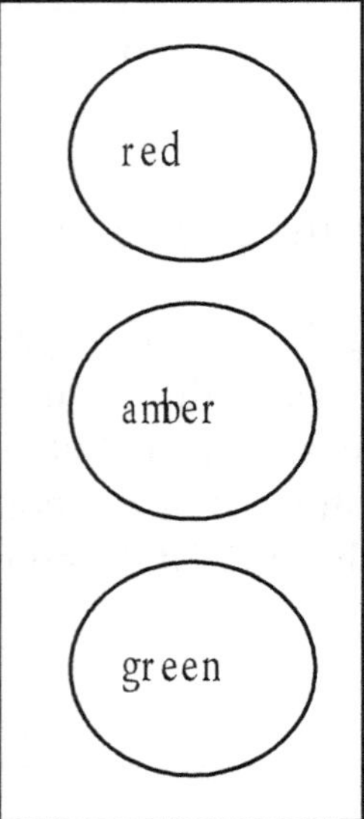

Fig 9-7 A set of Traffic Lights

(b) You should include procedures called red, amber, green, redamber to turn on the lights.

(c) Your program should call up these procedures so that the lights are turned on in the correct order with a 2 second delay between lights. The order is:

Green, Amber, Red, Red + Amber, Green, Amber, Red etc.

2. Write a program that can be used by a young child learning to use a keyboard for the first time. The idea is to print large letters corresponding to the keys pressed. The following criteria should be used:

(a) It will print large capital letters. These you will have to design yourself. You may consider using a 10×8 grid as in fig 9-8

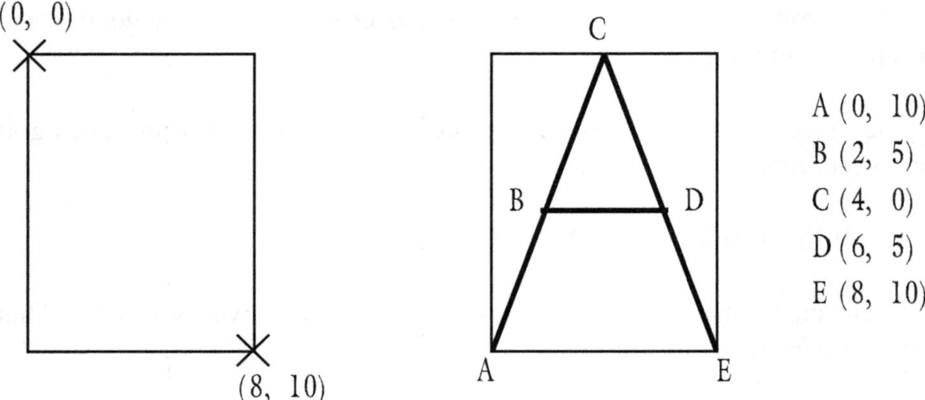

Fig 9.8 Using Vector graphics to create a letter.

(b) The letter can be produced by joining appropriate pairs of points. These points could be stored as follows in a DATA statement.

```
a:      DATA 0, 10, 4, 0, 4, 0, 8, 10, 2, 5, 6, 5, -1, -1, -1, -1
```

Here a data terminator -1 is used to indicate when there are no more points to read.

(c) You will need to have a DATA statement for each letter of the alphabet. The label a: is present so that a RESTORE statement can be used so that the appropriate data can be read for the letter you want to draw.

(d) You will need to write a procedure which will read data in a particular DATA statement and draw the letter.

(e) You will need to write some code that will accept input from the user. The key pressed will determine which letter to draw.

(f) Make sure that the next letter gets drawn to the right of the previous letter with a suitable gap. And when you reach the end of the line subsequent letters will be drawn on the next line. You can do all of this with LOCATE statements.

9.6 Drawing Polygons

Drawing regular polygons requires us to do some mathematics to calculate the position of each of the corners.

If you were to construct a polygon manually you would perhaps draw a circle first. Any regular polygon can be fitted around a circle. Its just a matter of calculating the size of the angle turned at the centre of the circle. Then marking the corners around the edge of the circle by measuring equal angles from the centre.

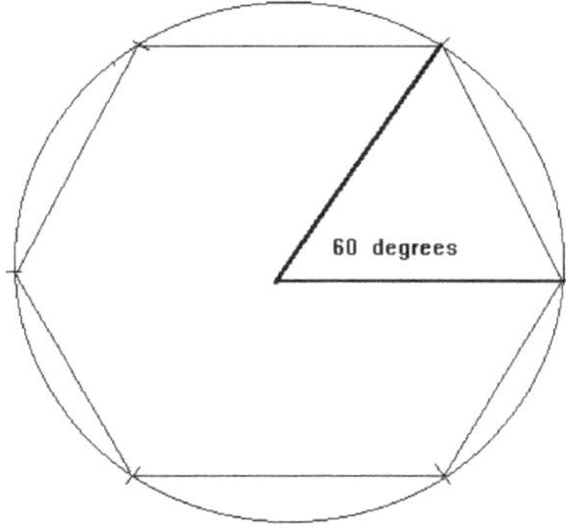

Fig 9-9 Constructing a hexagon Angle turned = 360 / 6

To draw a hexagon on the screen we need to be able to compute the co-ordinates of each point. This is just a matter of using standard trigonometry. See Fig 9-10

1. You need to remember your trig ratios sine, cosine and tangent.

2. The problem we need to solve reduces to solving right-angled triangles. Now stop and check out the mathematical working see Fig 9-10. Once you have done this you will end up with the following equations:

   (i) $\frac{x}{r} = \cos(60) \Rightarrow x = r \times \cos(60)$

   (ii) $\frac{y}{r} = \sin(60) \Rightarrow y = r \times \sin(60)$

   Which you can evaluate using the functions SIN and COS.

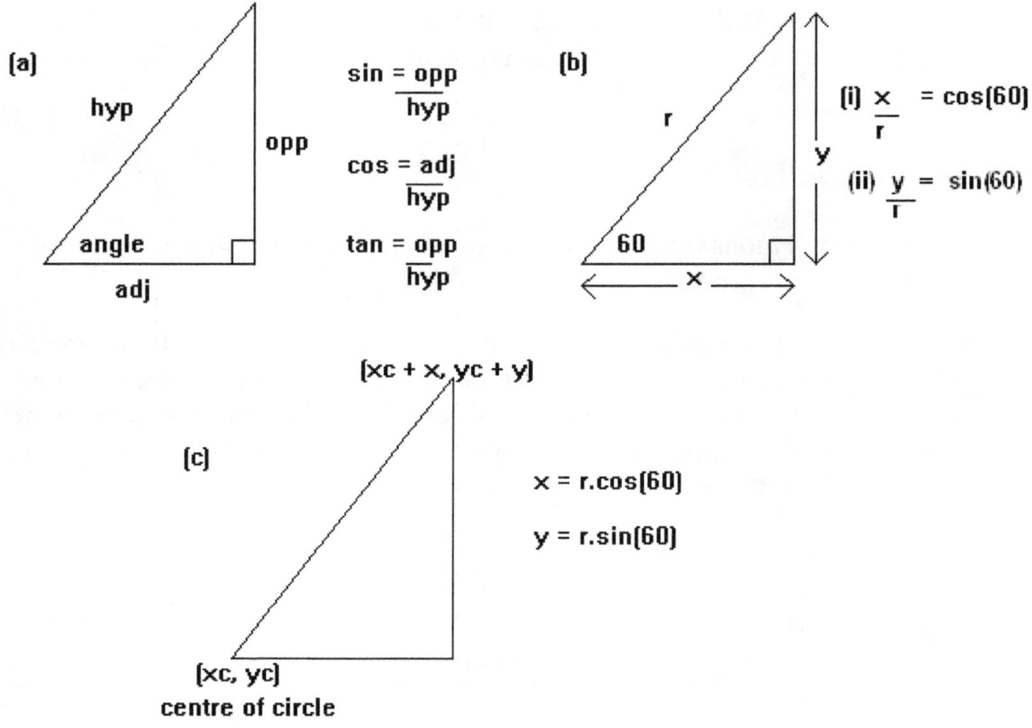

Fig 9.10 Use of Trigonometry to compute the next point

3. Having worked out distances x, and y we can now compute the new point by adding these values to the centre of the circle (xc, yc) to give:

   nextpoint = (xc + r × cos(60), yc + r × sin(60))

4. We cannot directly code this in QBASIC because the SIN and COS functions take an angle expressed in Radians not degrees.

$$360 \text{ degrees} = 2 \times 3.14159 \text{ radians}$$

$$\Rightarrow \quad 1 \text{ degree} = \frac{2 \times 3.14159}{360} \text{ radians}$$

$$\Rightarrow \quad 60 \text{ degrees} = \frac{2 \times 3.14159 \times 60}{360} \text{ radians}$$

5. To get successive points we have to turn through an angle of:

   60, 120, 180, 240, 300, 360 degrees

A simple program to plot a hexagon may now look like this:

```
REM -- Hexagon Plot
SCREEN 1
REM -- Centre of circle (xc, yc) , radius r.
pi = 3.14159 : xc = 100 : yc = 100 : r = 50
PSET (xc + r, yc)
FOR c = 0 TO 360 STEP 60
        angle = 2 * pi * c / 360        ' Convert angle to radians
        x = xc + r * COS(angle)
        y = yc + r * SIN(angle)
        LINE-(x, y)                     ' connect next corner to previous one
NEXT c
```

A more useful representation would involve writing a procedure to draw a hexagon. And rather than plot the polygons around the same centre point (xc, yc), and have the same constant size ; xc , yc, and size of radius should be passed as parameters.

Writing your programs in terms of procedures and functions also makes it easier for you to write more general and flexible programs. The hexagon program should be rewritten as:

```
DECALARE SUB hexagon ( xc!, yc!, r!)
SCREEN 1
REM -- draw a hexagon
CALL hexagon(100, 100, 50)

SUB hexagon(xc, yc, r)
        pi = 3.14159
        PSET(xc + r, yc)
        FOR c = 0 TO 360 STEP 60
                angle = 2 * pi * c / 360
                x = xc + r * COS(angle)
                y = yc + r * SIN(angle)
                LINE-(x, y)
        NEXT c
END SUB
```

Writing similar procedures you could draw pentagons, octagons and decagons etc. Even better would be the idea of creating a procedure called polygon which will take an extra parameter **s** (number of sides) and draw any polygon at all.

9.7 Styled Lines and Tiling

A styled line is made up of a sequence of dots and dashes. You can describe the type of line you want by appending a hexadecimal number to the end of a LINE command.

i.e LINE (x1, y1)-(x2, y2), , , &style

where &style is a 4 digit hexadecimal number.

To work out this number you will need to start with a 16 bit binary number. Here 1's are use to code for dots, and 0's for spaces. If you want a dash you get this by having a contiguous sequence of 1's. You may end up with a binary number such as:

1110110011101100

The first thing you need to do is split this up into groups of 4 binary digits

1110 1100 1110 1100

Each of these groups of digits represents a hexadecimal digit. You can translate these into hexadecimal by using the conversion table in fig 9.11 giving:

1110 1100 1110 1100
↓ ↓ ↓ ↓
E C E C

Binary	Hex	Binary	Hex	Binary	Hex	Binary	Hex
0000	0	0100	4	1000	8	1100	C
0001	1	0101	5	1001	9	1101	D
0010	2	0110	6	1010	A	1110	E
0011	3	0111	7	1011	B	1111	F

Fig 9-11 Conversion table Binary to Hexadecimal

You can now try this out with the following:

```
SCREEN 1
LINE (100, 100)-(200, 100), , , &HECEC
```

You can even draw rectangles using styled lines using statements such as:

```
LINE (100, 50)-(200, 150), , B, &HECEC
```

but unfortunately it won't work if you try and extend this idea to draw filled rectangles.

You can however create tiles, and fill a shape with these tiles. A tile is made up of a grid of pixels (8 pixels horizontally and between 1 and 64 pixels vertically). A tile is represented by a string. Each component of the string is a character that represents each horizontal element of 8 pixels. If a pixel is to be switched on it is coded as a 1, 0 otherwise. Each horizontal element then can be thought of as an 8 digit binary number which has to be converted to decimal.

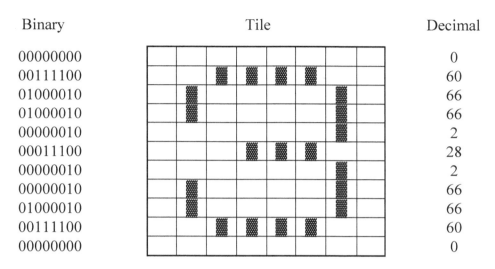

Binary	Tile	Decimal
00000000	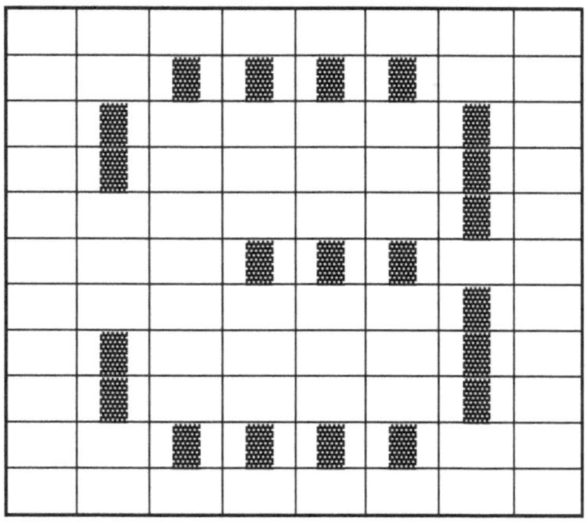	0
00111100		60
01000010		66
01000010		66
00000010		2
00011100		28
00000010		2
00000010		66
01000010		66
00111100		60
00000000		0

t$ = CHR$(60) + CHR$(66) + CHR$(66) + CHR$(2) + CHR$(28) + ...

Fig 9-12 Creating a Tile

You can test this out by running the following program:

```
SCREEN 2
t$ = ""
FOR c = 1 TO 11
        READ n                  ' Create tile string
        t$ = t$ + CHR$(n)
NEXT c
CIRCLE (300, 100), 100
PAINT (300, 100), t$            ' Fill circle with tiling pattern
'
DATA   0,60,66,66,2,28,2,66,66,60,0
```

You can create tiles in medium resolution using the same method as above. However each horizontal element must be 4 pixels instead of 8.

9.8 Business Graphics

Managers would much rather have a graphical interpretation of data rather then pages and pages of figures. The most common forms of graphical representation are illustrated in Fig 9-13

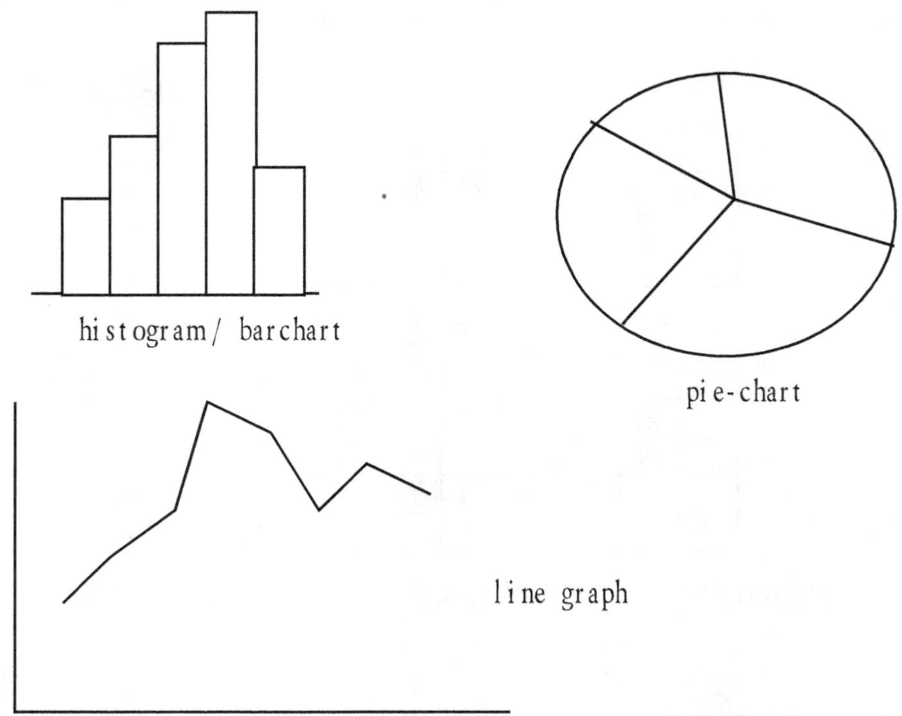

Fig 9.13 Bar-charts, Histograms, Pie-charts and line graphs

To create any of the above an appropriate scale needs to be worked out in advance. In the case of Bar charts, histograms and line graphs you should know the maximum and minimum values along the x and y axes. Make sure that you leave a suitably sized boundary and use the WINDOW command to set this up. This will simplify the program later.

To try out you business graphics ideally you want to use some real data. Either data that has been published or data you collect for yourself. The following examples should provide you with an insight as to the way that you may proceed and some of the problems you may encounter.

Year	Male	Female
1840	40	42
1870	41	45
1900	44	48
1930	59	63
1960	69	74

Fig 9-14 Life Expectancy in Years

We will first consider bar-charts and histograms. Technically there is a subtle difference between a bar-chart and a histogram. A histogram always has something plotted against frequency. In this example we are plotting date against Life

Expectancy (for men and women). The scale has been deliberately chosen so that the figures along the y axis do not need to be multiplied by a scale factor. The data is stored in data statements and used directly to compute the length of the columns etc.

```
REM -- Plot bar-chart
SCREEN 2
WINDOW (-30, -30)-(300, 120)
LINE (0, -10)-(0, 100)' Draw y axis
LINE (-10, 0)-(280, 0)' Draw x axis
FOR y = 10 TO 100 STEP 10
        LINE (-2, y)-(2, y)
NEXT y
'
' Print labels along y axis
LOCATE 3, 20
PRINT "Life expectation in years"
LOCATE 2, 3: PRINT "years"
LOCATE 4, 3: PRINT "100"
LOCATE 7, 3: PRINT "80"
LOCATE 11, 3: PRINT "60"
LOCATE 14, 3: PRINT "40"
LOCATE 17, 3: PRINT "20"
'
FOR x = 30 TO 260 STEP 60
        READ d, m, f
        LINE (x - 22, 0)-(x - 2, m), , BF       ' plot bar for men
        LINE (x + 2, 0)-(x + 22, f), , B        ' plot bar for women
        LOCATE 22, (x \ 4 + 5): PRINT d         ' label x axis with date
NEXT x
'
DATA  1840,40,42,1870,41,45,1900,44,48,1930,59,63,1960,68,74
```

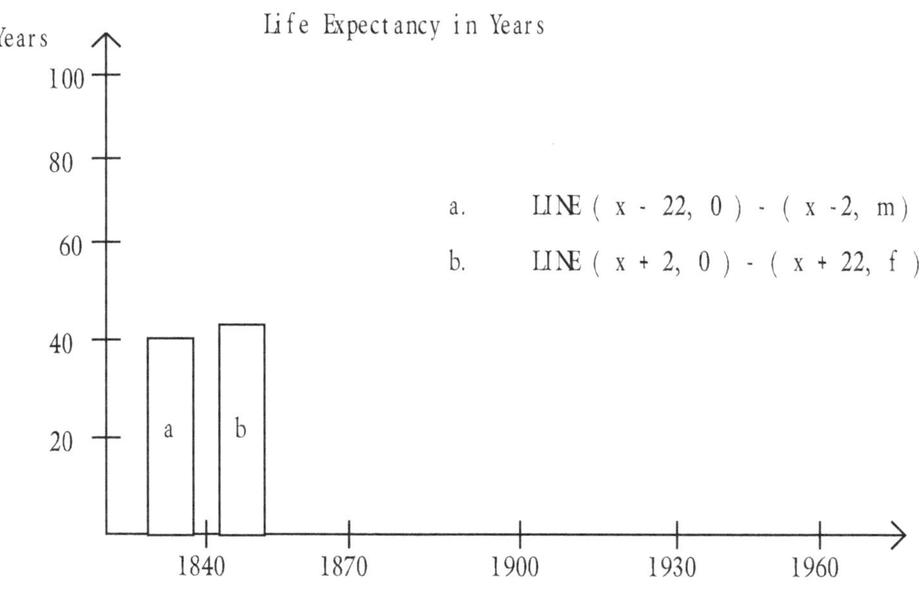

Fig 9-15 A plan of a bar-chart

A line-graph should fit using the same scale. You may find that unless there are significant differences in gradient between adjacent lines, you get a very uninteresting picture. In this situation bar-charts and histograms are much better. Below is a program to plot a line graph. You will notice that a significant part of the code has come from the previous program.

```
REM -- Draw Line graph for Life Expectation
SCREEN 2
WINDOW (-30, -30)-(300, 120)
LINE (0, -10)-(0, 100)
LINE (-10, 0)-(280, 0)
FOR y = 10 TO 100 STEP 10
        LINE (-2, y)-(2, y)
NEXT y
LOCATE 3, 20 : PRINT "Life expectation in years"
LOCATE 2, 3: PRINT "years"
LOCATE 4, 3: PRINT "100"
LOCATE 7, 3: PRINT "80"
LOCATE 11, 3: PRINT "60"
LOCATE 14, 3: PRINT "40"
LOCATE 17, 3: PRINT "20"
READ d, m, f
PRESET (30, m)
RESTORE
FOR x = 30 TO 260 STEP 60
        READ d, m, f
        LINE -(x, m)
        LOCATE 22, (x \ 4 + 5): PRINT d
NEXT x
DATA 1840,40,42,1870,41,45,1900,44,48,1930,59,63,1960,68,74
```

And finally we look at pie-charts to solve the same problem. You will find if anything the pie-chart is the most troublesome. This is because of the way circles are plotted in QBASIC. You will often find that when you want to divide the circle up, various lines especially along the vertical axis extend too far thus making the pie-chart very untidy. You can get round this problem by experimenting with the aspect ratio of the circle.

The CIRCLE statement has an extended form which includes the aspect ratio. The aspect ratio is the ratio of the horizontal radius to the vertical radius. In the next program the following was tried out:

```
CIRCLE (75, 100), 50, , , 0.49        ' problem is circle is now an ellipse
```

```
REM -- Use pie-charts to represent Life Expectancy
SCREEN 2
WINDOW (0, 0)-(300, 200)
LOCATE 3, 20
PRINT "Life expectation in years"
rev = 2 * 3.14159' 360 degrees = 2 pi radians
mtot = 0: ftot = 0
```

```
FOR c = 1 TO 5 '
        READ d, m, f
        mtot = mtot + m
        ftot = ftot + f
NEXT c
'    Pie-chart for male deaths
CIRCLE (75, 100), 50
RESTORE
LINE (75, 100)-(125, 100)
angle = 0
FOR c = 1 TO 5
        READ d, m, f
        angle = angle + (m / mtot) * rev
        x1 = 50 * COS(angle)
        y1 = 50 * SIN(angle)
        LINE (75, 100)-(75 + x1, 100 + y1)
NEXT c
'    Pie-chart for female deaths
CIRCLE (225, 100), 50
RESTORE
angle = 0
FOR c = 1 TO 5
        READ d, m, f
        angle = angle + (f / ftot) * rev
        x1 = 50 * COS(angle)
        y1 = 50 * SIN(angle)
        LINE (225, 100)-(225 + x1, 100 + y1)
NEXT c
DATA  1840,40,42,1870,41,45,1900,44,48,1930,59,63,1960,68,74
```

Exercise 9-3

1. Write a program to draw polygons. It should:

   (a) include a procedure polygon (x, y, r, sides) to draw a general polygon.

   (b) Test out the procedure by including procedure calls to draw:

   i. a pentagon
   ii. an octagon
   iii a decagon

   anywhere on the screen, and of different sizes.

2. Write a program which will produce bold patterned letters to be used on a banner or poster.

(a) Start by producing the following hollow letters in High Resolution mode.

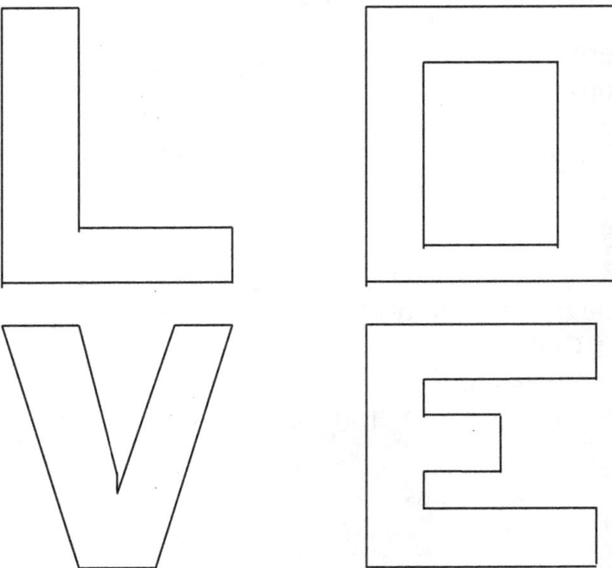

Fig 9-16 Hollow letters to be tiled for a poster or banner

(b) Design tiles for the letters L, O, V and E and use them to fill in your letters.

3. The following data records the number of deaths per 1000 population

Country	Deaths per 1000
USSR	7.7
Japan	6.7
Australia	9.1
Hong Kong	4.7
USA	9.5
France	11.3
West Germany	11.9
New Zealand	8.7
Hungary	11.3
United Kingdom	11.9
Italy	10.1
Sweden	10.4
Netherlands	8.3

Fig 9-17 Deaths per Thousand

Write a program that will:

(a) Store this data in data statements

(b) Will provide a procedure to produce the menu

1. Draw a histogram
2. Draw a line graph
3. Draw a pie-chart

(c) For each of the options on the menu implement a procedure to draw that choice.

(d) The pie-chart should use tiling to indicate which country the section of the pie-chart represents. You might consider making a tile that contains a letter that indicates the country.

(e) The histogram should use a also be filled in with tiles or another suitable method such as use of colour.

(e) You should also produce a key to indicate what the tile or colour represents.

(f) Another addition that you might consider is to sort the data in ascending order of deaths. For this you will need an array and a procedure to sort the array. You will probably use bubble sort.

9.9 Animation using GET and PUT

Computer animation can be achieved by continually redrawing parts of the screen in real-time. QBASIC offers the GET and PUT statements for this purpose.

The GET statement stores the pixels within a specified rectangle to an array. It has the following format:

```
GET (x1, y1)-(x2, y2), arrayname
```

The PUT statement is the opposite of GET and can be used to redraw the image stored in the array anywhere on the screen. Is has the following format:

```
PUT(x, y), arrayname, PSET
```

In place of PSET one of the following can be substituted:

PRESET, AND, OR, XOR. (See Fig 9-18 for details).

Plot Type	Characteristics
AND	Merges stored image with an existing image.
OR	Superimposes stored image on existing image.
PSET	Draws stored image, erasing existing image.
PRESET	Draws stored image in reverse colours, erasing existing image.
XOR	Draws a stored image or erases a previously drawn image while preserving the background.

Fig 9-18 Plot types for PUT statement

The array arrayname must be large enough to store all the pixel information within the specified rectangle. This size is calculated as follows:

1. **Pixels along horizontal side.**

   h = x2 - x1 + 1

2. **Pixels along vertical side**

   v = y2 - y1 + 1

3. **Number of bytes**

   p = 4 + INT ((h * bitsperpixel + 7) / 8) * v

4. **Bits per pixel**

Medium Resolution -- 2 bits per pixel, High Resolution -- 1 bit per pixel

Simple animation can be achieved by:

1. Plotting an image of the object to be moved
2. Using a GET statement to store information about all the pixels inside a specified rectangle that encloses the object into an array.
3. Using PUT statements to redraw the image, making use of the information in the array.

An illustration of this follows.

```
DECLARE SUB man ()
DIM pm%(1000)
SCREEN 1
WINDOW (0, 0)-(320, 200)
CALL man
GET (5, 8)-(25, 32), pm%
CLS
xc = 1:  yc = 1
FOR xc = 1 TO 300
        PUT (xc, yc), pm%, PSET
        FOR c = 1 TO 100: NEXT c  ' Slow down animation
NEXT xc
SUB man
        LINE (14, 25)-(18, 30), , BF
        LINE (12, 17)-(20, 25), , BF
        LINE (12, 10)-(16, 12), , BF
        LINE (18, 10)-(22, 12), , BF
        LINE (12, 12)-(14, 17), , BF
        LINE (18, 12)-(20, 17), , BF
        LINE (20, 21)-(25, 22), , BF
        LINE (6, 21)-(11, 22), , BF
END SUB
```

In this example a simple figure of a man is drawn and then made to move across the screen. To get a better illusion of walking you would need to have several images of a man in slightly different positions, and then drawn in turn while moving across the screen.

The next version of this program allows a user to interact with the program. It is inspired by games like Super-Mario. Keys are used to make the man move left, right or to jump.

```
DECLARE SUB man ( )
DIM pm%(1000)
SCREEN 1
WINDOW (0, 0)-(320, 200)
CALL man
GET (5, 8)-(25, 32), pm%
CLS
xc = 1:  yc = 1
PUT (xc, yc), pm%, PSET
DO WHILE a$ <> CHR$(27)
        a$ = INKEY$
        SELECT CASE a$
                CASE "K", "k"
                        CLS
                        IF xc > 5 THEN xc = xc - 5
                        PUT (xc, yc), pm%, PSET
                CASE "L", "l"
                        CLS
                        IF xc < 315 THEN xc = xc + 5
                        PUT (xc, yc), pm%, PSET
                CASE " "
                        CLS
                        PUT (xc, yc + 20), pm%, PSET
                        SLEEP 1
                        CLS
                        PUT (xc, yc), pm%, PSET
                CASE ELSE
                        PUT (xc, yc), pm%, PSET
        END SELECT
LOOP

SUB man
        LINE (14, 25)-(18, 30), , BF
        LINE (12, 17)-(20, 25), , BF
        LINE (12, 10)-(16, 12), , BF
        LINE (18, 10)-(22, 12), , BF
        LINE (12, 12)-(14, 17), , BF
        LINE (18, 12)-(20, 17), , BF
        LINE (20, 21)-(25, 22), , BF
        LINE (6, 21)-(11, 22), , BF
END SUB
```

Both of these programs will not work properly if a background is to be drawn. This is because every time the man is moved by issuing a PUT statement another part of the background gets erased. This can be overcome by using XOR in place of PSET.

XOR can be used to plot and restore the background as follows:

1. The first time a picture is drawn using a PUT statement, the man overwrites the background.

2. The second time a PUT statement is used with the XOR option at the same location it cancels out the image of the man leaving the background in tact.

This is illustrated in the next version of the program.

```
DECLARE SUB man ( )
DIM pm%(1000)
SCREEN 1
WINDOW (0, 0)-(320, 200)
' Store image of man and clear screen
CALL man
GET (5, 0)-(25, 30), pm%
CLS
REM -- draw background
COLOR 2
LINE (200, 0)-(250, 50), 1, BF
' Start of demo
PUT (200, 0), pm%, XOR
LOCATE 20, 5: PRINT "Now I'm here"
SLEEP 4
PUT (200, 0), pm%, XOR
LOCATE 20, 5: PRINT "Now I'm gone"

SUB man
        LINE (14, 25)-(18, 30), , BF
        LINE (12, 17)-(20, 25), , BF
        LINE (12, 10)-(16, 12), , BF
        LINE (18, 10)-(22, 12), , BF
        LINE (12, 12)-(14, 17), , BF
        LINE (18, 12)-(20, 17), , BF
        LINE (20, 21)-(25, 22), , BF
        LINE (6, 21)-(11, 22), , BF
END SUB
```

9.10 Sound

Sound is caused by vibrating columns of air. The number of waves per second is called the frequency and is measured in hertz (Hz). 1 Hz = 1 wave per second.

In QBASIC the SOUND statement can be used to produce sound through the computers internal speaker. It has the format:

```
SOUND frequency, duration
```

Frequency can be a number in the range 37 to 32,767, but most humans can't detect a frequency higher than 20,000 Hz.

The duration parameter can take a value from 1 to 65535 and is measured in clock ticks. There are 18.2 clock ticks to the second.

The most obvious motivation for using the SOUND statement is the ability to provide sound effects for computer games etc. You will find that you will need to experiment a lot to get the desired sound. Some examples follow:

```
REM -- Demo sound effects
'
REM  -- Alarm
FOR c = 1 TO 30
        SOUND 40, 2
        SOUND 60, 2
NEXT c
'
REM -- Bleep
FOR c = 1 TO 30
        SOUND 500, 1
        SLEEP 1
        SOUND 100, 1
NEXT c
'
REM -- Crackle
FOR c = 1 TO 500
        SOUND 37, .2
        SOUND 40, .2
        SOUND 43, .2
NEXT c
'
REM -- Space Invaders
FOR f = 600 TO 500 step -10
        SOUND f, 2
NEXT f
'
REM -- Siren
FOR c = 1 TO 10
        SOUND 1600, 10
NEXT c
```

```
REM -- takeoff
FOR f = 200 TO 400
        SOUND f, 2
NEXT f
```

As well as using the SOUND statement for creating sound effects you can use it to play music. You do however need to know the frequency of the notes required.

All musical notes are split up into octaves. The frequency of a corresponding note in the next octave is obtained by multiplying by 2. To illustrate this the frequency of the note C is given using the Physicists Standard.

$C_1 = 32$, C = 64, c = 128, c' = 256, c'' = 512

There is no universal standard for the frequency of notes. However musicians tend to use 'Concert Pitch' which sets middle c as 264 rather than 256.

Within a given octave the frequency of a note can be calculated by multiplying by a fixed ratio. Such a scale of notes is called a diatonic scale.

Note	C	D	E	F	G	A	B	c
ratio	1	9/8	5/4	4/3	3/2	5/3	15/8	2
frequency	64	72	80	85 1/3	96	120	106 2/3	128

Fig 9-19 diatonic scale

This information can be used to generate the correct frequency for desired notes as can be seen in the following program:

```
cnote = 132
music$ = "CEGCBAGFEDCEGCBAGFG"
FOR c = 1 TO LEN(music$)
        n$ = MID$(music$, c, 1)
        SELECT CASE n$
                CASE "C"
                        r = 1
                CASE "D"
                        r = 9 / 8
                CASE "E"
                        r = 5 / 4
                CASE "F"
                        r = 4 / 3
                CASE "G"
                        r = 3 / 2
                CASE "A"
                        r = 5 / 3
                CASE "B"
                        r = 15 / 8
        END SELECT
        n = cnote * r
        SOUND n, 10
NEXT c
```

9.11 Music and the PLAY statement

If you intend to play music rather than generate sound effects a more convenient method is to use the PLAY statement.

1. The simplest use involves just naming the notes to be used as in the following:

```
REM -- The beginners March -- Eleanor Franklin Pike
PLAY "ceg c bagfedceg c bagf+g"
```

   Here normal notes can be represented in either upper or lower-case. Sharps and flats can also be used as follows:

   sharp c# or c+
   flat c-

2. In QBASIC there are 7 octaves numbered 0 to 7. Unless you say otherwise the notes will be taken from octave 4.

   You can change the current by entering **o** followed by a number (0 - 7). All subsequent notes will now be taken from this octave until the octave is changed. A better rendition of the above tune would be:

```
PLAY "o3 ceg o4 c o3 bagfedceg o4 c o3 bagf+"
```

3. Length of note can be specified by appending a number after the note. If **n** is the number then the duration of the note is given by **1 / n**. The default duration is ¼. The tune with the correct beat now becomes:

```
PLAY "o3 ceg o4 c o3 b8a8g8f8edceg o4 c o3 b8a8g8f+8g2"
```

   An alternative method is to specify the duration of all subsequent notes.

   e.g L2 Each of the subsequent notes will be half a note. Tune becomes:

```
PLAY "o3 ceg o4 c o3 L8 bagf L4 edceg o4 c o3 L8 bagf+ L2 g"
```

4. Pauses can be introduced by entering P followed by a number n, where n is in the range 1 - 64.

   e.g P4 Pause for a quarter note.

5. Another important consideration is the tempo of the music. This can be specified using the standard musical tempos:

   MS -- Staccato Short and Sharp
   ML -- Legato Smoothly with no pause
   MN -- Normal

   With the appropriate tempo the march is played as:

```
PLAY "o3 MS ceg o4 c o3 ML b8a8g8f8ed MS ceg o4 c"
PLAY "03 ML b8a8g8f+8 MN g2"
```

6. An alternative method for specifying tempo is to use T**n**. Where **n** is a number in the range 32 - 255 and represents the number of quarter notes per minute.

   The default tempo is 120.

Musical Term	Meaning	Speed (n)
Largo	Very Slow	50
Adagio	Slow	70
Andante	Slow and Flowing	90
Moderato	Medium	110
Allegro	Fast	130
Vivace	Lively	150
Presto	Very Fast	170

Fig 9-20 Musical Tempo's

7. When the music gets complicated it is useful to be able to store different parts of the tune in string variables. Then include the value of the string variables in a PLAY statement. The following code demonstrates one way of doing this.

```
INPUT "Enter tempo (32 - 255) ", t
t$ = STR$(t)
a$ = "o3 ceg o4 c o3 b8a8g8f8ed ceg o4 c"
b$ = "03 b8a8g8f+8 g2"
music$ = "T" + t$ + a$ + b$
PLAY music$
```

   Or you could try the following:

```
PLAY "T Xt$; Xa$; Xb$"      ' Here the X is an instruction to substitute
                            ' the value of the string variable.
```

Exercise 9-4

1. Write a program to produce an animation of a moving ball,

   (a) It must contain a procedure called ball1 which draws a ball, so that one half is painted red and the other half is painted green.

   (b) Write furthur procedures called ball2, ball3, ball4 etc. which draw similar balls but rotated through angles of 90, 180 and 270^0.

   (c) Write a main procedure which will draw each of the balls in turn and store the pixel information into arrays called pic1, pic2, pic3 and pic4.

   (d) Continue the main body of the program by including appropriate PUT statements inside a loop such that the ball moves from left to right of the screen and back again, spinning as it goes.

   (e) Produce appropriate sound effects when the ball reaches the edge of the screen

2. Borrow from the library or a friend a book which includes some sheet music and play this music by writing a program which makes use of PLAY statements. Should you need some help with reading music refer to fig 9-21

Fig 9.21 C Major Scale

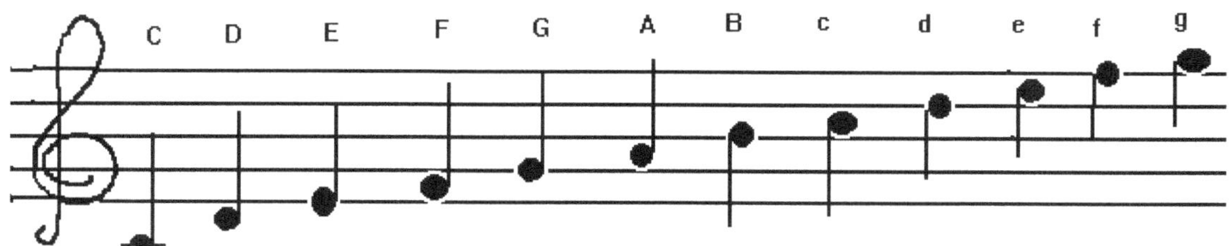

10 A Mathematical Interlude

10.1 Built in Mathematical Functions

This section explores the QBASIC built-in functions, and compares them with the arithmetic operators that have been used previously. Later on in the chapter they will be used again in the context of either using QBASIC as a tool to explore mathematics or for writing programs where some mathematics needs to be used. The table below lists the standard QBASIC mathematical functions.

Function	Description
ABS	Return the absolute value of a number
INT	Return the integer part of a number
FIX	Truncate a number leaving an integer
SGN	Return the sign of a number
SQR	Return the Square Root of a number
RND	Return a random number in the range 0 - 1
RANDOMIZE	Initialise the random number generator
SIN	Return the sine of an angle that is expressed in Radians
COS	Return the cosine of an angle that is expressed in Radians
TAN	Return the Tangent of an angle that is expressed in Radians
ATN	Return the angle in Radians for a given Tangent
LOG	Return the Logarithm to base e of a given number
EXP	Return the exponential or antilogarithm base e

Fig 10-1 Standard QBASIC Mathematical Functions

ABS always returns a positive number as can be seen from the following:

```
PRINT ABS(5), ABS(-4)        ' Returns 5      4
```

It is very useful for obtaining differences from a value (either positive or negative)

```
diff = ABS( x - average)
```

INT can be used in place of the integer division operator \.

To return the integer part of a number we have up until now used integer division.

For example:

```
a% = 5.17 \ 1          ' Returns 5
```

Another method that can be employed to output integer results is to use PRINT USING with a suitable format string.

```
PRINT USING " ##"; 5.17          ' returns 5
```

An equivalent result could be achieved using the function INT. a% = INT(5.17)

INT is possibly neater in situations where you want to test numbers. For instance if you want to test divisibility by 2, you could do the following:

```
IF n / 2 = INT(n / 2) THEN PRINT  "n is divisible by 2"
```

FIX and INT are very similar in operation. Both of them return an integer. You will only notice the difference if the argument is negative. Consider the following:

```
PRINT  INT (10.5),  FIX(10.5)       ' Returns  10     10
PRINT  INT (-10.5), FIX(-10.5)      ' Returns  -11    -10
```

SGN is used to determine whether a number is negative, zero or positive. Previously we would have done the following:

```
IF x < 0 THEN PRINT "x is negative"

IF x = 0 THEN PRINT "x is zero"

IF x > 0 THEN PRINT "x is positive"
```

SGN(x) returns -1, 0, or 1 depending on whether the number x is negative, zero or positive. In this example we are still in a position of having to test the return value to determine the sign of a number. It is however easier to code in a SELECT CASE statement as can be seen in the following example.

```
SELECT CASE SGN(x)
      CASE -1
            PRINT "Number is Negative"
      CASE 0
            PRINT "Number is Zero"
      CASE 1
            PRINT "Number is Positive"
END SELECT
```

Square Roots can be obtained using the power operator ^.

We know that $\sqrt{7}$ can be expressed as $7^{.5}$ which in QBASIC is coded as:

`7 ^ .5`   or as   `SQR(7)`   using the SQR function.

Random numbers can be generated using the RANDOMIZE and RND Functions. The function RND returns a real number in the range 0 - 1.

If a discrete integer value is required this can be achieved by multiplying by a scaling factor and then use INT to extract the integer part. Such an example follows:

```
REM  --  Generate 6 numbers in the range 1 - 49 for the National Lottery
'
RANDOMIZE  TIMER        ' Produce a Random seed
'
FOR n% = 1 TO 6
      PRINT  INT(RND * 49) + 1; "    ";
NEXT n%
```

Random numbers feature a lot in Statistics / Probability and other branches of mathematics. One such application is numerical integration. A simple example of this is given below to estimate the value of Pi. The technique being used is called a Montecarlo simulation. The area of the quadrant of the circle is assumed to be proportional to the ratio of random points falling inside Region A to the total number of random points falling inside the square (Regions A + B).

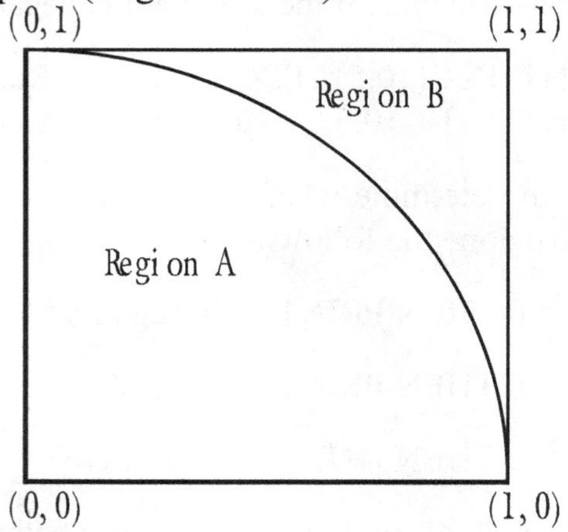

Fig 10-2 Montecarlo Estimate for Pi

A program to carry out this calculation follows:

```
RANDOMIZE TIMER
s = 1
FOR n = 1 to 1000
        x = RND
        y = RND
        IF x*x + y*y < 1 THEN s = s + 1 ' Point lies inside Region A
NEXT n
pi = 4*s / 100
Print "Estimate for Pi is "; Pi
```

QBASIC provides the following standard Trigonometric functions:

SIN , COS, TAN and ATN

All but ATN have been used in chapter 9. ATN or arctangent of an angle ($\tan^{-1}$) accepts as an argument a tangent and returns an angle expressed in Radians.

tan x = 3/4 = 0.75

x = arctan(0.75)

Written as :

x = ATN(0.75)

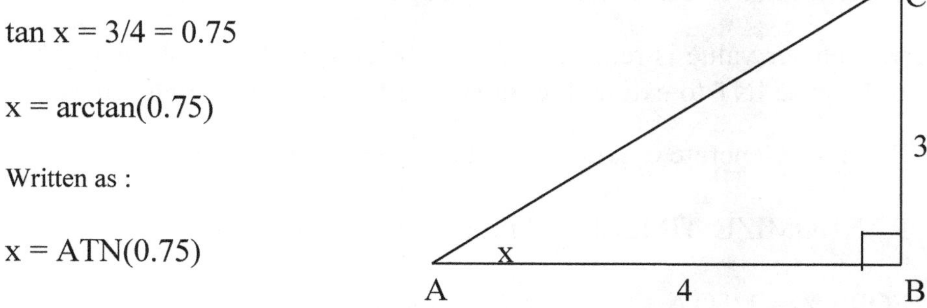

Fig 10-3 Using the ATN function

In the above example we can now convert the angle x (radians) to degrees as follows:

```
x = x *  180 / 3.14159
```

Exponentials and Logarithms are to the base e (2.718...). Presumably because many mathematical expansions use this base.

The EXP function returns the exponential of a number to the base **e** (2.718...) and can be used for evaluating the hyperbolic functions sinh, cosh, tanh.

Given $\sinh(x) = (e^{x} - e^{-x}) / 2$

then we can write a function sinh as follows:

```
FUNCTION sinh (x)
        sinh = (EXP(x) - EXP(-x)) / 2
END FUNCTION
```

For exponentials of bases other than **e** it is best to use the exponential operator ^ .

In many situations we wish to use logarithms to some other base besides **e**. This is made possible by using the following relationship:

$$\log_b(x) = \log(x) / \log(b)$$

To evaluate the right-hand-side of the expression it is not important what the base of logarithm is, because it will cancel. Because we only have the function LOG which is to the base **e**, we will have to use this.

Such a function for returning the base of a logarithm would look like:

```
FUNCTION logb (num, base)
        logb = LOG(num) / LOG(base)
END FUNCTION
```

10.2 Plotting Graphs

Graphs for any chosen mathematical expression can easily be plotted, especially if we have written a function to compute the value. It is important to be able to choose an appropriate scale and print both the x and y axes.

The scale can be determined by evaluating the maximum and minimum values for a given range of values x1 - x2.

The axes can easily be produced as follows:

```
LINE (x1, 0 ) - ( x2, 0 )      ' x axes
LINE (0, y1 ) - ( 0, y2 )      ' y axes
```

and the plot itself:

```
FOR x = x1 TO x2 STEP incr
        y = plotfn(x)
        PSET (x, y)     ' Will produce a scatter graph
NEXT x
```

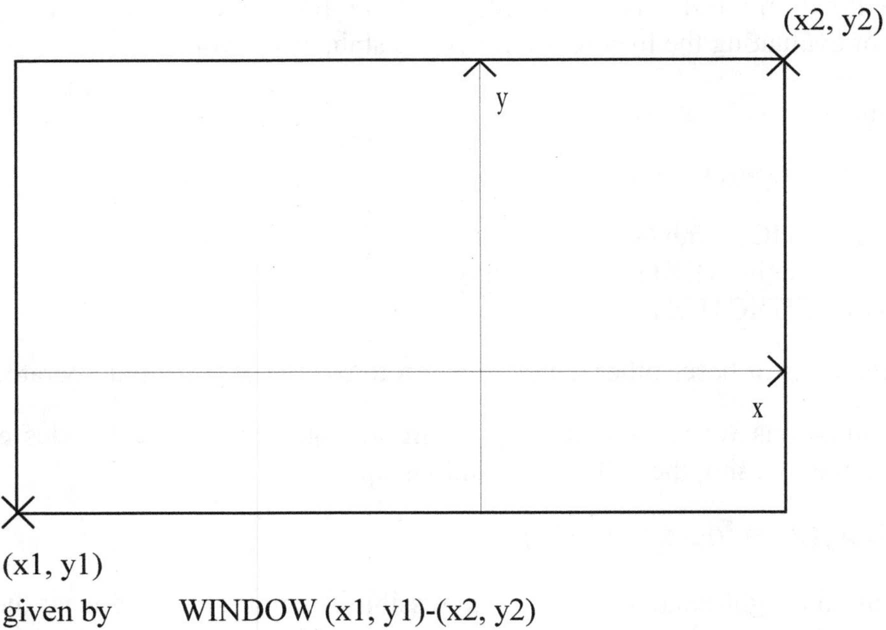

Fig 10-3 A suitably scaled screen with axes

10.3 Polar Curves

Graphs of curves whose equations are expressed in polar co-ordinates can also be plotted. If you were to do this manually you would expect to have to go out and buy some polar graph paper. This graph paper is made up of concentric circles to denote the radius, and these circles are partitioned by lines at say 10 degrees to mark the angle.

To plot such graphs in QBASIC the polar co-ordinates must be converted into Rectangular Cartesian form. This can be deduced by comparing the equation of a circle using both Rectangular Cartesian co-ordinates and Polar co-ordinates.

The Parametric form is the most useful tool for plotting curves expressed in Polar form. It means that the polar form can be converted to a pair of co-ordinates (x, y) simply by applying the transformations:

(i) x = r cos (theta)

(ii) y = r sin (theta)

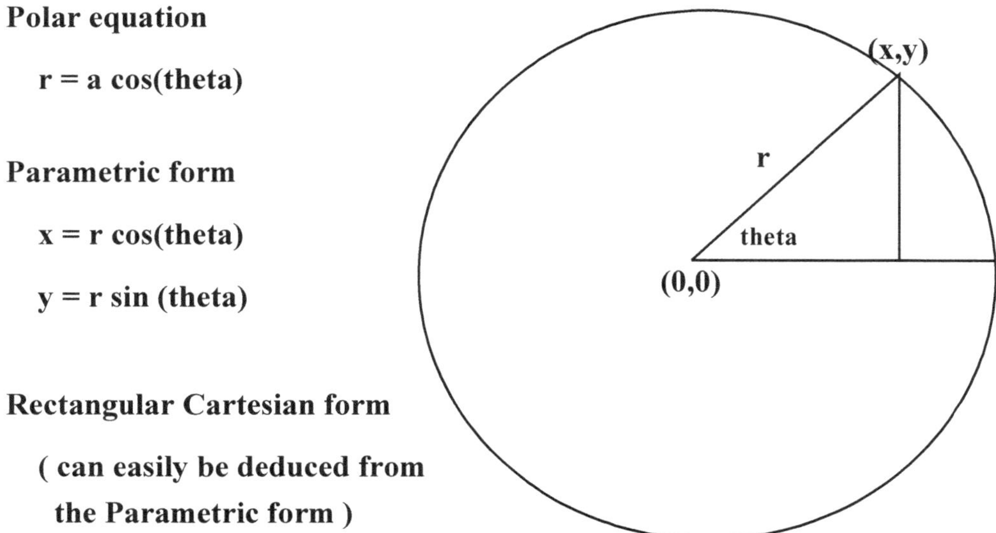

Polar equation
r = a cos(theta)
Parametric form
x = r cos(theta)
y = r sin (theta)
Rectangular Cartesian form
(can easily be deduced from
the Parametric form)
(x,y)
r
theta
(0,0)

Fig 10-5 Plotting a circle (polar form)

To illustrate this point consider plotting a Cardioid having the equation:

$$r = \frac{1}{2} a \, (1 + \cos\theta)$$

First we need to compute r for all theta between 0 and 360^0, then for each value of r obtained, we need to compute x and y to plot.

The full program follows below:

```
REM -- Plot a Cardioid
PI = 3.14159
INPUT "Enter value of a "; a
SCREEN 1
WINDOW (-10, -10) - (10, 10)
FOR theta = 0 TO 360
        ar = theta * PI / 180    ' Convert angle to Radians
        r = .5 * a * ( 1 + COS(ar))
        ' Evaluate x and y co-ordinates to plot
        x = r * COS(ar)
        y = r * SIN(ar)
        PSET(x, y)
NEXT theta
```

Exercise 10-1

1. Write a program to produce a page of a set of Mathematical tables for the Hyperbolic functions Sinh, Cosh and Tanh.

   Where:

   $$\text{Sinh } x = (e^{x} - e^{-x}) / 2$$

   $$\text{Cosh } x = (e^{x} + e^{-x}) / 2$$

   $$\text{Tanh } x = (e^{x} - e^{-x}) / (e^{x} + e^{-x})$$

   (a) Start by writing a function for each Hyperbolic Function

   (b) Then write a program that utilises these functions so that you end up with a printed table that has the following format:

x	Sinh x	Cosh x	Tanh x	x	Sinh x	Cosh x	Tanh x
0.00	0.0000	1.0000	0.0000	0.50	0.5211	1.1276	0.4621
0.01	0.0100	1.0000	0.0100	0.51	0.5324	1.1329	0.4699
.							
.							
.							
0.50	0.5211	1.1276	0.4621	1.00	1.1752	1.5431	0.7616

2. Write a program to compute the area of an irregular shape such as the one in fig 10-6. You will need to split the shape into strips of equal width and be able to measure the length of each strip. You should implement it using two functions. One for each rule.

Fig 10.6 Estimating the area of an Irregular shape

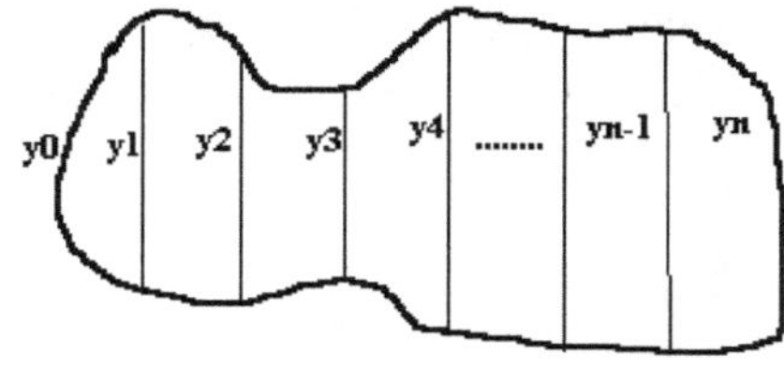

Trapezoidal Rule

A = h(0.5y0 + y1 + y2 + y3 + ... + yn-1 + yn)

Simpsons Rule

A = 1/3h(y0 + 4y1 + 2y2 + 4y3 + 2y4 + ... + 4yn-1 + yn)

3. Write a program that will plot a variety of curves of functions that have equations expressed in Polar co-ordinates.

Some examples follow:

(i) $r^2 = a^2 \cos 2\theta$ Lemniscate of Bernoulli

(ii) $r^2 = a^2 \sec 2\theta$ Rectangular Hyperbola

(iii) $r = \frac{1}{2}a(1 + \cos\theta)$ Cardioid

(iv) $r = a(\frac{1}{2} + \cos\theta)$ Limnaçon with loop

(v) $r = \frac{1}{2}a / (1 + \cos\theta)$ Parabola

10.4 Matrix Operations

An array of more than 1 dimension is often called a matrix. An m×n matrix is a two dimensional array made up of m rows and n columns. It can be declared in QBASIC using the statement:

DIM arrayname (1 TO m, 1 TO n)

It would be convenient to perform certain operations on matrices using a single statement. In deed some versions of BASIC have a set of built-in functions that add, multiply and invert matrices etc. For a complete list of what is typical for those versions of BASIC having such facilities refer to Fig 10-7

Statement	**Meaning**
MAT INPUT v	Input a list of numbers to populate an array v
MAT READ m(x,y)	Use data in DATA statements to populate an array m
MAT PRINT a	Print an entire matrix a
MAT c = a + b	Add two matrices
MAT c = a - b	Obtain the difference between two matrices
MAT c = (k)*a	Multiply by a constant (scalar)
MAT c = a * b	Multiply two matrices
MAT c = a	Copy a matrix
MAT c = TRN(a)	Transpose a matrix
MAT c = INV(a)	Invert a matrix

Fig 10-7 Matrix operations in BASIC

It would be useful if we could utilise these features in QBASIC. You will however have to write them yourself. You may want to start with functions like MAT INPUT and MAT PRINT.

MAT INPUT for instance could be implemented as a procedure as follows:

```
SUB matinput (a( ))
        CLS
        lb1 = LBOUND(a, 1)
        ub1 = UBOUND(a, 1)
        lb2 = LBOUND(a, 2)
        ub2 = UBOUND(a, 2)
        FOR r = lb1 TO ub1
                FOR c = lb2 TO ub2
                        PRINT r; " , " ; c ; " = " ;
                        INPUT a(r, c)
                NEXT c
        NEXT r
END SUB
```

Here two new standard QBASIC functions have been employed. LBOUND returns the lower bounds of an array, and UBOUND returns the upper bounds of an array. This information is obtained from the DIM statement itself which puts aside storage for the array before it can be used. So LBOUND and UBOUND are very useful for arrays of different sizes.

In particular for a two dimensional array declared as:

```
DIM a(1 TO 3, 1 TO 2)
```

will gives us:

```
lb1 = 1, ub1 = 3, lb2 = 1, ub2 = 2
```

A very simple implementation of MAT PRINT could also be implemented in a similar fashion using LBOUND and UBOUND.

The operations such as matrix addition, subtraction and multiplication would also have to be implemented as procedures or functions. The simplest to implement are addition and subtraction.

In the case of addition the rules are quite simple. Using the rules in Fig 10-8 we could write:

```
SUB matadd (a( ) , b( ) , c( ))
        la1 = LBOUND(a, 1)  :  la2 = UBOUND(a, 1)
        la2 = LBOUND(a, 2)  :  ua2 = UBOUND(a, 2)
        lb1 = LBOUND(b, 1)  :  ub1 = UBOUND(b, 1)
        lb2 = LBOUND(b, 2)  :  ub2 = UBOUND(b, 2)
        FOR rows = lb1 TO ub1
                FOR cols = lb2 TO ub2
                        c(rows, cols) = a(rows, cols) + b(rows, cols)
                NEXT cols
        NEXT rows
```

This has a lot to be desired. In particular a check should be made to ensure that all of the arrays a( ), b( ) and c( ) have the same dimensions.

Matrix Addition

$$\begin{bmatrix} c11 & c12 \\ c21 & c22 \end{bmatrix} = \begin{bmatrix} a11 & a12 \\ a21 & a22 \end{bmatrix} + \begin{bmatrix} b11 & b12 \\ b21 & b22 \end{bmatrix}$$

Where:

c11 = a11 + b11, c12 = a11 + b11, c21 = a21 + b21, c22 = a22 + b22

Matrix Multiplication

Here:

c11 = a11 × b11 + a12 × b21

c12 = a11 × b12 + a12 × b22

c21 = a21 × b11 + a22 × b21

c22 = a21 × b12 + a22 × b22

Fig 10-8 Matrix addition and multiplication for 2 × 2 matrices

Writing a procedure to perform matrix multiplication is rather more difficult. It is quite straight-forward in the case of a specific case such as multiplication of 2 × 2 matrices, but to write a more general procedure we need to formalise the operation.

Matrix multiplication is only possible if:

If matrix A has dimensions $I \times J$

and

If matrix B has dimensions $K \times L$

then $J = K$ and the resultant matrix has dimensions $I \times L$.

In general terms matrix multiplication can be defined as

$$c_{ij} = a_{i1}b_{ij} + a_{i2}b_{2j} + \ldots\ldots.. + a_{ip}b_{pj}$$

$$= \sum_{k=1}^{p} a_{ik}b_{kj}$$

This can be coded as:

```
FOR i = 1 TO rows1
        FOR j = 1 TO rows 2
                FOR k = 1 TO rows3
                        c(i, j) = c(i, j) + a(i, k) * b(k, j)
                NEXT k
        NEXT j
NEXT i
```

10.5 Solving Simultaneous Linear equations

This next section looks at one of the many applications of matrices. If we limit ourselves to 2 × 2 matrices we can use them to solve Simultaneous Linear equations.

The pair of simultaneous linear equations

$$2x + 5y = 9$$

$$x + 3y = 5$$

can be written as

$$\begin{bmatrix} 2 & 9 \\ 1 & 3 \end{bmatrix} \begin{bmatrix} x \\ y \end{bmatrix} = \begin{bmatrix} 9 \\ 5 \end{bmatrix}$$

The inverse of $\begin{bmatrix} 2 & 5 \\ 1 & 3 \end{bmatrix}$ just happens to be $\begin{bmatrix} 3 & -5 \\ -1 & 2 \end{bmatrix}$

If a matrix is multiplied by its inverse the result is the identity matrix $\begin{bmatrix} 1 & 0 \\ 0 & 1 \end{bmatrix}$

To solve the simultaneous equation we can pre-multiply both sides by the inverse.

$$\begin{bmatrix} 3 & -5 \\ -1 & 2 \end{bmatrix} \begin{bmatrix} 2 & 5 \\ 1 & 3 \end{bmatrix} \begin{bmatrix} x \\ y \end{bmatrix} = \begin{bmatrix} 3 & -5 \\ -1 & 2 \end{bmatrix} \begin{bmatrix} 9 \\ 5 \end{bmatrix}$$

$$\begin{bmatrix} x \\ y \end{bmatrix} = \begin{bmatrix} 3 & -5 \\ -1 & 2 \end{bmatrix} \begin{bmatrix} 9 \\ 5 \end{bmatrix} = \begin{bmatrix} 2 \\ 1 \end{bmatrix}$$

An inverse for a 2 × 2 matrix can be evaluated as follows:

$$A = \begin{bmatrix} a & b \\ c & d \end{bmatrix} \qquad A^T = \begin{bmatrix} a & c \\ b & d \end{bmatrix}$$

$$A^{adj} = \begin{bmatrix} d & -b \\ -c & a \end{bmatrix} \qquad \det A = a.b - b.c$$

$$A^{-1} = \frac{A^{adj}}{\det A} = \frac{\begin{bmatrix} d & -b \\ -c & a \end{bmatrix}}{a.b - b.c}$$

You will notice that there is a shortcut that only works for 2×2 matrices. That is to find an inverse you:

1. Obtain the adjoint matrix by interchanging elements a and d, and negate elements c and d.

2. Then obtain the inverse matrix by dividing the adjoint matrix by the determinant of the matrix.

This can be implemented as a function as follows:

```
FUNCTION inv( a( ), b( ) )
        det = a(1, 1) * a(2, 2) - a(2, 1) * a (2, 2)
        IF det <> 0 THEN
                b(1, 2) = a(2, 2) / det
                b(1, 2) = -a(1, 2) / det
                b(2, 1) = -a(2, 1) / det
                b(2, 2) = a(1, 1) / det
                inv = -1        ' Indicate inverse possible
        ELSE
                inv = 0         ' Indicate inverse is not possible
        END IF
END FUNCTION
```

10.6 Geometric Transformations

Transformations in the plane (2 dimensions), other than translations can be produced using 2×2 matrices.

Any point (x, y) can be mapped to another point (x', y') by multiplying by a 2×2 matrix which describes the transformation.

i.e

$$\begin{bmatrix} x' \\ y' \end{bmatrix} = \begin{bmatrix} a & b \\ c & d \end{bmatrix} \begin{bmatrix} x \\ y \end{bmatrix}$$

where $\begin{bmatrix} a & b \\ c & d \end{bmatrix}$ is the general transformation matrix

Some common examples of transformation follow :-

1. $\begin{bmatrix} 0 & -1 \\ -1 & 0 \end{bmatrix}$

   A reflection in the line y = -x

2. $\begin{bmatrix} 1 & 0 \\ 0 & -1 \end{bmatrix}$

   A reflection in the x axis

3. $\begin{bmatrix} -1 & 0 \\ 0 & 1 \end{bmatrix}$

   A reflection in the y axis

4. $\begin{bmatrix} 0 & -1 \\ 1 & 0 \end{bmatrix}$

   A rotation of +90 degrees about O

5. $\begin{bmatrix} \cos(a) & -\sin(a) \\ \sin(a) & \cos(a) \end{bmatrix}$

   A rotation about O.

   Where a is the angle rotated in radians.

Any given shape can be indicated as a set of points. Each of these points can be moved using a transformation of our choice such as rotation, reflection etc by pre-multiplying by an appropriate transformation matrix.

Exercise 10-2

1. Write a program which will include either procedures or functions to implement the following matrix operations:

   MAT INPUT, MAT PRINT, addition, subtraction, multiplication, MAT INV

   Refer to Fig 10-7 for a brief description.

   You can limit the scope of these to 2×2 matrices

2. Write a program to solve the following pairs of simultaneous equations.

(a)		(b)		(c)	
	$3x + 5y = 13$		$3x + y = 7$		$3x + 4y = 1$
	$x + 2y = 3$		$4x + 2y = 10$		$5x - 7y = -12$

   Use MAT INV, and a matrix multiplication function. Use MAT INPUT to enter the data, and MAT PRINT to print out the results.

3. Write a program that can be used to test out rotations

   (a) It should have a procedure called rotate, which given an argument in degrees will rotate a point (x, y).

   (b) Use the WINDOW command so that the screen area you use has the origin (0,0) at the centre of the screen.

   (c) Draw in and label the x and y axes.

   (d) Test the program by plotting a letter A drawn using vector graphics. See exercise 9-2 Fig 9-8. You could if you choose initially store the points in DATA statements.

10.7 Dealing with very large numbers

A calculator or for that matter any computer uses a limited amount of storage to store numbers. You may have discovered the problem of overflow while using a calculator. You try to perform a calculation and the result is too large to fit in the allocated space. Instead of obtaining the correct result you usually just get an error message.

In QBASIC there are 4 numeric datatypes. The size of the number you can use will depend on the data type chosen.

Data Type	**denoted by**	**description**	**largest number**
INTEGER	num%	16 bit signed integer	32767
LONG	num&	32 bit signed integer	2147483647
SINGLE	num!	32 bit real number	3.402823 E+38
DOUBLE	num#	64 bit real number	1.797693 D+308

Fig 10-9 Numeric data types in QBASIC

To appreciate the problem of numeric representation. Consider the following :

Q1. What is 720 factorial ?

A first attempt to solve this problem may use a simple function such as:

```
FUNCTION fac% ( num% )
        prod% = 1
        FOR c% = 1 TO num%
                prod% = prod% * c%
        NEXT c%
        fac% = prod%
END FUNCTION
```

Should you then use this function with the function call:

```
PRINT "720 factorial is ", fac%(720)
```

You will get the following error message:

```
Overflow
```

If you ask for Help, you will get the following extra information:

```
The result of a calculation or data-type
conversion is too large for the given data-types
ERR Code:  6
```

If you refer back to fig 10-9 you will see why. Perhaps if you use one of the other data-types to solve the problem, perhaps you will have better luck. You will in fact be able to calculate larger factorials, but will still not be able to calculate 720 factorial.

In fact the largest factorials you can calculate using the above method is as follows:

INTEGER	7 factorial	5040
LONG	12 factorial	479001600
SINGLE	34 factorial	2.952328 E+38
DOUBLE	169 factorial	4.269068009004703 D+304

We are still a long way from our target. If we think of how a real number is represented this should give us an idea to tackle this problem. A real number is made up of two parts a mantissa and exponent.

A real number such as a SINGLE or DOUBLE is then represented as:

$$\text{num} = \text{mantissa} \times 2^{\text{exponent}}$$

In our second attempt we could store our result in this way. use a variable to store the mantissa, and a variable to store the exponent. In the following program however there will be one major difference. We will work in base 10 instead of binary (base 2).

```
REM -- Factorial Program
'
CLS
PRINT "Computing factorials": PRINT
mantissa = 1
exponent = 0
INPUT "Enter number  ", num
FOR n = num TO 1 STEP -1
        mantissa = mantissa * n
        WHILE mantissa >= 10
                mantissa = mantissa / 10
                exponent = exponent + 1
        WEND
NEXT n
PRINT num; " factorial is "; mantissa; "E+"; exponent
```

One of the problems of working with real numbers on a computer is the fact that it is impossible to represent a real number exactly. If the program doesn't take this into account it is possible that the errors will be magnified and the resulting answer very inaccurate. The above program has taken us a step nearer to solving 720 factorial. But it is possible that the answer is only correct to say 10 decimal places.

10.8 Program for evaluating large factorials

If we want to have complete accuracy for the value of a factorial we may use long multiplication to solve this problem. It would be possible if we had a large enough piece of paper and a lot of patience to work out all the digits of a factorial. Most of us don't. We can however copy this method on the computer. Long multiplication involves breaking the problem down in to that of multiplying by single digits (hundreds, tens, and units) and then summing the results. This is what we will do in the next program. Here the intermediate results, and final answer to be printed will be store in arrays.

```
REM -- Program for evaluating large factorials
CLS
MAX = 2000
DIM current(2001), h(2001), t(2001), u(2001)
'
REM -- Initialize arrays
FOR i = MAX TO 0 STEP -1
        h(i) = 0          ' hundreds
        t(i) = 0          ' tens
        u(i) = 0          ' units
        current(i) = 0    ' answer and intermediate results
NEXT i
current(MAX) = 1: n = 1
'
INPUT "Enter number ", num
WHILE n <= num
        REM -- Sort out multipliers
        mul1 = n \ 100
        mul2 = n \ 10 - 10 * mul1
        mul3 = n - (100 * mul1 + 10 * mul2)


        REM -- Multiplication
        FOR i = MAX TO 1 STEP -1
                h(i) = current(i) * mul1
                t(i) = current(i) * mul2
                u(i) = current(i) * mul3
        NEXT i


        '    Summing
        FOR i = MAX TO 2 STEP -1
                current(i - 2) = h(i) + t(i - 1) + u(i - 2)
        NEXT i
        current(MAX) = u(MAX)
        current(MAX - 1) = u(MAX - 1) + t(MAX)
```

```
        REM -- Carries
        carry = 0
        FOR i = MAX TO 1 STEP -1
                IF current(i) > 9 THEN
                        carry = current(i) \ 10
                        current(i) = current(i) MOD 10
                        current(i - 1) = current(i - 1) + carry
                END IF
        NEXT i

        '

        PRINT ".";
        n = n + 1

WEND

'       Strip Leading zeros
x = 1
WHILE current(x) = 0
        x = x + 1
WEND

'       Print Result
PRINT
PRINT n - 1;
PRINT " factorial is "
PRINT
cnt = 0
FOR c = x TO MAX
        PRINT USING "#"; current(c);
        cnt = cnt + 1
NEXT c
PRINT : PRINT
PRINT "There are "; cnt; " digits"
```

10.9 Complex Numbers

The solution of a simple quadratic equation of the form $ax^2 + bx + c = 0$ can also give us problems. It is normal before solving such equations to perform a test $b^2 > 4ac$. If this is not true then there are no real solutions to this equation.

This problem can be overcome by accepting a new type of number into our number system. These are called complex numbers. Addition of complex numbers allows us to solve all quadratic equations.

A complex number has two components. A real part and an imaginary part. A complex number has the following format:

$x + iy$ (Where **i** is the square root of -1)

We can represent such numbers in QBASIC by creating a structure to hold both components. This can be done as follows:

```
TYPE complex
        re AS SINGLE          ' Real part of a complex number
        im AS SINGLE          ' Imaginary part of a complex number
END TYPE
```

Complex variables can now be created by means of DIM statements such as:

```
DIM x1 AS complex
DIM x2 AS complex
```

It is now east to write an improved program to compute the solution of quadratic equations. Without further comment such a program is given in its entirety for you to work through:

```
REM -- Solution of Quadratic equations
REM -- including those with complex roots
'
TYPE complex
        re AS SINGLE          ' Real part of a complex number
        im AS SINGLE          ' Imaginary part of a complex number
END TYPE
'
DIM x1 AS complex
DIM x2 AS complex

'
CLS
'
TRUE = -1: FALSE = 0
```

```
INPUT "Enter coefficients a, b, c ", a, b, c
'
IF b * b >= 4 * a * c THEN
        d = (b * b - 4 * a * c) ^ .5
        x1.re = (-b + d) / (2 * a)
        x1.im = 0
        x2.re = (-b - d) / (2 * a)
        x2.im = 0
        realsolution = TRUE
ELSE
        d = (4 * a * c - b * b) ^ .5
        x1.re = (-b) / (2 * a)
        x1.im = d / (2 * a)
        x2.re = (-b) / (2 * a)
        x2.im = -d / (2 * a)
        realsolution = FALSE
END IF
'
PRINT : PRINT "Solution"
'
IF realsolution THEN
        PRINT "x1 = "; x1.re; TAB(20); "x2 = "; x2.re
ELSE
        IF x1.im > 0 THEN
                PRINT "x1 = "; x1.re; " + "; ABS(x1.im); "i"
        ELSE
                PRINT "x1 = "; x1.re; " - "; ABS(x1.im); "i"
        END IF
        IF x2.im > 0 THEN
                PRINT "x2 = "; x2.re; " + "; ABS(x2.im); "i"
        ELSE
                PRINT "x2 = "; x2.re; " - "; ABS(x2.im); "i"
        END IF
END IF
```

Exercise 10-3

1. Write a program that will determine the largest factorial you can evaluate using the QBASIC numeric data types:

   INTEGER, LONG, SINGLE and DOUBLE

2. Rewrite the factorial program, so that you have a structure made of two components, a mantissa and an exponent.

3. Write a program that includes either functions or procedures to perform:

   complex addition, subtraction and multiplication

   Where the complex operations are defined as:

   addition: <x1, y1> + < x2, y2> = <x1+x2, y1+y2>

   subtraction: <x1, y1> - <x2, y2> = <x1 - x2, y1 - y2>

   multiplication: <x1, y1> * < x2, y2> = <x1*x2 -y1*y2, x1*y2 + x2*y1>

11. Dealing with Errors

11.1 Introduction

This chapter discusses Debugging, Testing, Validation and Verification, and Basic Error Handling.

Debugging is the process of removing faults (bugs) from a program. For debugging to take place a fault needs to be known about. Unless the fault is due to Syntax errors it is not always evident what caused the problem and where in the program that fault lies. There are however a number of traditional techniques and a built in Debugger which will help isolate the faults, so that they can be fixed.

Testing is the process of checking a program for correctness. It has to be systematic to increase the likelihood of finding all faults. Any moderately complex program cannot be tested exhaustively to prove the program is correct. You can however test it well enough to rid the program of most of the more blatant errors. Should the testing show up one or more errors, the program then has to be debugged.

Validation and **Verification** are techniques which are used to reject invalid data. These techniques make the program more robust so that instead of the program crashing if invalid data is entered, appropriate action can be taken (such as re-entering the data).

Error Handling is a catch-all phrase which covers anything else that can go wrong with the program. Despite the best intentions and efforts to produce a correct working program, there will always be the occasion when a certain set of circumstances make the program fail. Generally speaking if you have an error in your program, your program will crash with an error message. This topic deals with trapping these errors and taking appropriate action. Some of these errors may be due to hardware and so difficult to deal with until the error has been detected.

11.2 Review of Debugging Techniques

Debugging is the process of correcting errors which have been found while coding the program or by testing. It cannot occur unless you are aware of a program error.

Some of the errors are easy to detect as they are due to incorrect syntax. In this case the location of where the error occurs is highlighted and it is accompanied by an error message that describes the error.

Other errors are accompanied by error messages and a probable location. This time it is not a question of logic but having executed a forbidden action. An example of this is dividing by zero, or an out of bounds error caused by reading past the end of an array.

The most difficult to locate are logic errors. These errors don't necessarily produce error messages. They do however produce the wrong results.

There are many traditional techniques used by programmers to locate bugs in their programs. The simplest is to provide a trace in a portion of suspect code. In most cases this is achieved by addition of extra print statements which are used to dump the contents of all variables as they are updated. Also print statements are used to display a message whenever a certain portion of code is executed. This is useful to ensure that part of the program can be reached.

The flow of a program, and the name of each procedure that gets called can be verified by including a print statement within each statement that will display the name of the procedure each time it is called. An example of this follows:

```
REM -- Test program
INPUT "Enter parameter a", a
PRINT "Calling SUB demoproc"
CALL demoproc(a + 0)
PRINT "Returned to main program"

SUB demoproc( a )
        REM -- Demonstration of check
        PRINT "Entering SUB demoproc"

        ' Body of procedure

        PRINT "Leaving SUB demoproc"
END SUB
```

Termination of loops also need to be verified. Initially you may just want to display the number of iterations. In other situations you may need to check each iteration in detail to ascertain that both the action of the loop is carried out correctly and also that termination occurs correctly.

A manual variant of this is called a desk check or dry-run. This is achieved by filling in a blank table with the values of variables as they get updated.

Consider dry-running the following piece of code:

```
REM  -- Program to test function fac#
'
PRINT fac# (4)
'
END

FUNCTION fac# (n%)
        prod# = 1
        IF n% = 0 THEN
                fac# = 1
        ELSE
                FOR c% = n% TO 1 STEP -1
                        prod# = prod# * c%
                NEXT c%
                fac# = prod#
        END  IF
END FUNCTION
```

The desk check or table for dry-running this function should look something like this:

n%	c%	prod#	fac#
4	-	1	-
4	4	1	-
4	4	4	-
4	3	12	-
4	2	24	-
4	1	24	24

Fig 11-1 A sample dry-run table

Many versions of BASIC allow you to put a trace on program execution. When you run the program the line currently being executed gets highlighted. Should error situations arise you can easily determine where in the program the fault is located. You can also use a program trace to check loops. In particular you need to have an indication of how many times iteration takes place.

In QBASIC there are two statements you can use:

```
TRON     --    enables tracing
TROFF    --    disables tracing
```

These are equivalent to switching Trace On in the Debug Menu.

11.3 Using the Debugger

If you fail using the more traditional methods you may find it easier using the built-in debugger.

You can obtain the debug menu by pressing **Alt D**. You will now obtain the following options:

Step	F8
Procedure Step	F10
Trace on	
Toggle Breakpoint	F9
Clear all Breakpoints	
Set Next Statement	

Fig 11-2 Main debugger options

Normally when you run your program execution proceeds very fast. So fast that it is difficult to ascertain the statements currently being executed.

Stepping

When you use the debugger you can make use of this option to step through your program one statement at a time. Here you have a screen where your code is visible. The current statement being executed is highlighted.

Press **F8** to step to the next statement

If you now wish to view the value of a variable for instance you can press **F6**.

You will now get a split screen as in Fig 11-3

You can now examine the contents of a variable **varname** by typing in the command:

```
CLS : PRINT varname
```

You can also examine the effect of updating variables. In this case press **F6** and then enter the command:

```
CLS : varname = 10
```

Each time you want to progress to the next statement remember to press **F8**. If the next statement is a procedure or function call, each time you press **F8** you will proceed one statement within the procedure or function.

You can step over a function by pressing **F10**.

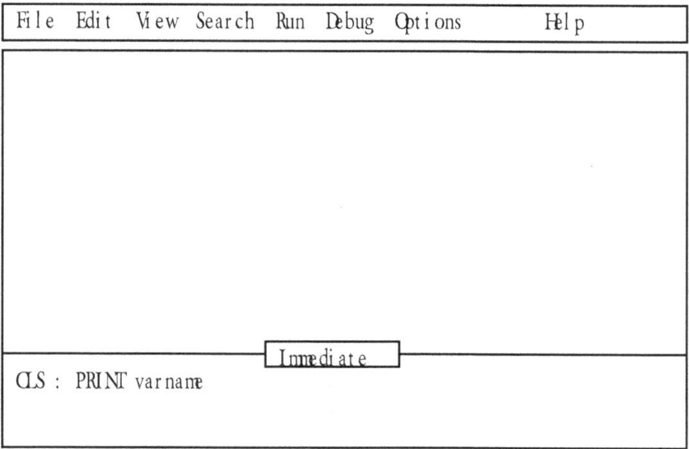

Fig 11.3 Displaying the contents of a variable while stepping

Breakpoints

As an alternative to stepping which is a rather tedious method of debugging, you can insert breakpoints into the program. A breakpoint is a place in the program where the program will pause. You can then continue running the program and the program will execute all the statements up to the next breakpoint.

You can inset a breakpoint by pressing **F9**. The current line will now be highlighted with a bold line across the screen. If at any time you wish to remove a breakpoint, you can do so by moving the cursor to that line and press **F9** again.

At the breakpoints you can stop and examine the value of variables etc, in the same manner as before.

Lastly when you have finished debugging you can remove all breakpoints with the **Clear all Breakpoints** option in the debug menu.

Trace On

Gives you the same facilities as using the TRON and TROFF statements within your QBASIC program.

Exercise 11-1

1. Referring to Fig 11-1

   (a) Perform a dry run with values 0, 1, 6

   (b) Modify the program to include TRON and TROFF. Run the program and examine the flow of the program. Compare what you see with the dry-run tables you produced previously.

   (c) Test the program by inserting breakpoints (Use the Debug Menu)

11.4 Designing a Test Plan

The aim of testing should be to intentionally create error conditions using both valid and invalid data. Invalid data should also be used to see if the program can handle them properly by validating the data etc.

For each module in the program a series of tests and test data for these tests should be determined in advance (often before the coding takes place). See Unit Testing.

The sorts of things you should consider when trying to make the modules fail are:

1. Input a number when the program is looking for a string.

2. Divide by zero.

3. Input a value outside the acceptable range.

All of these examples should be checked for within the modules itself. Reasonable input should be accomplished using validation and verification. Situations like divide-by-zero can in most cases be avoided by testing the value of the divisor before division takes place. Should the divisor equal zero, then instead of letting the program crash with a system error message, you should consider printing your own error message and other diagnostics before stopping the program gracefully.

You documentation for your test plan should consists of a list of each and every test that you intend to carry out. See fig 11-4 . For unit testing you will need a table like this for each module to be tested. Likewise when you want to test the overall performance of the program you will need to create a table to document tests which will test the running of several modules at once (Integration testing).

11.5 Unit Testing

Unit testing is the process of testing each module (Procedure or Function) in isolation. This should take place as each module is being coded.

Functional testing treats the module as a black box. It checks that for given inputs you get the desired outputs. It does not concern itself with the internal structure of the module, just whether you get the correct results.

It is normal to create a blank table to fill in, and compare the results you get with those that are expected. Such a table may look like this:

Test	Purpose	Test Data	Expected Results	Actual Results
1 2 3 4 . . .				

Fig 11-4 Table for Black Box testing

Another form of testing (White Box testing) looks at the internals of the module. Each part of the module is checked in detail. In particular the following must be tested:

- All computations
- Branching conditions are correct
- Loops terminate correctly
- No intermediate steps are missing
- Both valid and invalid data are used in testing

As well as testing for correctness, it is often a requirement that the program works efficiently. A measure of the efficiency of the program can be determined by maintaining a count of the number of assignments, and the number of comparisons, compared with the number of items of data being processed.

11.6 Integration Testing

Once Unit Testing is complete you need to test how well each of the modules integrate with the rest of the program. The logic of the program may dictate that certain modules call other modules etc. If you refer back to the design (a Structure Chart is possibly clearest), you will be able to see how the different modules interact.

It is up to you to test that the modules get called as they are supposed to. You must be sure that after the modules are called, program execution returns to the calling part of the program. This can be verified by either enabling a trace before running the program or by adding extra print statements in both the called modules and the line after the calling statements.

Exercise 11-2

1. Redo question 6 from exercise 8-1. Your new version should have:

    (a) a Program Design (such as a Structure Chart).

    (b) a Test Plan with suggested Test Data for each module (Unit Testing).

    (c) the output from each Test Run and expected results for comparison.

    (d) output from an Integration Testing that uses 10 employees in which all the test data is valid. To obtain hardcopy output place LPRINT statements in appropriate places in the program.

11.7 Using only valid data

The sorts of things you need to think about when checking for valid data are:

1. Sequence checking -- Data is presented in the correct order.

2. Testing fields to see if the have the correct format.

3. Checking for missing data

4. Replacing Tabs/Spaces with zero's. Have a notion of a default value if the data is missing.

5. Test for reasonableness
    - range tests
    - Limit tests

6. Checking coded fields for valid contents. Usually whatever is entered must match one of a small set of data.

11.8 Basic Error Handling

In QBASIC the ON ERROR command can be inserted at the top of the program to be used as a declarative to trap all errors anywhere in the program.

Having trapped the error, how do you deal with it. Some common procedures for dealing with error situations are as follows:

1. Abort the program and print your own error message.

2. Print error message containing the key fields and contents of erroneous fields.

3. Partially process or bypass erroneous records. Remember to include an error report of all by-passed records.

The format of the ON ERROR command is as follows:

ON ERROR GOTO [label | linenumber]

I have advocated that we don't use line-numbers, so for now we will use a label. The label marks the start of the error-handling routine for the program.

QBASIC also provides us with some functions that provide us with information about the nature of the error. They are:

ERR -- Returns an error-code which can be used to determine the type of error. (See appendix 3)

ERL -- Returns the line-number where the error occurred. (Must have line numbers in your program. Otherwise returns 0.

The following illustrates this:

```
ON ERROR GOTO ErrorHandler
REM -- Main body of program starts here
.
.
.
INPUT "Enter name of file to write to ", file$
file$ = "a:" + file$ + ".dat"
OPEN file$ AS OUTPUT FOR #1
.
.
.
REM   -- Main Body of program ends here
```

```
ErrorHandler:                  ' Label marking beginning of error handler
'
' Check for type of error using the function ERR
'
SELECT CASE ERR
        CASE 71
                CLS
                PRINT "Disk not ready"
                PRINT
                PRINT "Insert Disk and press a key"
                a$ = INPUT$(1)
                RESUME        ' Go back and try again
        CASE 72
                PRINT "Disk Media Failure"
                PRINT
                PRINT "Aborting operation"
                STOP
END SELECT
```

You will notice for each type of error detected There must be a RESUME command or STOP.

The RESUME command has one of 3 formats that follow:

1. RESUME ' go back to where the error occurred

2. RESUME NEXT ' go back to the next line after the line where the error occurred.

3. RESUME NEXT [label | line-number]

There are also special functions that specifically test for device errors.

They are:

ERDEV	--	Returns the error code indicating the type of device error.
ERDEV$	--	Returns the device name.

You may want to try the following using the above functions:

```
ON ERROR GOTO DisplayError

DisplayError:
'
PRINT "Error code on "; ERDEV$; " is "; ERDEV
```

Exercise 11-3

1. Continue question 1 from exercise 11-2

   (a) Add validation functions to test:

   hours worked
   rate of pay
   Job position is one from a short list of possible jobs

   You should choose appropriate test data to test for out of range and invalid data.

   (b) Test for divide-by-zero errors when computing the average salary. Write two versions:

   (i) Check number of employees before calculating average salary.

   (ii) Use ON ERROR to trap an error condition. Then test the value of ERR. (i.e. ERR = 11)

12. Using sequential Files

12.1 Introduction to File Handling

For large amounts of data it is not practical to store the data in memory using any of the techniques discussed in previous chapters. The data has to be stored on disk, and the container that holds this data is called a file.

Files tend to have a fixed structure. A file can be considered to be a collection of records. Each record is made up of a fixed number of data items or fields. Such a record might look like this.

Field 1 = Name	Field 2 = Address	Field 3 = TelNo.
Fred Bloggs	12A New Street	567 7892
Andy Pandy	23 Enid Close	567 8905
Bill Benn	42 Enid Close	567 3456
....	......	......

Fig 12-1 A simple file

In QBASIC we could give these fields names such as name$, addr$ and tel$ to indicate that they are going to be stored as strings. This might be an advantage as we don't need to calculate how big each field is.

QBASIC provides 3 ways to organise data in files. These are:

1. Sequential files
2. Random-access
3. Binary Files.

Sequential files provide the simplest organisation and also use up less space. The disadvantage is that when you want to search the file for a particular record the file has to be scanned record by record starting at the beginning of the file. In simple terms this makes access slow unless you know that you want to access most of the records most of the time. It makes sense to ensure that such a file is sorted. The rest of the chapter is now going to be devoted to how you can use sequential files in QBASIC.

12.2 Creating a Sequential File

Creating a file consist essentially of 3 stages:

1. **Opening a file** for output by using a statement such as:

```
OPEN "file.dat" FOR  OUTPUT AS #1
```

or

```
INPUT "Enter filename "; file$
OPEN file$ FOR OUTPUT AS  #1
```

Both of these examples create a new file for writing to and establishing a connection between the program and the actual data file. #1 is referred to channel 1. When ever we use a statement which includes this channel number QBASIC knows that we are referring to this file.

The statement has a general format:

```
OPEN filename FOR OUTPUT AS #n
```

where n (the channel number) can take a value between 1 and 255

2. **Store the data**

This is typically achieved by accepting input from the keyboard and then writing it to the file using a WRITE #1 statement. Remember the statements that write to the file must include the correct channel number. An example of how to store a single record is included below.

```
INPUT "Enter Name:     "; name$
INPUT "Enter Address: "; addr$
INPUT "Enter Tel No. : "; tel$
'          Write data to file
WRITE #1, name$, addr$, tel$
```

This block of statements will only store one record. If you want to store more you will need to put these statements inside a loop. You will now need to decide how you are to terminate the loop. i.e. how do you indicate that you have stored all the records.

(i). You could consider prompting the user to see if they want to enter another record and use the value entered as a condition to terminate the loop.

```
INPUT "Enter another record ? (y/n) ", ans$
```

(ii). You could use a data terminator. For example enter "ZZZZ" for name$ and let this be used to terminate the loop.

3. **Close the file**

Sequential files need to be closed when you have finished with them. If you forget you won't be able to open the file to perform some other operation. It is achieved with the statement:

```
CLOSE #1
```

12.3 Adding records to a sequential file.

You will often need to go back to a file and add records to the end of it. This is achieved in a similar manner to creating a file and adding records. But in this case the file is opened in a different mode.

```
OPEN filename FOR APPEND AS #n
```

The APPEND keyword indicates that any output is going to the end; rather than the beginning of a file. Should you use OUTPUT in place of APPEND you will wipe out your file.

To summarise. Appending records to the end of a file consists of the following stages:

1. Open the file

   ```
   OPEN "file.dat" FOR APPEND AS #1
   ```

2. Writing records to the file

   ```
   INPUT "Enter Name:    "; name$
   INPUT "Enter Address :"; addr$
   INPUT "Enter TelNo:   "; tel
   WRITE #1, name$, addr$, tel$
   ```

3. Closing the file when you have finished

   ```
   CLOSE #1
   ```

Exercise 12-1

1. Design a simple record Structure to catalogue the contents of your video or tape collection.

2. Write a simple program or sub program to create a file.

3. Run your program and store some records.

4. Check the contents of the file to see how the data has been stored.

   e.g. type the following at the DOS prompt

   ```
   TYPE  FILE.DAT
   ```

   You will see something like this:

   ```
   "Blade Runner", "Science Fiction", "Harrison Ford", "112 min", "1982"
   ```

12.4 Reading a Sequential File

Data read from a sequential file is read in order starting from the beginning of the file. You should make sure that the statements that read the file, read the fields in the same order that they were written to the file and that you stop reading when the end of file is reached.

To summarise. Reading a sequential file consists of the following stages:

1. **Open the file** for reading

   ```
   OPEN "file.dat" FOR INPUT AS #1
   ```

2. **Read records** from the file

   ```
   INPUT #1, name$, addr$, tel$        -- will read an entire record
                                          and store the results in string variables

   PRINT "Name:    "; name$            -- print out values to screen in an
   PRINT "Address: "; addr$               appropriate format
   PRINT "TelNo:   "; tel$
   ```

   You will need to place these statements inside a loop. But how do you know when it is time to finish reading. You can test for End-of-file using the EOF function. You might use it like this:

   ```
   DO UNTIL EOF(1)
   ' Read a record
   ' Print it out
   LOOP
   ```

   This is the sort of thing that you would do if you wanted to display the entire file. Often you are only interested in certain records.

3. When all processing has been done. Close the file

   ```
   CLOSE #1
   ```

12.5 Searching for a record

Even if you are only interested in certain records you still have to start at the beginning of the file and read a record at a time in order. The idea is to read the file a record at a time and only print out those records which satisfy your requirements.

A simple program to do this might look like this:

```
INPUT "Enter file to Search"; file$
INPUT "Enter name to search for "; s$
OPEN file$ FOR INPUT AS #1
DO UNTIL (s$ = name$) OR EOF(1)          -- Two conditions to test for
        INPUT #1, name$, addr$, tel$
LOOP
IF s$ = name$ THEN                        -- Need to check which condition
        PRINT "The details are"              terminated the loop
        PRINT "name:    "; name$
        PRINT "address: "; addr$          -- If the record was found
        PRINT "tel:     "; tel$              print it out.
ELSE
        PRINT "Name not found"            -- otherwise indicate record
END IF                                       not found.
CLOSE #1
```

Exercise 12-2

(a) Choose an application such cataloguing a video or tape collection and design a record format.

(b) Write a subprogram which will produce a menu with 5 options

MENU
----

1. Create a File
2. Add additional records to a file
3. Display entire file
4. Search for a record
5. Quit Menu

(c) Write a sub program for each item on the menu and test them out individually before you include them in the program.

(d) Discuss any problems you found with your program and any improvements that could be made.

12.6 Example Program

```
REM  -- Program to demonstrate use of Sequential Files
'
'Declaration of Sub Programs -- done for you by QBASIC
'
DECLARE SUB add ( )
DECLARE SUB menu ( )
DECLARE SUB create ( )
DECLARE SUB display ( )
DECLARE SUB search ( )
'
CALL menu
'
'       Sub Programs to follow
'


SUB add
        REM  -- Add additional records to end-of-file
        CLS
        PRINT "Adding records to a file"
        INPUT "Enter filename"; file$
        OPEN file$ FOR APPEND AS #1
        ans$ = "y"
        WHILE ans$ = "y"
                INPUT "Enter Name "; name$
                INPUT "Enter Address "; addr$
                INPUT "Enter Telephone number "; tel$
                INPUT "Another record ? (y/n) "; ans$
                WRITE #1, name$, addr$, tel$
                SLEEP 4
                CLS
        WEND
        CLOSE #1
        PRINT "Records added"
        PRINT "Returning to menu"
        SLEEP 4
        CLS
        CALL menu
END SUB
```

```
SUB create
	REM  --  Create a file and add records to it
	CLS
	PRINT "Creating a file"
	INPUT "Enter filename "; file$
	OPEN file$ FOR OUTPUT AS #1
	ans$ = "y"
	WHILE ans$ = "y"
		INPUT "Enter Name "; name$
		INPUT "Enter Address "; addr$
		INPUT "Enter Telephone Number "; tel$
		WRITE #1, name$, addr$, tel$
		INPUT "Another Record ? (y/n) "; ans$
		SLEEP 4
		CLS
	WEND
	CLOSE #1
	PRINT "File created"
	PRINT "Returning to Menu"
	SLEEP 4
	CLS
	CALL menu
END SUB

SUB display
	REM -- Display contents of entire file
	CLS
	PRINT "Displaying a file"
	INPUT "Enter name of file to display "; file$
	rec = 1
	OPEN file$ FOR INPUT AS #1
	DO UNTIL EOF(1)
		PRINT
		PRINT
		INPUT #1, name$, addr$, tel$
		PRINT "Data from record "; rec
		PRINT "Name: "; name$
		PRINT "Addr: "; addr$
		PRINT "Tel:  "; tel$
		rec = rec + 1
		SLEEP 2
		CLS
	LOOP
	CLOSE #1
	PRINT
	PRINT "End of file "; file$
	SLEEP 2
	CALL menu
END SUB
```

```
SUB menu
	REM -- produce menu
	CLS
	PRINT "                    Menu"
	PRINT "                     -----"
	PRINT
	PRINT " 1.                          Create a file"
	PRINT
	PRINT " 2.                          Add records to file"
	PRINT
	PRINT " 3.                          Display a file"
	PRINT
	PRINT " 4.                          Search for an entry"
	PRINT
	PRINT " 5.                          Quit Menu"
	PRINT
	PRINT
	PRINT " Enter your choice 1 - 5.  ";
	INPUT choice
	SELECT CASE choice
		CASE 1
			CALL create
		CASE 2
			CALL add
		CASE 3
			CALL display
		CASE 4
			CALL search
		CASE 5
			PRINT "Quitting menu. "
			SLEEP 4
			CLS
		CASE ELSE
			PRINT
			PRINT "invalid choice"
			PRINT "Try a number between 1 and 5"
			SLEEP 4
			CLS
			CALL menu
	END SELECT
END SUB
```

```
SUB search
        REM -- Search for a record
        CLS
        PRINT "Search for an Entry"
        PRINT
        INPUT "Enter file to Search"; file$
        INPUT "Enter name to search for "; s$
        OPEN file$ FOR INPUT AS #1
        DO UNTIL (s$ = name$) OR EOF(1)
                INPUT #1, name$, addr$, tel$
        LOOP
        IF s$ = name$ THEN
                PRINT "The details are"
                PRINT "name:    "; name$
                PRINT "address: "; addr$
                PRINT "tel:     "; tel$
        ELSE
                PRINT "Name not found"
        END IF
        CLOSE #1
        SLEEP 2
        PRINT
        PRINT "Search completed"
        PRINT "Returning to menu"
        SLEEP 2
        CLS
        CALL menu
END SUB
```

12.7 Joining Files

In this section we are going to look at some methods of joining two files.

Concatenation is the process of joining two files by appending one file to the end of another file.

Merging is the process of taking two sorted files and interleaving the records according to the sort order of a particular key field. This should result in a sorted file created using the contents of two smaller sorted files. In file maintenance terms merging is a very important feature which we will look at in detail later.

By far the easiest to discuss and implement is concatenation

This involves opening two files. The first will be opened in APPEND mode so that the file pointer will be pointing to the end of the file. This allows us to write to the end of the file. The second will be opened for INPUT. The idea is that we now read records from the second file and write them to the end of the first file.

```
REM  --   Program to concatenate two files
CLS
INPUT "Enter first filename "; file1$
INPUT "Enter second filename "; file2$
OPEN file1$ + ".dat" FOR APPEND AS #1
OPEN file2$ + ".dat" FOR INPUT AS #2
WHILE NOT EOF(2)
        '       Read a record
        INPUT #2, name$, addr$, tel$
        '       Write it to end of second file
        WRITE #1, name$, addr$, tel$
WEND
CLOSE #1 : CLOSE #2
PRINT "Concatenation complete"
```

If two files are to be merged, they must themselves be sorted and opened for INPUT. A third file must be opened for OUTPUT. The algorithm for a first attempt at merging might look like this:

```
open file1 and file2 for input
open file 3 for output
read an initial record from file1 and file2
repeat until end-of-file is reached for both files
        if key1 < key2
                write record 1 to file3
                read record from file 1
        else
                write record 2 to file 3
                read a record from file 2
        end if
```

But this would obviously fail because there is nothing taken into account when one of the file pointers reaches the end-of-file marker. A trick that COBOL programmers use is they assign the key a value of **highvalues,** where highvalues is the highest possible value that that field can take. There is no **highvalues** in QBASIC but we can do something very similar. As we a comparing alphabetic characters all we need to do is find a character with a higher ASCII code than any other character stored in the file. How about CHR$(255)?

A version of the program which follows, uses this algorithm and also includes the last feature.

```
REM -- First attempt at merging files
CLS
INPUT "Enter name of first file to merge"; f1$
INPUT "Enter name of second file to merge"; f2$
INPUT "filename for output"; f3$
OPEN f1$ + ".dat" FOR INPUT AS #1
OPEN f2$ + ".dat" FOR INPUT AS #2
OPEN f3$ + ".dat" FOR OUTPUT AS #3
highvalue$ = CHR$(255)        ' highest value for a character
'     Read a record from each file
INPUT #1, name1$, addr1$, tel1$
INPUT #2, name2$, addr2$, tel2$
DO until EOF(1) and  EOF(2)
        IF name1$ < name2$ THEN
                WRITE #3, name1$, addr1$, tel1$
                INPUT #1, name1$, addr1$, tel1$
                IF EOF(1) THEN name1$ = highvalue$
        ELSE
                WRITE #3, name2$, addr2$, tel2$
                INPUT #2, name2$, addr2$, tel2$
                IF EOF(2) THEN name$ = highvalue$
        END IF
LOOP
CLOSE #1: CLOSE #2: CLOSE #3
PRINT "Merging complete"
```

Unfortunately it still doesn't work properly. Can you say why?

To get round the problem of the program ignoring the last two records of each file we need to be more careful when we read the file.

In the example program that follows a subprogram is written to read a record from each file. Rather than leave the DO condition to check for end-of-file, all of the end-of-file checking is done by the readfile routine. If the readfile routine does detect an end-of-file it sets a flag which can be detected by the DO condition and assigns a high value to the key. Doing this will ensure that this key will have a higher value than any key in the other file. A routine to accomplish this follows below:

```
SUB readfile (name$, addr$, tel$, eof$, n)
        SHARED highvalue$
        IF NOT EOF(n) THEN
                eof$ = "f"
                INPUT #n, name$, addr$, tel$
        ELSE
                eof$ = "t"
                name$ = highvalue$
        END IF
END SUB
```

And this is what the complete program looks like:

```
REM -- A merge program that works properly
DECLARE SUB readfile (name$, addr$, tel$, eof$, n)
CLS
INPUT "Enter name of first file to merge"; f1$
INPUT "Enter name of second file to merge"; f2$
INPUT "filename for output"; f3$
OPEN f1$ + ".dat" FOR INPUT AS #1
OPEN f2$ + ".dat" FOR INPUT AS #2
OPEN f3$ + ".dat" FOR OUTPUT AS #3
highvalue$ = CHR$(255)
'     Read a record from each file
CALL readfile(name1$, addr1$, tel1$, eof1$, 1)
CALL readfile(name2$, addr2$, tel2$, eof2$, 2)
DO WHILE eof1$ = "f" OR eof2$ = "f"
        IF name1$ < name2$ THEN
                '     Process file 1
                WRITE #3, name1$, addr1$, tel1$
                 CALL readfile(name1$, addr1$, tel1$, eof1$, 1)
        ELSE
                '     Process file 2
                WRITE #3, name2$, addr2$, tel2$
                CALL readfile(name2$, addr2$, tel2$, eof2$, 2)
        END IF
LOOP
CLOSE #1: CLOSE #2: CLOSE #3
PRINT "Merging complete"

SUB readfile (name$, addr$, tel$, eof$, n)
        SHARED highvalue$
        IF NOT EOF(n) THEN
                eof$ = "f"
                INPUT #n, name$, addr$, tel$
        ELSE
                eof$ = "t"
                name$ = highvalue$
        END IF
END SUB
```

12.8 Suggested Project

A college has started to make extensive use of multiple choice testing and wants this to be automated. It is proposed that the contents of each test will reside in a sequential file. A program will be written to read these files and test each student. In addition to these there will be a student score file which will record the name of the student, date, answers and scores achieved for each test taken.

Write a program to implement this so that it includes:

(a) A Procedure called MainMenu which includes the options

1. Take a test
2. Display Scores and grades for a Test
3. Produce retake list for students who fail
4. Produce a Test file.
5. Quit the system

It is a further requirement that options 2, 3 and 4 are password protected.

(b) A function called SelectTest which will print on the screen a menu of up to 20 options. Each option corresponds to a test to take. The function will return a filename identifying the file to open for reading.

(c) Each data file will have Topic heading and 20 questions. Each question will have 4 choices of possible answer. Corresponding to each question there will also be a letter that identifies the correct choice.

An Example of the required format follows:

```
          " Topic test name"
          "Q1.   First question goes here"
choices → "A. First choice", "B. Second choice", "C. Third ", "D. Fourth", "B"

                                                           Correct answer
```

(d) You will need to create some test files. One way to do this would be to use the DOS editor. Another alternative would be to write a procedure to do it.

(e) A procedure called Taketest which will allow a student to take a topic test. To help you an outline has been included to indicate the scope of the procedure.

```
SUB Taketest
        Enter student-name
        Obtain System-date
        set score = 0
        file$ = SelectTest       ' Choose topic test
        OPEN file$ FOR INPUT AS #1
        OPEN "score.dat" FOR APPEND AS #2
        Write Student-name and System-date to score file
        foreach question {
            read question, choice1, choice 2, choice 3, choice 4, answer
            display question, choice 1, choice 2, choice 3, choice 4
            Enter student-answer
            If student-answer = correct-answer   add 1 to score
            Add student-answer to list-of-answers     }
        Write list-of-answers and score to score file.
        close all files
END SUB
```

(f) Write a function that will return a grade given a student score. The grades are awarded as follows:

$15 \leq$ score ≤ 20	Distinction	(D)
$12 \leq$ score ≤ 14	Merit	(M)
$9 \leq$ score ≤ 11	Pass	(P)
Score < 9	Fail	(F)

(g) Write a procedure that will given a topic test number, will display the name, score and grade of all students taking that test.

(h) Write a procedure that will read the score file and display the topic test name, name of student and score of all students that fail a test.

13. Random Access files

13.1 Introduction

We have seen that Sequential files are rather inflexible. In particular they :

1. Have to be accessed in order starting from the beginning of the file. This often means that a large proportion of the file has to be read even to find a single item.

2. They are difficult to modify. You can only easily append items to the end of a file. You cannot without much effort delete records, modify fields of records, insert records etc. All of these operations require that a new file be created and data from the old file gets copied to the new.

A Random Access or Direct Access file overcomes all of these problems. To acquire this degree of flexibility the records and fields therein need to be a fixed length. This can be achieved by creating a record structure using the TYPE statement, as mentioned in chapter 7.

A random access file can be visualised as a chunk of disk storage made up of a number of slots or cells. Each of these slots is uniquely identified by a number in the range 1 to n and either contains one record or is empty.

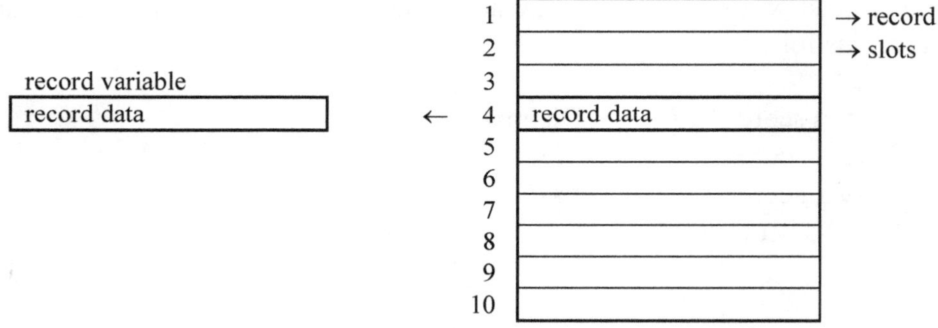

Fig 13-1 A random access file. Visualised as a collection of slots

When accessing it is normal to have a record variable corresponding to each of the record slots in the file. Data can then be transferred from the record variable to a slot in the file in one go. The slots can be both written to and read from in any order.

Writing to the file involves transferring data from the record variable to a named slot in the file using a statement of form:

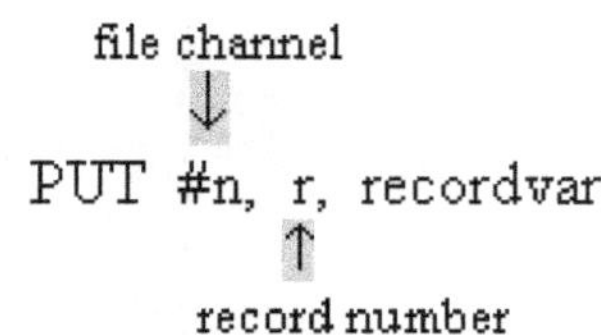

Reading a file involves transferring data from a named slot in the file to the record variable using a statement of form:

```
GET #n, r, recordvar
```

13.2 Fixed length record variables

As a reminder you will remember there are 5 simple data types STRING, INTEGER, LONG, SINGLE and DOUBLE. Each of these can be used in a DIM statement to specify the size and type of a variable as follows:

	Size in bytes
DIM age AS INTEGER	2
DIM SecondsInDay AS LONG	4
DIM mysalary AS SINGLE	4
DIM SizeOfUniverse AS DOUBLE	8
DIM PersonsName AS STRING * 20	20

An aggregate data type can be created using the TYPE statement. This will be our record structure. To solve a problem in the last chapter we could use:

```
TYPE scoredata
        studentname AS STRING * 20
        date AS STRING * 10
        answers AS STRING * 20
        score AS INTEGER
END TYPE
```

You can even nest your data types. For instance you may want to define name as follows:

```
TYPE sname
        firstname AS STRING  * 10
        initial AS STRING * 1
        lastname AS STRING * 10
END TYPE
```

and then use this type definition inside another type definition.

```
TYPE scoredata
        studentname AS sname
        date AS STRING * 10
        answers AS STRING * 20
        score AS INTEGER
END TYPE
```

You can now create a record variable as follows:

```
DIM recvar AS scoredata
```

This record variable is either going to be used to store data prior to writing to a file, or is going to be used for reading from a file.

The following code would suggest how values can be assigned to the record variable.

```
INPUT "First name: ", recvar.studentname.firstname
INPUT "Initial :", recvar.studentname.initial
INPUT "Last name: ", recvar.studentname.lastname
recvar.date = DATE$
recvar.answers = "ABCBABAAABCAAAAB"
score = 8
```

When you assign a value to a field that is a fixed length string you don't need to make sure that it is the right size as it will be truncated if too long, or padded with spaces if too small.

The record variable is also used to create the random access file. The length of the record variable is used to determine how big each slot will be.

e.g. `OPEN "scorefil.dat" FOR RANDOM AS #n LEN = LEN(recvar)`

13.3 Accessing Random Access files

A statement of form:

```
OPEN filename FOR RANDOM  AS #n LEN = LEN(recvar)
```

opens a random access file for any purpose. i.e Creating a file, reading a file, writing to the file, appending records, modifying records etc.

If this is done for the first time it will create a file and that file will remain open for any purpose you choose.

Writing records to the file

Records can be written to a random access file as follows:

1. Prepare the record for writing by assigning values to the fields of the record variable.

2. Write the contents of the record variable to the file.

```
PUT #n, r, recvar        ' will write the contents of recvar to slot n.
```

You can write the records to any slot you choose. You do not need to write in sequence slot 1, 2, 3 ... etc. However many people still choose to do so. This is because the records are often accessed sequentially and they are conscious of wasting space by having empty slots.

If this is the case all new records will be appended to the end of a file. This can be achieved by calculating how many records have already been stored and then store the record in the next position.

The following code is used to do this:

```
' Prepare a record for writing
'
INPUT "firstname: ", recvar.studentname.firstname
INPUT "Initial: ", recvar.studentname.initial
INPUT "Lastname: ", recvar.studentname.lastname
recvar.date = DATE$
ans$ = ""
FOR c = 1 TO 20
        '    Read a question from the question file
        INPUT "Enter answer A, B, C, D or - :", ch$
        ans$ = ans$ + UCASE$(ch$)
NEXT c
recvar.answers = ans$
'
' Determine how many records present in file
num = LOF(2) / LEN(recvar)
'
' Write record to next slot
PUT #2, num + 1, recvar
```

You will notice the use of the LOF function. LOF(2) returns the number of bytes storage in the file identified by channel 2. If you divide this number by the size of the record length you get the number of records in the file.

Reading the file

Reading records from the file is the reverse process of using PUT.

```
GET #2, 4, recvar
```

Here the GET statement is used to locate a specified slot and copy the contents to the record variable. Any slot position can be read in any order. The problem is knowing what is in a particular slot. Another problem is comparing the value of a field with the value of an item you are looking for. This is because all fields are fixed length and so the values assigned if less than the field length will always be padded with spaces.

If you don't like the idea of doing the following for instance:

```
IF recvar.studentname.firstname = "Tony      "
```

another alternative would be to strip off the trailing spaces.

e.g.

```
IF RTRIM$(recvar.studentname.firstname) = "Tony"
```

Another way to deal with this problem is to perform partial comparisons. You could for instance compare only the first 4 characters as in

```
IF LEFT$(recvar.studentname.firstname, 4) = "Tony"
```

Should the records be stored with no gaps in between the slots, displaying the entire file just involves computing the number of records stored and using a FOR loop as follows:

```
numrecords = LOF(2) / LEN(recvar)
'
FOR n = 1 TO numrecords
        GET #2, n, recvar
        PRINT "record #"; n
        PRINT recvar.studentname.firstname,
        PRINT recvar.studentname.initial,
        PRINT recvar.studentname.lastname
        PRINT recvar.date
        PRINT recvar.answers
        PRINT recvar.score
        SLEEP 2
        CLS
NEXT n
```

An alternative method would be to test for End-of-file.

i.e.

```
WHILE NOT EOF(2)
        GET #2, recvar
        .
        .
        .
WEND
```

You will notice that the statement **GET #2, recvar** doesn't specify a slot number. This is the relative format. It will get the next occupied slot. So the strategy above will work even if there are gaps. First time round GET #2, recvar will obtain the first occupied slot. There after the GET statement will obtain the next record and so on until end-of-file is detected.

If the file has no particular sort order, to locate a record you would have to scan the entire file. A preferable method would be a bisection search (previously mentioned for searching arrays). For this to be a possibility the file needs to be maintained in a sorted state. This can be done by inserting new records in the sort order. This will be discussed in the next section.

Closing Random Access files

The nice thing about random access files is that they do not have to be closed in between different operations like reading and writing to the file.

Exercise 13-1

1. Rewrite Q2 (Exercise 4-2). This time store the Country, Currency Rate, and Currency of each record in a record of a Random Access file. Your program should have procedures to perform the following:

   (a) Store a new currency record

   (b) Modify the currency rate for a given country

   (c) Search for a particular record given the name of the country

   (d) Given the name of the country, and an amount of money in pounds perform a currency conversion and print out the results in a suitable format.

   (e) Produce a menu which will provide the following options:

   Menu
   ------

   1. Store a new record
   2. Modify a currency rate
   3. Display the currency rate
   4. Perform a currency conversion
   5. Quit the system

13.4 DOS File System Commands

It is often useful to be able to interract with the operating system from within a program. This is especially useful when the program is manipulating one or more files. This capability is made available to QBASIC programs by means of the inbuilt DOS File System commands.

CHDIR	--	Change Directory
MKDIR	--	Create a Directory
RMDIR	--	Remove a Directory
KILL	--	Delete a File
FILES	--	List Files in a Directory
NAME	--	Rename a File
SHELL	--	Execute a DOS command

Fig 13-2 DOS File System Commands

The following examples illustrate how they can be used:

Manipulating Directories

```
' Create a new directory
INPUT "Enter name of directory ", dirname$
MKDIR dirname$

' Move to the new directory
CHDIR dirname$

' Delete a directory
INPUT "Enter name of directory to delete ", dirname$
RMDIR dirname$
' Note to achieve this successfully the directory needs to be empty
```

Accessing Files

```
' List Files of current directory
FILES

' List Files in another directory
INPUT "Enter directory you wish to view ", dirname$
FILES dirname$

' List specific file types
FILES "*.TXT"          ' Lists all .TXT files in current directory

' Delete a File
INPUT "Enter name of File to delete ", file$
KILL file$
```

```
' Rename a file
oldfile$ = "a:\p13\temp.dat"
newfile$ = "a;\p13\file.dat"
NAME oldfile$ AS newfile$
```

Other DOS commands

```
' SHELL statement can be used to execute any DOS command, batch file
' or executable file.
'
SHELL "DATE"
'
INPUT "Enter DOS command ", command$
SHELL command$
'
SHELL          ' With no parameters you are given a DOS prompt
```

13.5 More File Access Operations

The following are examples of more advanced file operations that you may want to use on a regular basis.

Inserting records

We have already seen that inserting a record into a vacant slot is an easy matter. It only involves using a statement of the form:

```
PUT #1, m, recvar
```

If we do this and slot number m is not vacant then the record will be overwritten. We may have the records written to the file so that there are no gaps. So to avoid overwriting the record it is necessary to move all the records with slot number greater than or equal to m, down one. This can be achieved as follows:

```
FOR c = n TO m STEP -1
        GET #1, c, recvar
        PUT #1, c + 1, recvar
NEXT c
' Slot number m can now be overwritten
CALL getdetails(recvar)        ' Procedure to New record
PUT #1, m, recvar
```

Deleting Records

One way to delete a record is to carry out the process of inserting a record in reverse. That is the slot number of the record to be deleted needs to be obtained, possibly by means of a search function. The records below this slot are now copied up one slot, thus overwriting the record to be deleted. We have however overlooked one flaw in this method. It leaves us with two copies of the last record. This can be wiped out by overwriting the record with spaces, and zeros in the case of numeric data.

A more satisfactory method is to mark the records that are to be deleted. Then copy only the unmarked records to a new file before renaming the new file name to the old file name. This is also much more efficient if multiple records are to be deleted.

An example of how this could be done is given in the next program fragment.

```
DIM records$(100)     ' Array to indicate marked records
' Indicate marked records by storing "*" in the appropriate elements
'
INPUT "Enter name of oldfile ", oldfile$
INPUT "Enter name of newfile" newfile$
OPEN oldfile$ FOR RANDOM AS #1 LEN = LEN(recvar)
OPEN newfile$ FOR RANDOM AS #2 LEN = LEN(recvar)
c1 = 1  ' Initialize slot position of oldfile
c2 = 1  ' Initialize slot position of newfile
WHILE NOT EOF(1)
        IF record$(c1) = "*" THEN
                GET #1, c1, recvar
                PUT #2, c2, recvar
                c2 = c2 + 1
        END IF
        c1 = c1 + 1
WEND
' Rename newfile
NAME newfile$ AS oldfile$
```

Searching for a record

Both inserting a record and deleting a record require that we are able to find a record to insert above or delete. If the records are not maintained in any particular sort order it is necessary to scan the file sequentially before the slot number of the required record can be returned.

An example of such a function follows:

```
FUNCTION findrecord(recvar AS recorddata, name$)
        true = -1 : false = 0 : found = false
        n = 1
        name$ = RTRIM$(name$)
        WHILE (NOT found) AND (NOT EOF(1))
                GET #1, n, recvar
                IF name$ = RTRIM$(recvar.name$) THEN
                        found = true
                ELSE
                        n = n + 1
                END IF
        WEND
        IF found THEN
                findrecord = n
        ELSE
                findrecord = 0 ' Indicates no record found
        END IF
END FUNCTION
```

The function can now be use to delete a record:

```
INPUT "Enter name to delete", n$
n = findrecord(recvar, n$ + "")
IF n <> 0 THEN
        GET #1, n, recvar
        ' Check that you have got the correct record
        CALL displayrecord(recvar)
        INPUT "Is this the record to delete (y/n)", ans$
        IF UPPER$(ans$) = "Y" THEN
                CALL deleterecord(n)
        END IF
END IF
```

Modifying a record

This is perhaps the easiest operation of all. First locate the record to be modified as in the example above.

```
GET #1, n, recvar
```

will read the record to be modified. Now overwrite the fields to be modified, and then write the record back to the file with:

```
PUT #1, n, recvar
```

13.6 Suggested Project

Write a program to create, update and access a 'Desk Diary' system. In this system you could have a file for each month, and allow 10 slots for each day. One slot for each hour between 8am and 6pm. These slots can be used to store an appointment.

Each slot should have the following structure:

```
TYPE appointment
        company AS STRING * 20
        contact AS STRING * 20
        purpose AS STRING * 30
        time As  STRING * 5
END TYPE
```

To store an appointment you might use the following code:

```
DIM recvar AS appointment
INPUT "Enter Company name ", recvar.company
INPUT "Enter Contact name ", recvar.contact
INPUT "Enter purpose ", recvar.purpose
INPUT "Enter date dd/mm/yyyy ", d$
day = VAL(LEFT$(d$, 2))
month = VAL(MID$(d$, 3,2))
INPUT "Enter appointment time hh:mm ", recvar.time
hours = VAL(LEFT$(recvar.time, 2))
'
file$ = "month" + month + ".dat"
OPEN file$ FOR RANDOM AS #1 LEN = LEN(appointment)
'
' Store record
slot = 10 * day + (hours - 7)
PUT #1, slot, recvar
```

Here the appropriate file is chosen using the given month, and the appropriate slot is computed given the day and time.

(a) Start by implementing the above code. Then rewrite the above so that the routine to store a record is contained in a procedure.

(b) Write further procedures for:

i. Searching for all appointments on a certain day
ii. Searching for all appointments for a given customer

(c) Given a time, date and customer name write a procedure which will enable you to change an appointment.

14. Binary Files

14.1 Introduction to Binary files.

A binary file can be thought of as an unstructured sequence of characters. The only structure that such a file has is the structure imposed on it by the program that reads it.

Any file at all can be opened as a binary file. If for instance you opened a sequential as a binary file, you would have to know details of how many fields in each record, and make use of the fact that fields are separated by commas etc.

A file can be opened in binary mode by issuing a statement such as:

```
OPEN "file.dat" FOR BINARY AS #2
```

This file can then:

1. be written to and read
2. accessed in any order by moving to a specific character position
3. Can read 1 or more characters at a time depending on the size of the record variable being used.

To access a binary file you can use the following statements and functions:

Statements	**Functions**
SEEK -- Change current file position	SEEK -- Return current position
GET -- Read from the file	LOF -- Return length of file
PUT -- Write to the file	LOC -- Return current position

Fig 14-1 Statements and Functions used for Binary files

A file is read by means of a GET statement such as:

```
GET #n, r, var
```

The number of characters read is determined by the size of the variable **var**, and the position to start reading from by the value of **r**.

In a similar manner characters can be written to a file by means of a PUT statement such as:

```
PUT #n, r, var
```

Here a number of characters determined by the size of **var** are inserted into the file starting at position **r**. If r is not the end of the file then characters are going to be overwritten.

In both of the commands GET and PUT, there is a relative format. That is the position to start reading or writing in the file can be missed out. In which case the position to be used will be the last file position accessed.

This file position can be changed by means of the SEEK statement. The statement:

```
SEEK #n, r
```

will move the current file position to character number r. In which case the following statements can be used.

```
GET #n, var    ' Read a number of characters  starting at the current position

PUT #n, var    ' Write the contents of var starting at position r
```

The functions are there to provide us with information.

The function SEEK returns the current file position and can be used as follows

```
PRINT "The current file position is ", SEEK(n)
```

The function LOF returns the total number of characters in the file and is likely to be used as follows:

```
REM -- Display contents of a small text file
DIM character AS STRING * 1
INPUT "Enter name of text file to view ", file$
OPEN file$ FOR BINARY AS #1
FOR c = 1 TO LOF(1)
        GET #1, c, character
        PRINT character
NEXT c
CLOSE #1
```

Here LOF is used to determine when the end of file has been reached. The same technique can be used to display other types of file but we need to make 2 amendments. They are:

1. Avoid printing anything but the normal printable characters.

2. Provide a means of stopping when there is a screen full of information, so that the user has time to read it.

You would now be able to use the program to view a variety of files which have some text in it.

Such a program may look like this:

```
DIM character AS STRING * 1
CLS
INPUT "Enter Filename: ", file$
OPEN file$ FOR BINARY AS #1
charcnt = 0: linecnt = 1
FOR c = 1 TO LOF(1)
        charcnt = charcnt + 1
        IF charcnt > 80 THEN
                charcnt = 0
                linecnt = linecnt + 1
        END IF
        IF linecnt > 20 THEN
                linecnt = 1
                SLEEP 2
                CLS
        END IF
        GET #1, c, character
        a = ASC(character)
        IF (a > 31) AND (a < 127) THEN
                PRINT character;
        ELSE
                PRINT ".";
        END IF
NEXT c
CLOSE #1
```

In addition to the listed amendments, a check has been made to make sure that there are no lines greater than 80 characters in length. If an unprintable character is detected a fullstop is printed to mark this character.

14.2 A Text File Browser

A useful utility to use within MS-DOS is the **more** command. This utility allows you to browse through a file a screen-full at a time. It does however lack the features that you would have in a similar utility within UNIX. It does not have in-built commands to go backwards and forwards, and quit when you want to finish. Instead it just goes forward through the file 24 lines at a time each time you press a key.

How can we write such a utility within QBASIC? If we are to open the text file as a binary file we need to know where each line of text begins and ends. A good starting point would be to create an index indicating where each line begins. We can then write out this line by starting at the beginning and continuing until we reach the next carriage return. The starting point for the first line will be character position number 1, and that of the second line will be one more than the character position of the next carriage return. This is illustrated in the following fragment of QBASIC code:

```
DIM character AS STRING * 1
DIM linepos(1 TO 1000)
CLS
INPUT "Enter name of file ", infile$
OPEN infile$ FOR BINARY AS #1
linepos(1) = 1  ' First line of text starts at character position 1
n = 2           ' Set index ready for next line
FOR c = 1 TO LOF(1)
        GET #1, c, character
        IF character = CHR$(13) THEN
                linepos(n) = c + 1
                n = n + 1
        END IF
NEXT c
lastline = n - 1
```

Here you will note that an array called linepos( ) has been set up to store the position of the character position of the start of up to 1000 lines of text. Having obtained this information it is now quite easy to print out the desired lines of text.

Lets start by writing a procedure to write a line of text given the start of the line. This could be achieved as follows:

```
SUB printline(n)
        DIM character AS STRING * 1
        WHILE character <> CHR$(13)
                GET #1, n, character
                PRINT character;
                n = n + 1
        WEND
        PRINT
END SUB
```

We now need a means of printing up to 20 contiguous lines of text. There is of course a possibility that there are less than 20 lines to print, and this must be tested for. The following procedure makes use of printline to do this:

```
SUB printscreen(lc)
        SHARED lastline, linepos()
        c = lc : p =1
        WHILE  lc <  c + 20 AND lc < lastline
                m = linepos(lc)
                LOCATE p, 1
                CALL printline(m + 0)
                lc = lc + 1
                p = p + 1
        WEND
END SUB
```

Using these two procedures it is an easy matter to scroll through the file 20 lines at a time in the same manner as **more** under MS-DOS. What we need to be able to do is prompt for a command and test for one character commands such as:

b	--	Scroll up 1 screen (20 lines)
SPACE	--	Scroll down 1 screen (20 lines)
<RET>	--	Scroll down one line
h	--	help
q	--	quit

This will be left to the reader as an exercise which will follow.

Exercise 14-1

1. Implement the code illustrated above, and test that it works by making suitable procedure calls.

2. Write a looping statement which will:

   (a) Prompt with the character :

   (b) Allow a user to enter SPACE, b, Return, q, h.

   (c) Will terminate if q is entered.

   (d) For each of the commands entered write code to implement appropriate actions. Remember to check to see whether it is possible to carry out these actions. i.e. can't scroll down if you have reached the end of the file etc.

   (Print CHR$(7) to indicate an impossible action)

14.3 Another example application

Up until now I have discouraged the use of line numbers altogether. There is one situation where line numbers are useful. That is for debugging purposes. Should your program have a fault and you wish to use the debugger to locate the fault it would be nice to have a tool that would add line numbers to your program.

Conceptually this is a very simple problem. You need to read a line of text from the program file and insert a line number at the beginning of the line before writing the entire line to another file. This can be achieved by using an array to read the line into before writing a line number at the beginning. The contents of the array can now be written to another file

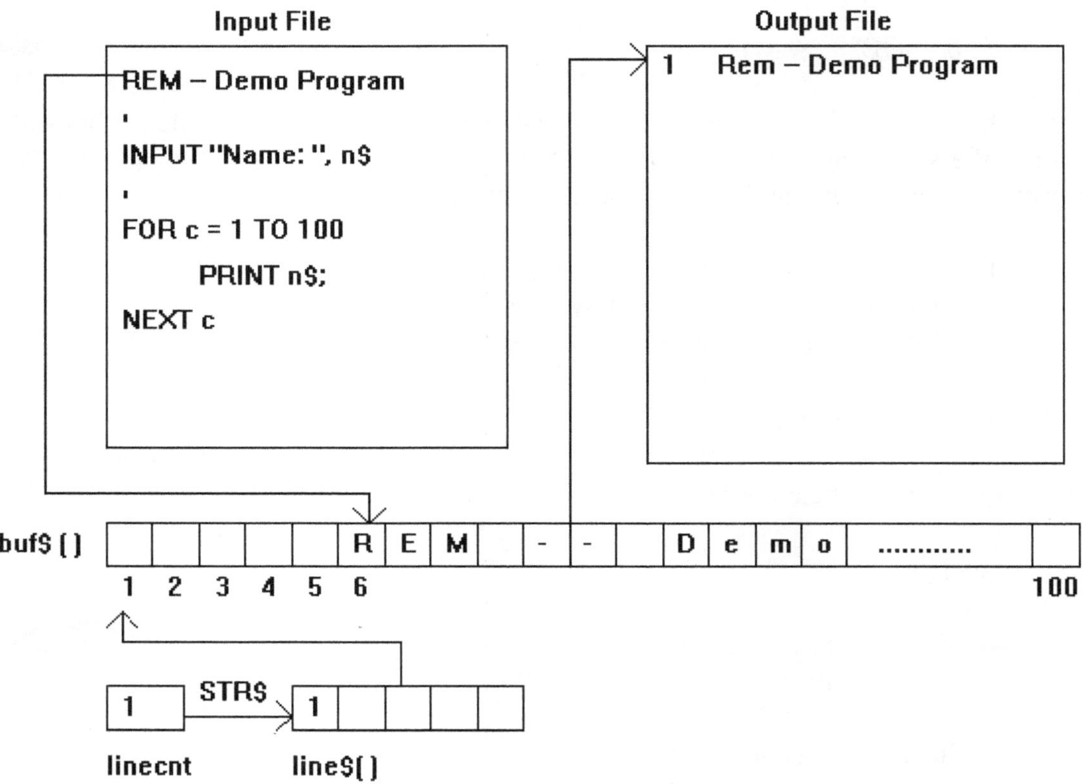

Fig 14-2 Algorithm for adding Line numbers

See at Fig 14-2. Here buf$( ) is an array capable of storing up to 100 characters. The first 5 characters are reserved for storing a line number. A line at a time is read from the input file and copied to the array buf$ one character at a time. The value of the current line number is converted to a string before being copied to the beginning of the array buf$. Once this has been done the contents of the array up to the last character copied is written to the output file. Both of the files are opened as binary files and a record of the current character position must be kept. The line count is then incremented ready for the next line of text to be read from the input file.

A complete version of the program may look like this:

```
DECLARE SUB initbuf (buf$())
DIM buf$(1 TO 100)
DIM character AS STRING * 1
linecnt = 1
bufptr = 6
outptr = 1
'
CLS
PRINT "These files are available"
FILES
PRINT
INPUT "Enter name of input file   ", infile$
INPUT "Enter name of output file  ", outfile$
OPEN infile$ FOR BINARY AS #1
OPEN outfile$ FOR BINARY AS #2
CALL initbuf(buf$())
FOR c = 1 TO LOF(1)
        GET #1, c, character
        IF ASC(character) <> 13 THEN
                ' Add a character to buffer
                buf$(bufptr) = character
                bufptr = bufptr + 1
        ELSE
                buf$(bufptr) = character ' Store carriage return
                ' Write line to outfile
                FOR p = 1 TO bufptr
                        PUT #2, outptr, buf$(p)
                        outptr = outptr + 1
                NEXT p
                ' Set up buffer for next line
                linecnt = linecnt + 1
                bufptr = 6
                CALL initbuf(buf$())
        END IF
NEXT c
CLOSE

SUB initbuf (buf$())
        SHARED linecnt
        line$ = STR$(linecnt)
        FOR c = 1 TO 100: buf$(c) = " ": NEXT c
        FOR l = 1 TO LEN(line$)
                buf$(l) = MID$(line$, l, 1)
        NEXT l
END SUB
```

14.4 Reading dBASE III files

Software applications such as Spreadsheets, databases, graphics etc all make use of files. And each of them have a specific file structure and programs that can interpret that structure. dBASE III is a popular database management system that has been around for several years now. The package enables the user to create databases and also make queries that will access the database. Other software products can also read dBASE format data files. If you know what the format is you can write your own programs to do the same thing.

The structure of a dBASE data file is made up of a header and data records. The header contains such information as the number of records, the number of fields, time of last update etc. Each data record is made up of a number of fixed length records, each of which has a corresponding field descriptor in the data file header.

Byte	Contents	Meaning
1	1 character	dBASE III version number
2 - 3	3 characters	date of last update (yy mm dd)
5 - 8	32 bit number (LONG)	number of records in data file
9 - 10	16 bit number (INTEGER)	length of header structure
11 - 12	16 bit number (INTEGER)	length of each record
13 - 32	20 characters	Reserved
33 - n	Each 32 characters	Field descriptor array (Each element corresponding to a field)
n + 1	1 character	Field terminator = 0DH

Fig 14-3 dBASE III file header

Byte	**Contents**	**Meaning**
1 - 11	11 characters	Field name
12	1 character	Field Type (C, N, L, D, or M)
13 - 16	32 bit number (LONG)	Field data address (in memory)
17	1 character	Field length
18	1 character	Field decimal count
19 - 32	14 character	Reserved

Fig 14-4 A field descriptor

For each of the components in the file header it is necessary to create a variable that is big enough to store the contents. This is best done using DIM statements, and will be used later in GET statements.

In each of the field descriptors there is a component that describes the datatype. The following datatypes are available in dBASE III:

1.	C	Character	(ASCII characters)
2.	N	Numeric	(Numeric digits)
3.	L	Logical	(Y, y, N, n, T, t, F, f or ? if not initialised)
4.	M	Memo	(10 digits representing a .DBT block number)
5.	D	Date	(8 digits in YYYYMMDD format)

To get you started there follows a program that will read a dBASE III data file and extract header information from it. As an exercise you may wish to continue the program and access the data records as well.

```
DECLARE SUB fdes (recvar AS ANY, n!)
CLS
' Create type for a field descriptor
TYPE fdescr
        fieldname AS STRING * 11
        fieldtype AS STRING * 1
        dataaddr AS LONG
        fieldlen AS STRING * 1
        fieldcnt AS STRING * 1
        reserved AS STRING * 14
END TYPE
' Create a variable to store a field descriptor
DIM recvar AS fdescr
' Record Variables for file header
DIM ver AS STRING * 1
DIM y AS STRING * 1
DIM m AS STRING * 1
DIM d AS STRING * 1
DIM numrec AS LONG
DIM headerlen AS INTEGER
DIM reclen AS INTEGER
DIM reserved AS STRING * 20
'
OPEN "books.dbf" FOR BINARY AS #1
'
' Read File Header
GET #1, 1, ver
GET #1, 2, y
GET #1, 3, m
GET #1, 4, d
GET #1, 5, numrec
GET #1, 9, headerlen
GET #1, 11, reclen
GET #1, 13, reserved
```

```
' Output info about data file
PRINT "Version is ", ASC(ver)
yy = ASC(y): mm = ASC(m): dd = ASC(d)
PRINT "Last update", dd; "/"; mm; "/"; yy
PRINT "Number of records is ", numrec
PRINT "Length Header Structure is ", headerlen
PRINT "Length of each record is ", reclen
numfields = (headerlen - 1) / 32
PRINT "Number of Fields is ", numfields
SLEEP 4
CLS
'
'       Get Field Descriptors
FOR c = 1 TO numfields
        CALL fdes(recvar, c + 0)
        SLEEP 4
        CLS
NEXT c


SUB fdes (recvar AS fdescr, n)
        start = 32 * n + 1
        GET #1, start, recvar
        PRINT "Field "; n
        PRINT "Fieldname ", recvar.fieldname
        f$ = recvar.fieldtype
        SELECT CASE f$
                CASE "C", "c"
                        PRINT "Fieldtype is Character"
                CASE "D", "d"
                        PRINT "Fieldtype is Date"
                CASE "L", "l"
                        PRINT "Field type is Logical"
                CASE "N", "n"
                        PRINT "Field type is Numeric"
        END SELECT
        PRINT "Data address ", recvar.dataaddr
        l = ASC(recvar.fieldlen)
        PRINT "Field length", l
        c = ASC(recvar.fieldcnt)
        PRINT "Field Count ", c
END SUB
```

14.5 Design for a faster database system

For larger databases especially Hierarchical and Network databases, speed is of the utmost importance. These days it is possible that you have one or more large hard disks (1-2 Giga Bytes) on you PC. You now have the resources to create large databases. If you use products such as dBASE the records are stored sequentially and they have to be of a fixed size. Here a B-Tree (or Multi-way balanced tree) is used as an index to locate the records easily.

In databases that store a lot of text, it is undesirable to have fixed length records, as much space is potentially wasted. For data to be accessed efficiently from the hard disk, you want to read large chunks of data at a time into memory. Once in memory you can then access individual records. For us to do this it is necessary to have a unit of transfer which may contain one or more records. I would suggest a minimum I/O transfer of 1024 bytes (1K). I propose we call this unit of storage 1 database page.

So a database then is made up of 1024 byte database pages. The initial amount of storage to be allocated should then be num_pages × size_of_page. To access a record we only need a means of evaluating which page it should be on, and then read in the entire page before looking for the record.

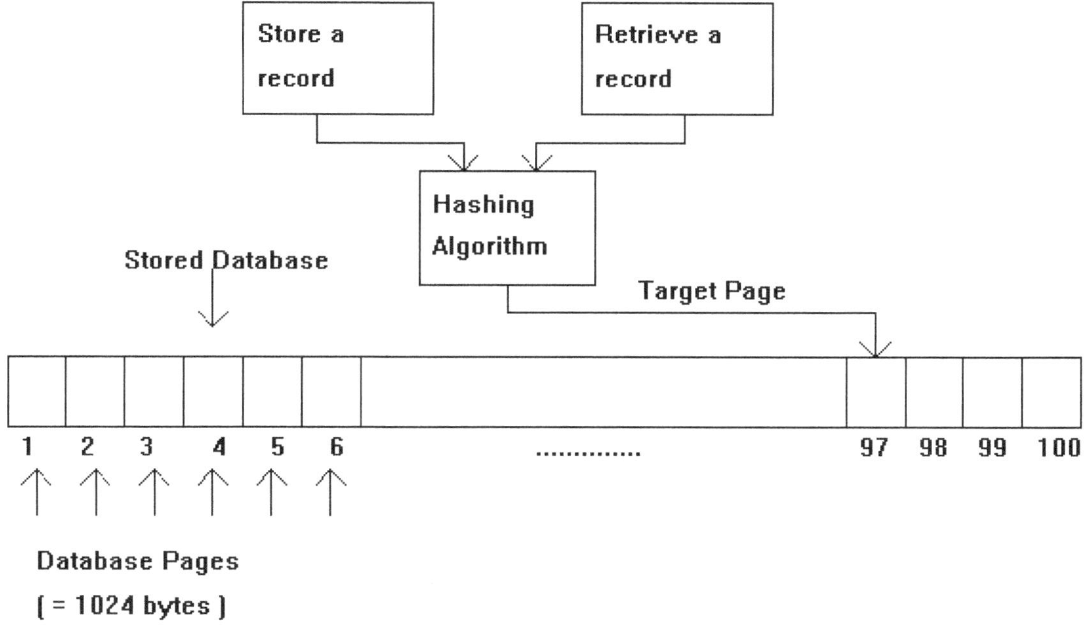

Fig 14-5 Design for a Database Architecture

The method illustrated in Fig 14-5 is called Dynamic Hashing and is used by large DBMS's such as VAX DBMS, and VAX Rdb, which are typically used on VAX Mini-computers.

Dynamic Hashing is the process of locating a target page to store a record. The page number is determined by supplying a Hash-key to a Hashing Algorithm. The hashing algorithm uses the key, operates on this key and returns a page number within the range of pages available in your database. The same hash-key can be used to locate the record later on.

The hashing algorithm should be able to disperse the records evenly amongst the database. One way of ensuring this happens is if the hashing algorithm uses prime numbers, or uses a random number generator (which makes use of random numbers).

A hashing function could be implemented in QBASIC as:

```
FUNCTION hash% ( hashkey%, numpages% )
        RANDOMIZE hashkey%
        hash% = INT( RND * numpages% ) + 1
END FUNCTION
```

This one function can then be used to both store and locate records.

How are we going to organize out data? Especially if we are to use variable format records. We could use a delimiter such as the character \ to separarate each field, and store the size of the record. This can be achieved by storing an index for each record on the database page. This index to the records could contain an offset and a size. The offset indicates where the record starts from the beginning of the page, and the size can be used to determine where it ends.

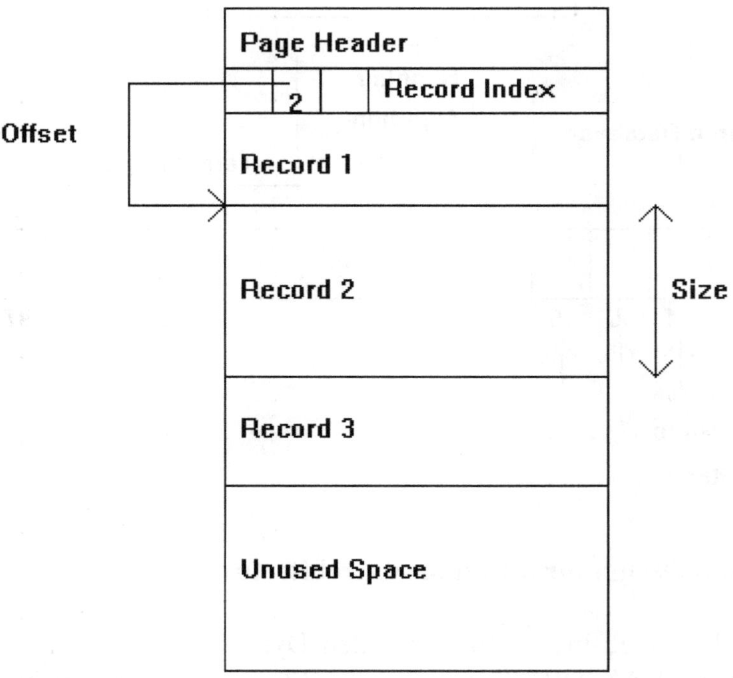

Fig 14-6 A database page structure

In fig 14-6 The pageheader occupes the beginning of the structure. This should be of a fixed length, and can be used to store such things as:

Page number, date last updated, number of records, amount of unused space

There can be a fixed number of indices (lets say 5). Each index is made up:

1. an offset that points to the beginning of the record.

2. a record size, indicating the size of record in bytes.

This is followed by zero or more records and some unused space.

The above page structure could be represented as:

```
TYPE Pageheader
        Pagenum AS INTEGER
        DateLastModified AS STRING * 10
        NumRecs AS INTEGER
        UnusedSpace AS INTEGER
END TYPE

TYPE IndexItem
        offset AS INTEGER
        size AS INTEGER
END TYPE

TYPE PageIndex
        p1 AS IndexItem
        p2 AS IndexItem
        p3 AS IndexItem
        p4 AS IndexItem
        P5 AS IndexItem
END TYPE

TYPE DatabasePage
        PHeader AS PageHeader
        PIndex AS PageIndex
        RecordStorage AS STRING * 988
END TYPE
```

A variable to store such a structure could be created as follows:

```
DIM dbpage as DatabasePage
```

A record structure for an employee record could for instance be represented as:

Employee(EmpNum, FirstName, Initial, LastName, Dept, DateOfBirth)

And because we want to have a variable length field format it will not be possible to define a record structure using a TYPE statement.

Instead we could set up string variables to contain the varible length fields. You may for instance have the following:

```
' Enter details for a variable length Record
'
INPUT "Employee Number: "; EmpNum$     ' Easier to store as a string
INPUT "full name: "; name$
INPUT "Address line 1: "; addr1$
INPUT "Address line 2: "; addr2$
INPUT "Address line 3: "; addr3$
INPUT "Telephone Number: "; tel$
INPUT "Department: "; dept$
'
' Obtain Target Page
'
num% = VAL(Empnum$)
pagenumber% = hash%( num%, 100)' Assumes 100 pages in database
'
' Store record
'
recorddetails$ = Empnum$ + "\" + name$ + "\" + addr1$ + "\" + addr2$ + "\"
recorddetails$ = recorddetails$ +  "\" addr3$ + "\" + tel$ + "\" + dept$
'
reclen = LEN( recorddetails$ )
'
' Assuming this is the first record on the Target Page
'
dbpage.PIndex.p1.offset = 0   ' easier if take offset at beginning of record
                              ' storage area
dbpage.PIndex.p1.size = reclen
dbpage.PIndex.p2.offset =  reclen
'
' Write record to record storage area of dbpage
'
FOR c = 1 TO  reclen
        dbpage.RecordStorage(c) = MID$(recorddetails$, c, 1)
NEXT c
'
' Write whole page to file
'
OPEN file$ FOR BINARY AS #1
start% = (pagenumber% - 1) * 1024
PUT #1,  start%, dbpage
'
```

14.6 Suggested Project

1. A company wants to create a database to store information about all of their employees. The information about each employee is of variable length format. In addition to this it is required to store a Job-History record for each year of employment and if possible these records should be stored on the same database page.

   Given that:

   (1) The Employee Record has the following format:

   Employee(Empnum, Name, addr1, addr2, addr3, tel, dob)

   (2) The Job-History record will have the following format:

   Jobhistory(EmpNum, Year, dept, JobDescr, salary)

   (3) No employee has been employed for more that 3 years

   (a) Calculate a reasonable Page size so that you can fit one employee record and 3 Job-History records on the same page. Remember this size must be a multiple of 1024 bytes.

   (b) Write a record structure, so that you can read in a page at a time.

   (c) Write a procedure to create an empty database, based on the size of each database page and the number of pages.

   (d) Write a procedure to store a record

   (e) Write a procedure to retrieve a record

   (f) Modify each of the procedures so that you can time how long each operation takes.

Appendix 1

Keywords by programming Task

Programming Task	**Keywords included in this List**
Control Program Flow	DO ... LOOP, END, EXIT, FOR ... NEXT, IF ... THEN ... ELSE, GOSUB ... RETURN, GOTO, ON ... GOSUB, ON ... GOTO, SELECT CASE, STOP, SYSTEM
Declare Constants and Variables	CONST, DATA, DIM, ERASE, OPTION BASE, READ, REDIM, REM, RESTORE, SWAP, TYPE ... END TYPE
Define and Call BASIC Procedures	CALL, DECLARE, EXIT, FUNCTION, RUN, SHELL, SHARED, STATIC, SUB
Device Input/Output	CLS, CSRLIN, INKEY$, INP, INPUT, KEY (assignment), LINE INPUT, LOCATE, LPOS, LPRINT, LPRINT USING, OPEN COM OUT, POS, PRINT, PRINT USING, SPC, SCREEN function, TAB, VIEW PRINT, WAIT, WIDTH
Display graphic Images	CIRCLE, COLOUR, GET (graphics), LINE, PAINT, PALETTE, PCOPY, PMAP, POINT, PRESET, PUT (graphics), SCREEN statement, VIEW, WINDOW
DOS File System commands	CHDIR, KILL, MKDIR, NAME, RMDIR
File Input/Output	CLOSE, EOF, FILEATTR, FREEFILE, GET (File I/O), INPUT, INPUT$, LINE INPUT, LOC, LOC$, LOF, OPEN, PUT (File I/O), SEEK function, SEEK statement, UNLOCK, WRITE,
Manage Memory	CLEAR, FRE, PEEK, POKE

Manipulate Strings	ASC, CHR$, HEX$, INSTR, LCASE$, LEFT$, LEN, LSET, LTRIM, MID$ function, MID$ statement, OCT$, RIGHT$, RSET, RTRIM$, SPACES$, STR$, STRING$, UCASE$, VAL
Perform Mathematical calculations	ABS, ASC, ATN, CDBL, CINT, CLNG, COS, CSNG, CVDMBF, CVSMBF, EXP, INT, LOG, RANDOMIZE, RND, SGN, SIN, SQR, TAN, TIME$ function
Set Traps for Events and Errors	COM, ERDEV, ERDEV$, ERL, ERR, ERROR KEY (Event trapping), ON COM, ON ERROR, ON KEY, ON PEN, ON PLAY, ON STRIG, ON TIMER, PEN, PLAY (Event trapping), RESUME, RETURN, STRIG, TIMER function, TIMER statement

Appendix 2

ASCII Codes

Code	Character	Code	Character	Code	Character	Code	Character
0	NUL	32	Space	64	@	96	`
1	SOH	33	!	65	A	97	a
2	STX	34	"	66	B	98	b
3	ETX	35	#	67	C	99	c
4	EOT	36	$	68	D	100	d
5	ENQ	37	%	69	E	101	e
6	ACK	38	&	70	F	102	f
7	BEL	39	'	71	G	103	g
8	BS	40	(	72	H	104	h
9	Tab	41	)	73	I	105	i
10	NL	42	*	74	J	106	j
11	Home	43	+	75	K	107	k
12	FF	44	'	76	L	108	l
13	CR	45	-	77	M	109	m
14	SO	46	.	78	N	110	n
15	SI	47	/	79	O	111	o
16	DLE	48	0	80	P	112	p
17	DC1	49	1	81	Q	113	q
18	DC2	50	2	82	R	114	r
19	DC3	51	3	83	S	115	s
20	DC4	52	4	84	T	116	t
21	NAK	53	5	85	U	117	u
22	SYN	54	6	86	V	118	v
23	ETB	55	7	87	W	119	w
24	CAN	56	8	88	X	120	x
25	EM	57	9	89	Y	121	y
26	SUB	58	:	90	Z	122	z
27	ESC	59	;	91	[	123	{
28	Rt Arr	60	<	92	\	124	|
29		61	=	93	]	125	}
30	RS	62	>	94	^	126	~
31	US	63	?	95	_	127	DEL

Appendix 3

Extended ASCII character set

Code	Character	Code	Character	Code	Character	Code	Character
128	Ç	160	á	192	└	224	α
129	ü	161	í	193	┴	225	ß
130	é	162	ó	194	┬	226	Γ
131	â	163	ú	195	├	227	π
132	ä	164	ñ	196	─	228	Σ
133	à	165	Ñ	197	┼	229	σ
134	å	166	ª	198	╞	230	µ
135	ç	167	º	199	╟	231	τ
136	ê	168	¿	200	╚	232	Φ
137	ë	169	⌐	201	╔	233	Θ
138	è	170	¬	202	╩	234	Ω
139	ï	171	½	203	╦	235	δ
140	î	172	¼	204	╠	236	∞
141	ì	173	¡	205	═	237	ø
142	Ä	174	«	206	╬	238	ε
143	Å	175	»	207	╧	239	∩
144	É	176	░	208	╨	240	≡
145	æ	177	▒	209	╤	241	±
146	Æ	178	▓	210	╥	242	≥
147	ô	179	│	211	╙	243	≤
148	ö	180	┤	212	╘	244	⌠
149	ò	181	╡	213	╒	245	⌡
150	û	182	╢	214	╓	246	÷
151	ù	183	╖	215	╫	247	≈
152	ÿ	184	╕	216	╪	248	°
153	Ö	185	╣	217	┘	249	•
154	Ü	186	║	218	┌	250	·
155	¢	187	╗	219	█	251	√
156	£	188	╝	220	▄	252	n
157	¥	189	╜	221	▌	253	2
158	₧	190	╛	222	▐	254	■
159	ƒ	191	┐	223	▀	255	Blank ff

Appendix 4

Error Codes

code	message
1	NEXT without FOR
2	Syntax error
3	RETURN without GOSUB
4	Out of data
5	Illegal function all
6	Overflow
7	Out of memory
8	Label not defined
9	Subscript out of range
10	Duplicate definition
11	Division by Zero
12	Illegal indirect mode
13	Type mismatch
14	Out of string space
16	String formula too complex
17	Cannot continue
18	Function not defined
19	No RESUME
20	RESUME without ERROR
24	Device timeout
25	Device Fault
26	FOR without NEXT
27	Out of paper
29	WHILE without WEND
30	WEND without WHILE
33	Duplicate label
35	Subprogram not defined

code	message
37	Argument count mismatch
38	Array not defined
40	Variable required
50	Field overflow
51	Internal error
52	Bad file name or number
53	File not found
54	Bad file mode
55	File already open
56	FIELD statement active
57	Device I/O error
58	File already exists
59	Bad record length
61	Disk full
62	Input past end of file
63	Bad record number
64	Bad filename
67	Too many files
68	Device unavailable
69	Commuinication buffer overflow
70	Permission denied
71	Disk not ready
72	Disk-Media failure
73	Feature unattainable
74	Rename across disks
75	Path/file access error
76	Path not found

Appendix 5

Selected Bibliography

MS-DOS

1. Noel Kantaris
   A concise Users Guide to MS-DOS 5
   Bernard Babani (Publ) 1993

BASIC Programming

1. Russell Borland
   Microsoft WORDBASIC Primer
   Microsoft press 1991

2. John Clark Craig
   The Microsoft Visual Basic Workshop
   Microsoft press 1991

.3. N. Kantaris
   Programming in QuickBASIC
   Bernard Babani (Publ) Reprinted 1992

4. John G. Kemeney + Thomas E. Kurtz
   BASIC Programming
   Wiley (3rd ed) 1980

5. David I. Schneider and the Peter Norton Computing group
   QBASIC Programming
   Brady 1991

Other Programming Languages

1. Leendert Ammeraal
   C for Programmers
   Wiley (2nd ed) 1991

2. Luis Castro, Jay Hanson + Tom Retig
   Advanced Programmers Guide (Featuring dBASE III and dBASE II update)
   Ashton Tate 1985

3. Lawrie Moore
Foundations of Programming with Pascal
Ellis Horwood reprinted 1982

4. J.S. Rohl
Writing Pascal Programs
Cambridge University press 1983

Computer Graphics

1. Donald Hearn and M. Pauline Baker
Computer Graphics
Prentice Hall 1986

2. Richard Kinslake
An Introductory Course in Computer Graphics
Chartwell-Bratt 1986

3. S. Laflin
Two-dimensional Computer Graphics
Chartwell-Bratt 1987

General Computing

1. P. M Heathcote
Computing (An Active-Learning approach)
D P Publications (2nd ed) 1994

2. P. M Heatcote
Tackling Computer Projects
D. P. Publications 1993

Mathematics

1. Ian Bradley and Ronald L. Meek
Matrices and Society
Penguin 1986

2. COMAP
FOR ALL PRACTICAL PURPOSES
(Introduction to Contemporary Mathematics)
Freeman 1988

3. H.M. Cundy and A.P. Rollet
Mathematical Models
Oxford (reprint) 1976

4. Duncan Graham, Christine Graham + Allan Whitcombe
Mathematics (A-level course companion)
Letts (2nd ed) 1988

5. Graham Hoare and Martin Powell
Mathematics with a Microcomputer
Ward Lock Educational 1985

General

1. Alan F. Sillitoe
Britain in Figures (A handbook of social statistics)
Pelican 1971

Index

www.ingramcontent.com/pod-product-compliance
Lightning Source LLC
Chambersburg PA
CBHW081226050326
40689CB00016B/3690